Positive Organizational Scholarship

Foundations of a New Discipline

Kim S. Cameron,
Jane E. Dutton,
Robert E. Quinn

Volume 2 of 2

EasyRead Large

Copyright Page from the Original Book

Positive Organizational Scholarship

Berrett-Koehler Publishers, Inc.
235 Montgomery Street, Suite 650
San Francisco, California 94104-2916
Tel: (415) 288-0260, Fax: (415) 362-2512
www.bkconnection.com

Ordering information for print editions
Quantity sales. Special discounts are available on quantity purchases by corporations, associations, and others. For details, contact the "Special Sales Department" at the Berrett-Koehler address above.
Individual sales. Berrett-Koehler publications are available through most bookstores. They can also be ordered directly from Berrett-Koehler: Tel: (800) 929-2929; Fax: (802) 864-7626; www.bkconnection.com
Orders for college textbook/course adoption use. Please contact Berrett-Koehler:
Tel: (800) 929-2929; Fax: (802) 864-7626.
Orders by U.S. trade bookstores and wholesalers. Please contact Ingram Publisher Services, Tel: (800) 509-4887; Fax: (800) 838-1149; E-mail: customer.service@ingram publisherservices.com; or visit www.ingrampublisherservices.com/Ordering for details about electronic ordering.

Berrett-Koehler and the BK logo are registered trademarks of Berrett-Koehler Publishers, Inc.

First Edition
Hardcover print edition ISBN 978-1-57675-232-6
PDF e-book ISBN 978-1-57675-966-0

2008-1

Interior production by Westchester Book Group.
Cover design by Ark Stein/The Visual Group.

ReadHowYouWant partners with publishers to provide books for ALL Kinds of Readers. For more information about Becoming A **RHYW** Registered Reader and to find more titles in your preferred format, visit:
www.readhowyouwant.com

TABLE OF CONTENTS

Part 3

POSITIVE MEANINGS AND POSITIVE CONNECTIONS

The chapters in this part offer an important window into how positive connections with others and how positive meaning engage processes and produce outcomes that help to explain extraordinary experience and performance in organizations. As we look across these six chapters, we see several important generative ideas that offer important insights for researchers interested in positive organizational scholarship.

First, several chapters invite inquiry into understanding how energy and vitality are created and spread in organizations. The authors use energy both to register the life and vitality in the system and to explain the causal dynamics that undergird different kinds of extraordinary performance. They imply that this vitality is a type of variable and renewable resource that contributes to understanding why and how people and groups thrive. Baker, Cross, and Wooten, as well as Dutton and

Heaphy use energy to characterize differences in how people feel when in relationship with others at work. They argue that these experienced differences of energy in relationship are consequential for individuals, groups, and organizations as a whole. Feldman and Khademian use energy or vitality to describe differences in both individual and organizational capacities to expand, grow, and develop.

Second, these chapters reveal how organizational conditions create information and opportunities, and engage people in ways that facilitate the construction of positive meaning and the coordination of work in ways that contribute to vital individual and group functioning. They help us to see that organizational conditions alter the micro-contexts in which people function and the meaning that people make of their own experience. These different meanings in turn, increase or decrease the type and level of resources available to individuals, as well as activate processes and structures that people find enabling or disabling. Wrzesniewski as well as Pratt and Ashforth both view organizational practices as consequential in providing motivation and freedom for individuals to construct the meaning of jobs in ways that are consequential. Gittell highlights how communication patterns and the quality of connection between people in a context enable or disable the execution of coordination in highly interdependent work. Feldman and Khademian reveal how empowerment enables capacity-building by allowing individuals to utilize connections and information as resources. Rather than seeing context as fixed, several of the authors describe how context enables action, but is also transformed by action, contributing to positive dynamics in organizational systems.

Third, the chapters uncover new ways of characterizing the connections between people that help to explain their power in fostering different forms of extraordinariness. They infuse connection with physiological significance—when in different forms of connection, people feel and are more alive (e.g., Dutton and Heaphy). They infuse connection with emotional significance by highlighting how connection relates to experienced vitality and engagement (Baker, Cross, and Wooten; Feldman and Khademian). They infuse connections with existential significance, emphasizing that different connections facilitate the crafting of different identities (Pratt and Ashforth; Wrzesniewski). Finally, they infuse connections with material significance in reminding organizational researchers that in different connections, people have access to different information, which endows them with differing amounts of power and differing choice points for action.

Fourth, the authors construe organizational members as active creators of their own fate and the fate of organizations by how they construe the meaning of work, how they cultivate energy-enhancing connections between people, as well as how they share and use power. The agentic construal of individuals in organizations helps to uncover how contexts enable flourishing and positive deviance through how they unlock individuals' capacities to act, and endow them with resources (like understanding, connections, information, energy) that are used to accomplish work (e.g., coordination, Gittell; planning, Feldman and Khademian), shape jobs (Wrzesniewski; Pratt and Ashforth), and perform more generally (Baker, Cross, and Wooten; Dutton and Heaphy).

The chapters invite organizational scholars to engage a number of important questions that help to explain positively deviant processes and outcomes in organizations. How do positive, energy-creating connections with other people contribute to extraordinary performance? What are the underlying mechanisms? How do conditions in organizations (e.g., strategy, culture, design) enable or disable the creation of these energy-generating connections? Similarly, what are the underlying mechanisms through which the construal of positive meaning about work affects individuals' beliefs, emotions, and behaviors? How does the cultivation of positive meaning contribute to extraordinary behavior for individuals, groups, units, and the organization as a whole? Why and how do features of organizations and features of organizational environments shape the construction of positive meaning about work, about self, and about the organization? How do organizational features enable the enhancement of capabilities and resources that individuals can use to empower others inside and outside the organization? New domains of inquiry and insight in organizational studies are opened through active pursuit of these questions.

Chapter 17

The Power of High-Quality Connections

Jane E. Dutton and Emily D. Heaphy

Human connections in organizations are vital. Whether they form as part of long-term relationships or brief encounters, all connections leave indelible traces. Organizations depend on individuals to interact and form connections to accomplish the work of the organization. Connections formed in work contexts, therefore, have a significant effect on people just by virtue of the time spent there (Hochschild, 1997). The quality of the connections, in turn, impacts how organizations function. Theories of human behavior in organizations need to take seriously the quality of connections between people to understand why people flourish or flounder and to unpack how they affect organizational functioning. In this chapter we respond to positive organizational scholarship's call to better understand how to build contexts that enable human flourishing by understanding the power of high-quality connections.

We define the quality of the connection in terms of whether the connective tissue between individuals is life-giving or life-depleting. Like a healthy blood vessel that connects parts of our body, a high-quality connection between two people allows the transfer of vital nutrients; it is flexible, strong, and resilient. In a low-quality connection, a tie exists (people communicate, they interact, and they may even be involved in interdependent work), but the connective tissue is damaged. With a low-quality connection, there is a little death in every interaction (Dutton, 2003).

In this chapter, we develop this definition and unpack the theoretical bases for the power of high-quality connections (HQCs) in work organizations in three steps. In the first step, we define HQCs. In the second step, we describe four theoretical lenses for seeing how HQCs affect people at work. Finally, we develop a research agenda for organizational studies that puts understanding the power of HQCs as a keystone for positive organizational scholarship.

HIGH-QUALITY CONNECTIONS

When people are at work, connections with others compose the fabric of daily life. A connection is the dynamic, living tissue (Berscheid & Lopes, 1997) that exists between two people when there is some contact between them involving mutual awareness and social interaction. The existence of some interaction means that individuals have affected one another in some way, giving connections a temporal as well as an emotional dimension. Connections can occur as a result of a momentary encounter, and can also develop and change over a longer time period (Gabarro, 1987). Other scholars have called this relationship feature the bond (e.g., Baumeister & Leary, 1995) or "space between" (Josselson, 1996) two individuals. In our definition, connection does not imply an enduring (Reis, 2001) or recurring (Gutek, 1995) bond, nor does it assume intimacy or closeness.[1]

Understanding the quality of the connection is critical to understanding why and how people thrive at work. Hallowell (1999), for example, describes the power of a connection created in a matter of minutes:

> A five-minute conversation can make all the difference in the world if the parties participate actively. To make it work, you have to set aside what you're doing, put

down the memo you were reading, disengage from your laptop, abandon your daydream and bring your attention to bear upon the person you are with. Usually, when you do this, the other person (or people) will feel the energy and respond in kind, naturally. (p.126)

Gersick, Bartunek, and Dutton (2000) describe one person's expression of the power of a more long-lasting work-based connection:

I haven't chosen this relationship to be important to me. It just—is. She is always there in the back (of my mind).... She has had such an impact on how I should run my life—how I should be a female faculty member. (p.1025)

In both examples, the power of high-quality connections is felt and sensed, with lasting implications for the individual, and often for the organization.

In contrast, low-quality connections leave damage in their wake. As one manager explained, "Corrosive connections are like black holes: they absorb all of the light in the system and give back nothing in return" (Dutton, 2003: 15). Studies of work incivility (Pearson, Andersson, & Porath, 2000) and minority employees (Blake, 1999) document the long-lasting damage done by corrosive connections at work. A low-quality, toxic connection depletes and degrades (Frost, 2003). It imposes a damaging emotional and physiological toll on individuals in work organizations (Williams & Dutton, 1999). Incidents like the one below, in which an executive sales consultant explains why he left a high-status job after eighteen months, happen frequently in all kinds of work contexts.

> The day he hired on, his assigned mentor showed him his new office and walked away without a word—no tour of the office, no introductions to co-workers, "in short, no information," the consultant says. Later, in a meeting, a partner treated him like a piece of furniture. Pointing him out as a new hire, the partner said, "I don't know if he's any good. Somebody try him out and let me know," he recalls. (Shellenbarger, 2000: B1)

Despite its importance organizational, researchers have not consistently defined connection quality. Some imply quality is relationship strength (Mills & Clark, 1982). Others define connection strength (and by implication, quality) in terms of the emotional weight of the attachment (Kahn, 1998) or by emotional weight coupled with reciprocity and frequency of communication (Granovetter, 1973). Researchers focusing on leader-member exchange relationships treat the quality of connection using a broad array of definitions (e.g., Schriesheim,

Castro, & Cogliser, 1999). Mentoring researchers often gauge connection quality by relationship satisfaction (e.g., Ragins, Cotton, & Miller, 2000). Other times, they use a broader definition, including emotional affect, reciprocity, mutuality, interdependence, and mutual motivation to be responsive (e.g., Higgins & Kram, 2001). Many imply connection quality is important, but leave the construct undefined (e.g., Uzzi, 1997). All in all, the concept of connection quality needs work (Berscheid & Lopes, 1997).

We define and gauge the quality of connection between people by three clusters of indicators. One cluster directly focuses on features of the actual connection between two people. Two clusters tap the experience of each individual in the connection. While we represent the quality of a connection using a static picture of the life-giving features of the tie, in reality quality is dynamic and processual, and is affected by changes in the individual and the social context.

Features of the Tie in a High-Quality Connection

To distill high-quality connections we focus on the features of the connection between two people, though connections occur in larger groups. We have identified three defining characteristics of the connection itself when it is defined as high quality.

First, HQCs have greater strength as indicated by *higher emotional carrying capacity.* Greater emotional carrying capacity of a connection is evidenced by both the expression of more emotion when in the connection and the expression of both positive and negative emotions. Connections with higher quality have capacity to withstand the expression of more absolute emotion and more emotion of varying kinds. We know we are in an HQC by the safety we feel in displaying different emotions:

> I can say anything to Art and he will be understanding. I am able to get frustration and anger out in a more constructive fashion with him. We do that for each other. (Kram & Isabella, 1985: 121)

The *tensility* of the tie is related to the capacity of the connection to bend and withstand strain and to function in a variety of circumstances. It is the feature of the connection that indicates its resilience or the capacity to bounce back after setbacks. Work in psychology (Reis, 2001; Gottman, 2001) has shown that meaningful connections are indicated by how the connection responds to conflict. In a connection with greater tensility, the connection alters form (while maintaining strength) to accommodate changes in the conditions of either individual, or conflict and tensions in the joint circumstances of the dyad.

The third characteristic of the tie, the *degree of connectivity,* developed by team researchers working from complex adaptive systems theory (Losada, 1999), is a measure of a relationship's generativity and openness to new ideas and influences, and its ability to deflect behaviors that will shut down generative processes. These researchers found that teams with a high degree of connectivity display an atmosphere of buoyancy, creating expansive emotional spaces that open possibilities for action and creativity. Stated in terms of complex adaptive systems, an HQC has the ability to dissolve attractors that close possibilities and evolve attractors that open possibilities (Losada, 1999: 190).

Subjective Experience of a High-Quality Connection

We propose that people in HQCs share three subjective experiences.[2] First, HQCs are sensed by *feelings of vitality and aliveness.* People in HQCs are more likely to feel positive arousal and a heightened sense of positive energy (Quinn & Dutton, 2002). The subjective experience of vitality is of interest to psychologists who study well-being and health (Nix,

Ryan, Maly, & Deci, 1999; Ryan & Frederick, 1997). It has been documented by researchers who study networks and energy at work (Baker, Cross, & Wooten, 2003).

Second, being in an HQC is also felt through a heightened sense of *positive regard* (Rogers, 1951). People in HQCs experience a feeling of being known or being loved. This sense can be instantaneous. It does not imply romantic attachment, nor does it imply a relationship of long duration. Sandelands (2002: 250) calls this the first moment of social life and describes it as the feeling of "living presence, a state of pure being, in which isolating worries, vanities and desires vanish within a single vital organism." Quinn calls the subjective experience of deep connection "profound contact" (Quinn & Quinn, 2002). Kahn (1998) uses emotional weight to indicate this kind of attachment. At the physiological level it is a form of unconscious resonance of neural engrams between two people (Lewis, Amini, & Lannan, 2000).

Finally, the subjective experience of being in an HQC is marked by felt *mutuality*. Mutuality captures the sense that both people in a connection are engaged and actively participating. Miller and Stiver describe mutuality as "a way of relating, a shared activity in which each (or all) of the people involved are participating as fully as possible" (1997: 43). While positive regard captures a "momentary feeling" of love at rest, mutuality captures the feeling of potential movement in the connection (Miller & Stiver, 1997) born from mutual vulnerability and mutual responsiveness. Miller and Stiver distinguish felt reciprocity from mutuality by the presence of mutual empathy. All three subjective experiences are important barometers of the quality of connection between people.

Physiological Experience of a High-Quality Connection

Physiological indicators mark a high-quality connection and positive interactions (Reis & Gable, 2003). However, most studies connecting high-quality connections and physiology are not designed to capture instantaneous correlates of the quality of connections. Instead, research has been focused on longer-term effects. There is diverse evidence that having highquality relationships with others is central to optimal living (Ryff & Singer, 1998) and associated with well-being in higher social animals (Mendoza, 1991) and humans (Uvnäs-Moberg, 1997).

First, people with more positive connections in their life have a lower allostatic load (Seeman et al., 1997) or a lower physiologic to responses to environmental stressors (Adler, 2002).

Allostatic load refers to the cumulative effects of activation of physical systems in responding to environmental demands (McEwen, 1998). Second, HQCs are associated with a longer lifespan (House, Landis, & Umberson, 1988) and lower risk of death (Seeman, 1996). Third, HQCs are associated with a stronger immune system (Cohen, 2001; Ornish, 1998) and lower blood pressure (Uchino, Cacioppo, & Kiecolt-Glaser, 1996), helping people cope more effectively with stress. Thus the cumulative effects of being in HQCs are clearly positive and life-enhancing.

Going beyond these longer-term effects, research suggests that people are instantaneously more alive and healthy in HQCs and that this state is indicated by three sets of physiological changes. First, in HQCs there is a *release of oxytocin,* which reduces anxiety and increases activity of the sympathetic nervous system (Altemus et al., 1997), at the same time that it fuels further affiliative behavior (Taylor, Dickerson, & Klein, 2002: 561). Second, HQCs are associated with a *release of endogenous opiad peptides,* which down-regulate the sympathetic and hypothalamic-pituitary-adrenocortical (HPA) response to stress. Previous studies have shown that their release is associated with positive social contact (Taylor, Dickerson, & Klein, 2002). Third, an instantaneous effect of being in a high-quality connection is *reduced systolic blood pressure.* In one experimental study that demonstrated this effect, people's cardiovasicular reaction was assessed under three conditions that varied in terms of the strength of social support present when participants had to give a six-minute speech. When HQCs were present, there was an attenuated blood pressure and heart response, suggesting immediate cardiovascular effects of being in an HQC (Lepore, Mata-Allen, & Evans, 1993).

FOUR THEORETICAL LENSES ON THE POWER OF HIGH-QUALITY CONNECTIONS

Four rich veins of theory inform how HQCs leave their imprint on people at work. The theories are interrelated and the boundaries blurred, but for now we will present them as four separate lenses: exchange, identity, growth, and knowledge. The exchange lens argues that HQCs matter by endowing individuals with resources that are useful and valuable. The identity perspective highlights the role that HQCs play in co-creating the meaning that employees can and do make of themselves and of the organization. A growth perspective showcases how relationships with others literally develop employees in the direction of their potentiality and health as human beings. Finally, a learning perspective focuses on relationships as micro-contexts for knowing. By putting these theoretical explanations and research communities side by side, we can better see the generative capacity of HQCs at work.

An Exchange Lens

An important way that organizational scholars explain the effects of HQCs is through a social exchange lens. In this perspective, work connections are vehicles for resource and reward exchanges. Rooted in sociology (e.g., Blau, 1964; Homans, 1974) and social psychology (Thibaut & Kelley, 1959), social exchange theory suggests that social relations involve the exchange of valued commodities between people. These commodities include money, advice, political opportunities, trust, social support, and even positive feelings (e.g., Lawler & Yoon, 1998). If people in a social relation acquire valuable resources, then that relationship is likely to endure and be strengthened (Emerson, 1976).

There are numerous examples within this paradigm for how HQCs enliven. We sample two. First, network theory asserts that relationships exist, survive, and thrive when ties in the network gain utility from their connection

(Baker, 2000). For example, studies of power in organizations typically use an exchange logic to explain what gives and what sustains power. For example, Brass (1984) found that employees acquired influence in the eyes of supervisors and nonsupervisors through their relative position in a social network. Different positions gave people access to resources that other people value, increasing interdependence and influence. These studies emphasize that organizational structures shape the connecting potential between people at work, and if people are in HQCs they may benefit from access and flows of valued resources, which in turn create and strengthen power.

Leader-member exchange theory illustrates how HQCs between leaders and their subordinates create value through how they deliver valued goods to both parties. The theory assumes that the dyadic linkage between leaders and subordinates is negotiated through a series of interactions over time in which both people exchange resources (Graen & Scandura, 1987). In a high-quality connection, a member may receive discretion and development from a leader, and in return, a leader may receive strong commitment and high effort from the subordinate. The leader-member exchange paradigm uses the exchange of valued resources and the building of trust to show how these relationships develop over time (Bauer & Green, 1996). The building of HQCs improves the flow and rate of valued resource exchange, which further cements and deepens the dyadic connection.

Through an exchange lens, we see how HQCs enliven through the mutual passing of valued resources. We see how repeated inter-actions create new and valued resources (such as trust and power or influence), which shape patterns of future exchange. This perspective stands in stark contrast to an identity lens on HQCs.

An Identity Lens

Other people are active players in the co-creation of who we are at work. Our work identities, and selves more generally, are created, deployed, and altered in social inter-actions with others (Potter & Wetherell, 1998; Prus, 1996; Reicher, 1995; Sampson, 1993; Schlenker, 1985; Swann, 1987). Cooley's idea of the looking-glass self (1902) and symbolic interactionists' claims that self-reflections from others compose the self (Blumer, 1966; Mead, 1934) undergird the idea that the quality of connections matters to the content and evalu-ation of the identity that employees form, claim, and express at work.

High-quality connections with others allow for the co-constructions of identities that are valued by organizational members themselves. Highquality connections afford the opportunity and the psychological safety (Kahn, 1990) to explore alternative identities, to make claims, and to craft an identity that a person feels is worthwhile and that fits who employees are or who they wish to become. In addition, HQCs help to make employees intelligible to them-selves and to others through talk and through storytelling (Gergen, 1994).

Ibarra (1999, 2003) has written about the process that individuals deploy to reinvent their career and to craft a viable and desired work identity. Her stories of how individuals invent themselves as a work in progress highlight the role that HQCs play. Other people encourage actions that are the seed corn for revising one's identity in the direction of a desired and valued possible self. Thus June, the literature professor who becomes a broker in Ibarra's book, relies on HQCs to give her feedback, to help her experiment and transition, and to affirm her new work identity (Ibarra, 2003). Through relationships with others she enters a type of holding environment for playing with elements of the new identity, and she acquires real information that helps her to understand and legitimately claim this new self. She imagines new possibilities for herself, which then motivates action consistent with this new self (Markus, 1977).

HQCs help employees create valued identities by helping people derive positive meaning about what they are doing. For example, we found that coworkers and supervisors play pivotal roles in helping temporary workers see their value:

> The boss I had was extraordinary at taking me under his wing. He did things for me as a temp that I wasn't used to. It was as if the minute I walked through the door I was you know, I ... was a permanent employee, even if I really wasn't. He took me to lunch the first day. I mean he went over everything [the company] did in detail, he brought out all the materials, and he even talked about the political relationships of everyone in the department—his allies, management, this person and that person. This was the most delightful experience I've ever had. (Bartel & Dutton, 2001: 126)

Thus, HQCs with others can make positive aspects of one's current identity salient (Ashforth & Johnson, 2001). They can play a significant role in converting ambivalence into positive meaning that helps people make positive sense of who they are and what they are doing at work (Pratt, 2000).

In certain cases, HQCs facilitate the expression of identities that are more authentic and genuine, at the same time that identity expression mobilizes change. Creed and Scully (2000) describe how gay, lesbian, bisexual, and transgendered (GLBT) employees deploy their identities in ways that allow them to contribute more fully to their work organization. At the same time, this form of identity claiming facilitates a self-narration that is in greater alignment with how someone sees themselves. High-quality connections enable this process by providing subtle and not so subtle support for marginal identity displays. One lesbian speaker talked about the effect this way:

> That right there is your validation. Among these friends are people that make the workplace a safe environment. They've been the driving force behind this network. I think a lot of it is [that for] a lot of gay and lesbian employees, there is still some fear to be out there in the front and to be a friend and supporter, though that takes a lot of risk too. So many of them have just been right out there. (Creed & Scully, 2000: 403)

Through an identity lens, we see that HQCs enliven people at work by facilitating employees' experimentation with new possible selves, by helping employees construct positive meaning about the current work that they do, and by creating support and possibility for identity displays at work.

A Growth and Development Lens

Scholars in this perspective view connections with others as fundamental to human development and growth. In contrast to theories that view separation and the drawing of boundaries around the self as humans' primary developmental task, in this perspective humans' growth is enabled or stunted by the quality of connections with others. Through HQCs, people at work can realize and activate new developmental trajectories.

Three veins of theory contribute to this perspective. First, scholars at the Stone Center argue that human growth occurs and action is enabled through mutually empathic and mutually empowering connections (Miller & Stiver, 1997). Second, building on attachment theory (e.g., Bowlby, 1969) and Winnicott's work on holding (1960, 1965), researchers show relationship systems are central to individuals' physical health, growth and development, and meaningfulness in life (Josselson, 1996; Kahn, 1998). The third stream views humans as driven toward satisfying the need to belong through connections characterized by frequent interaction and persistent caring (Baumeister & Leary, 1995).

Miller and Stiver (1997) illustrate how this theory of high-quality connection works. Psychological growth occurs in mutually empathic interactions, where both people engage with authentic thoughts, feelings, and responses. Through this process they experience mutual empowerment, which is characterized as a feeling of zest, effectiveness of the other person, greater knowledge, sense of worth, and a desire for more connection. The connection becomes a micro-context that fosters growth and development. For example, Phyllis was able to engage in a growth-fostering connection with her boss during a time of tough layoffs:

> She was able to let her boss know how hard it must be for him to have everyone angry at him but she told him that she thought he could make a difference if he more actively engaged with his employees and listened to their concerns. Phyllis created a forum for meeting with all the people involved and facilitated an energetic exchange among them. In the process, she encouraged her boss to be responsive to his staff through "not being defensive" and letting them know he did

not have all the answers but truly wanted them to participate in the company's problem-solving endeavors.... People responded with energy and high motivation, and morale was greatly improved. (Miller & Stiver, 1997: 192)

HQCs become contexts for growth and development through organizational caregiving. Building on the work of Bowlby (1973), Kahn (1993) uses caregiving to understand how role-related interactions produce a sense of security for employees. When one or more caregiving behaviors are part of a connection, they can become the basis for personal growth and development.

Finally, the quality of connection is a cornerstone of the literature on developmental relationships. We see this in an early mentoring definition: "Mentoring is defined not in terms of formal roles but in terms of the *character of the relationship* and the functions it serves" (Levinson et al., 1978: 98, italics added). Mentoring relationships foster growth by helping protégés gain promotions, demonstrate competence, and decipher organizational norms. A mentor can help protégés with integrating their professional and personal identities through role modeling, counseling, acceptance, confirmation, and friendship (Kram, 1985).

In sum, with a growth lens we see that HQCs enliven by providing growth-fostering connections, secure bases of attachment for organizational caregiving, and developmental relationships. In the next section, we look at how HQCs enable learning.

A Learning Lens

There are two theoretical explanations for how HQCs affect learning. First, connections can function as vessels in which knowledge is passed from one person to another; in an HQC, knowledge is absorbed faster, more completely, and with the quality of the connection intact or enhanced (Wenger, 2000; Lave & Wenger, 1991; Lampert, 2001). Second, knowledge is constituted in interaction between people, with HQCs being more generative, heedful, and flexible (Miller & Stiver, 1997; Losada, 1999; Weick & Roberts, 1993).

Studies of communities of practice demonstrate how HQCs enable employees to join, participate in, and learn from groups of people organized around a socially defined competence. Learning occurs as individuals engage with a novel experience and alter or elaborate social practices (e.g., Brown & Duguid, 1991). We see this form of relational learning in Orr's study of Xerox technical representatives (1996), which showed how HQCs facilitated developing tacit knowledge for fixing copiers. The vitality of the connective tissue facilitated story-telling, made question-asking safe, and created a context in which practitioners could elaborate and develop their practice.

HQCs also enable people to expand their knowledge about the self, the relationship, and the world. When mutual empathy and mutual empowerment characterize relationships, both people elaborate their own thoughts and feelings, and build a new shared understanding (Miller & Stiver, 1997). When people demonstrate care in HQCs, they create an enabling context, which facilitates the creation of new knowledge (von Krogh, Ichijo, & Nonaka, 2000).

People who study relational practice in organizations also provide a learning lens for HQCs (Fletcher, 1997; Jacques, 1993). These studies uncover the micromoves in interactions that simultaneously increase the quality of connection and enable learning. For example, Fletcher (1999) describes a set of practices she calls empathic teaching in which the "teacher" takes the emotional context, intellectual context, or both, into account when interrelating. This practice increases learning by preserving the dignity and respect for the other while communicating information about needed changes in behavior. For example, one female engineer who was teaching a young male technician, who was a junior to the engineer by several job grades, said:

> Statistics is an expertise that people are interested in and they want to know it, but they are getting negative feedback from their managers when it takes them a long time to do an analysis or to design an experiment. So they have a lot of discouragement to learning. So if you turn them off at all, you've lost them. So in that case I always teach things so I try not to bruise an ego. (Fletcher, 1999: 56)

In this instance, the engineer teaches in a way that preserves and possibly improves the quality of the connection, while presenting the statistical information in a way that enables the technician to act, enhancing her teaching competence.

A learning lens on the power of HQCs reminds us that these forms of ties are micro-contexts in which people acquire, develop, and experiment with new knowledge or ways of being. HQCs enable people to learn how to be practitioners and enable competence. Mutual empathy and mutual empowerment provide a relational context to safely navigate and learn about unfamiliar thoughts and feelings. Finally, relationally competent people can use HQCs to design effective learning situations for others.

HQCS AND POSITIVE ORGANIZATIONAL SCHOLARSHIP

Focusing on the quality of connection between people at work is pivotal to understanding individual and organizational behavior. It weaves together theories of growth, identity, learning, and exchange to improve our understanding of how and why connections at work matter. Focusing on connection quality adds a critical new dimension to our understanding of people's behavior at work: it puts individuals in context, but in a context that is alive, dynamic, and embodied, making it a rich reservoir of possibilities for human behavior and accomplishment. The focus on HQCs invites us to engage three important venues for positive organizational scholarship.

HQCs and Positive Individual Outcomes

High-quality connections literally and figuratively enliven people. We think this claim is critical for expanding the set of outcomes to which organizational scholars attend. A focus on HQCs reopens very important and basic questions about how work affects human health and well-being. While there have been noteworthy and critical developments in understanding how social relationships affect basic human health in psychology (Ryff & Singer, 1998) and behavioral medicine (e.g., Ornish, 1998), organizational scholars barely touch the subject. When they do, the typical focus is on stress and physiological damage done by the conditions of work. We have given far less attention to how work contexts affect human flourishing, from a psychological or a physiological perspective.

Our brief review of how HQCs at work affect people unlocks all kinds of new research possibilities.[3] For example, do employees with HQCs at work have more energy, zest, and vitality as measured by actual physiological indicators, in addition to subjective perceptions? Do they demonstrate more resilience (Sutcliffe & Vogus, 2003; Worline et al., 2002)? Do they learn more and at a faster rate? Do they experience more authenticity and craft identities that better fit who they are? Do they find better, more workable paths for their own development through organizations? Are they more effective change agents? There is evidence from our brief review that the answer to each of these questions is a resounding *yes!* Posing these questions opens up exploration of how work organizations enable the development of human strengths and virtues, which is at the heart of positive organizational scholarship. Research awaits, however.

HQCs and Positive Dynamics

If we back up from outcomes and focus on process, we see that a focus on HQCs reveals productive paths for developing scholarship about positive dynamics. Understanding how HQCs unleash human resourcefulness (e.g., energy, Baker et al., 2003; Quinn & Dutton, 2002) uncovers the human potentiality in organizational systems. By identifying the quality of connections as a pivotal construct, we begin to explore basic questions about how HQCs enable employees to create positive spirals of meaning about projects and the organization. For example, if organizations create fertile ground for building HQCs, employees may be able to display authentic identities more often, engage each other more fully, be more vulnerable in the process of learning, and experience more interpersonal valuing through positive regard, all of which cultivate positive meaning about being an organizational member. These positive meanings and constructive interactions in turn may create positive emotions and cultivate trust, which contribute to higher coping, greater resilience in the face of setbacks, more creativity, greater attention and a broadening of the thought-action repertoire (Fredrickson, 1998), and a greater probability of the experience of flow (Csikszentmihalyi, 1990).

These are just some of the imagined effects that are part of the nonlinear dynamics that compose what Fredrickson (2002) calls the upward spirals of human functioning. Our hope is that by understanding better how these dynamics and spirals work, and how they are stimulated, sustained, and nourished through HQCs, we can unlock new forms of theory and intervention that help people thrive at work.

HQCs and Positive Organizational Outcomes

A focus on HQCs affords new insights for understanding positive organizational-level behavior and actions. On the one hand, a focus on HQCs sheds new light on "old" mechanisms that undergird processes of heedful interrelating (Weick & Roberts, 1993), absorptive capacity (Zahra & George, 2002), relational coordination (Gittell, 2001), intra- and inter-organizational collaboration (Uzzi, 1997; Powell, Koput, & Smith-Doerr, 1996), and organizational learning and resilience (Weick, Sutcliffe, & Obstfeld, 1999). A focus on HQCs as a mechanism helps us to see the synergies possible from linking studies of these critical organizational-level processes. At the same time, using HQCs to understand these processes provides a window into understanding organizations' dynamic capabilities (Eisenhardt & Martin, 2000). We see real yield from linking HQCs to strategic processes and outcomes for the firm.

A focus on HQCs also invites consideration of collective-level outcomes that focus on organizational-level strengths and virtues. For example, organizational intelligence or wisdom (Srivastva & Cooperrider, 1998), organizational compassion (Dutton, Worline, Frost, & Lilius, 2002), organizational integrity, and forgiveness as ongoing collective accomplishments and competencies are just some of the possible outcomes that can draw on HQCs as a foundation. Cameron, Caza, and Bright (2002) call these collective behaviors "virtuousness" and show their positive effects on performance in the wake of organizational downsizing. These topics are fertile territory for future organizational scholarship. If explored, they will surely reveal how and why organizations create value at a much more profound and sustainable level, over and above the production of financial returns.

LOOKING FORWARD TO COMING ALIVE!

In this chapter we hope to have equipped you to embark with us on mapping a new direction in organizational studies. There are calls in a number of fields to develop a greater understanding of relationships (e.g., Baron & Pfeffer, 1994; Berscheid, 1999; Bradbury & Lichtenstein, 2000; Emirbayer, 1997; Duck, 1990). We join them and add three important elements. First, we provide a definition and operationalization of connection and connection quality. Second, we provide researchers with four rich theoretical approaches to begin to map the territory. Third, our focus on positive potentialities of HQCs challenges us to deepen our knowledge about building human and organizational strength, health, and flourishing in work organizations. Currently, we simply don't know very much about these processes. We hope that this chapter enables many of us to begin the process of accumulating knowledge about this vital construct.

ACKNOWLEDGMENT

Thanks to Rob Cross, Joyce Fletcher, Rachel Hsuing, Jason Kanov, Lou Lukas,

Sally Maitlis, Giovanna Marchio, Jean Baker Miller, Leslie Perlow, Ryan Quinn, Cara Sandelands, and Leslie Sekerka for comments on earlier drafts of this chapter.

NOTES

[1] We also use the word "connection" differently than Jean Baker Miller and colleagues, who define connections as positive and growth-fostering (Miller & Stiver, 1997; Kaplan et al., 1991; Miller, 1988). We wish to allow for the possibility that connections can be growth-fostering (life-giving) or growth-depleting (lifedepleting).

[2] We define subjective experience as "thoughts together with their accompanying emotions" (Miller & Stiver, 1997: 27).

[3] This section only addresses positive effects of HQCs, but there may be negative direct and indirect effects as well that also deserve consideration. We also wonder if what limits, if any, might apply to people's capacity to handle HQCs. Thanks to Rob Cross for these suggestions.

Chapter 18

A Theory of Relational Coordination

Jody Hoffer Gittell

The theory of relational coordination argues that the coordination of highly interdependent work is most effectively carried out through highquality communication and relationships, particularly through relationships of shared goals, shared knowledge, and mutual respect (Gittell, 2001, 2002, 2003). Coordination is not a mechanistic process, in this view, but rather a relational one. High-quality communication and relationships together give rise to high-quality connections—connections that are life giving rather than life depleting (Dutton & Heaphy, 2003). High-quality connections are characterized by recognition of and responsiveness to the other, and therefore are critical for coordinating highly interdependent work, where actions taken by each participant potentially require a response by each of the others. The theory of relational coordination thus offers a positive organizational scholarship perspective on coordination, arguing that organizations can move from less positive states to more positive states by developing high-quality communication and relationships among their members.

In this chapter I take a traditional body of theory—organization design—and reconceptualize it from the perspective of relational coordination. The role of organization design has traditionally been to create structures through which information can flow, to facilitate the coordination of work. From the perspective of relational coordination, however, we come to see the role of organization design in a new light. It becomes apparent that the role of organization design is not merely to create the structures through which information can flow. Rather, organization design is called upon to create structures that foster both high-quality communication and high-quality relationships. These high-quality connections are life giving, providing a source of new energy. This perspective thus suggests a more transformative role for organization design, consistent with positive organizational scholarship.

ORGANIZATION DESIGN THEORY

Organization design theory identifies coordination as a fundamental design challenge encountered by all organizations. Lawrence and Lorsch (1968) argued that to perform effectively, organizations must coordinate the specialized activities of people in different but interrelated organizational functions. Their research suggested that performance differences among organizations can be attributed to their differential ability to coordinate these specialized activities. In organization design theory, coordination is conceptualized as an information-processing problem (Galbraith, 1973; Tushman & Nadler, 1978). According to Tushman and Nadler (1978: 614):

> Organizations can fruitfully be seen as information processing systems. Given the various sources of uncertainty, a basic function of the organization's structure is to create the most appropriate configuration of work units (as well as the linkages between these units) to facilitate the effective collection, processing and distribution of information.

More recent developments in organization design theory have elucidated the set of organizational structures through which coordination can be achieved (Argote, 1982; Galbraith, 1977, 1995; Mohrman, 1993; Nadler & Tushman, 1988; Van de Ven, 1975), including routines, boundary spanners, team meetings, and so forth. Despite its focus on structures that support coordination, however, organization design theory has not developed a way to conceptualize the connections through which coordination is carried out, nor how to think about coordination as potentially occurring through high-quality communication and relationships rather than simply through the processing of information. The theory of relational coordination has sought to fill this gap.

THE THEORY OF RELATIONAL COORDINATION

When work processes are highly interdependent (that is, reciprocally interdependent rather than sequential or pooled), any action taken by one participant potentially requires a response by one or all of the other participants (Thompson, 1967). High levels of task interdependence would therefore appear to benefit from high-quality connections and in particular from the responsiveness and sensitivity to the needs of the other that characterize high-quality connections (Dutton & Heaphy, 2003). The theory of relational coordination suggests that coordination of highly interdependent work is facilitated by high-quality connections, specifically by high-quality communication carried out through relationships of shared goals, shared knowledge, and mutual respect (Gittell, 2003, 2002, 2001). The following sections describe the dimensions of relational coordination.

High-Quality Communication

Frequent Communication

The information needed to manage task interdependencies is exchanged through communication. But the role of communication is not merely informational. Frequent communication helps to build relationships through the familiarity that grows from repetition. Indeed, in network theory, strong ties are defined primarily and sometimes solely in terms of frequency (Granovetter, 1973). While recognizing the importance of frequent communication for the coordination of highly interdependent work (e.g., Argote, 1982), relational coordination encompasses far more than simply the frequency of communication.

Timely Communication

Communication can be frequent and still be of poor quality. For one thing, it can lack timeliness. In coordinating highly interdependent work, timing can be everything. Delayed communication may result in errors or delays, with negative implications for organizational outcomes. Research supports the importance of timely communication for successful task performance (e.g., Orlikowski & Yates, 1991; Waller, 1999), although timely communication has not been widely recognized as essential to the coordination of highly interdependent work.

Accurate Communication

The coordination of highly interdependent work depends not only on the frequency and timeliness of communication, but also on its accuracy. If updates are given frequently and in a timely way, but the information is inaccurate, the consequences for error or delay are apparent. Research has shown the importance of accurate communication for supporting effective group process (e.g., O'Reilly & Roberts, 1977), although it has not been widely linked to the coordination of highly interdependent work.

Problem-Solving Communication

Task interdependencies often result in problems that require joint problem solving. Hence, effective coordination of interdependent work requires that participants engage in problem-solving communication. However, the more common response to interdependence is conflict (Pondy, 1967) as well as blaming and the avoidance of blame (Donnellon, 1994; Gittell, 2000). The resort to blaming rather than problem solving reduces opportunities to solve problems, with negative consequences for performance (Deming, 1984). Others have recognized the role that problem solving plays in the coordination of highly , 2000).

High-Quality Relationships

Relational coordination depends on high-quality communication among participants, but it also depends upon high-quality relationships—in particular the strength of shared goals, shared knowledge, and mutual respect—among them. Although shared goals, shared knowledge, and mutual respect are not the attributes of relationships that organizational scholars have traditionally explored, the theory of relational coordination argues that they are integral to the effective coordination of highly interdependent work.

Shared Goals

Relational coordination depends on the strength of shared goals among participants in a given work process. With shared goals for the work process, participants have a powerful bond and can more easily come to compatible conclusions about how to respond as new information becomes available. However, shared goals are often lacking among those from different functional areas who are involved in the same work process. In their classic work on organizations, March and Simon (1958) described the potentially disintegrative effects that occur when participants pursue their own functional goals without reference to the overarching goals of the work process in which they are engaged. More recent scholars have identified shared goals as playing an important role in the coordination of highly interdependent work (Saavedra, Earley, & Van Dyne, 1993; Wageman, 1995).

Shared Knowledge

Furthermore, relational coordination depends upon the degree of shared knowledge that participants have regarding each other's tasks. When participants share knowledge of each other's tasks and how they fit together, they have a powerful bond that provides a context for knowing who will be impacted by any given change and therefore for knowing who needs to know what and with what urgency. But shared knowledge is often lacking among participants in highly interdependent work processes. Dougherty (1992) showed that participants from different functional backgrounds often reside in different "thought worlds" due to differences in their training, socialization, and expertise. She showed that these thought worlds create obstacles to effective communication and therefore undermine the effective coordination of work processes. Weick's "sense-making" theory suggests that collective mind, or shared understanding of the work process by those who are participants in it, can connect participants from these distinct thought worlds and therefore enhance coordination (Weick, 1993; Weick & Roberts, 1993).

Mutual Respect

Finally, relational coordination depends upon the respect that participants have for the roles played by other participants in the same work process. Members of distinct occupational communities are divided by differences in status and may bolster their own status by actively cultivating disrespect for the work performed by others (Van Maanen & Barley, 1984). When members of these distinct occupational communities are engaged in a common work process, the potential for these divisive relationships to undermine coordination is apparent. Respect for each other's competence creates a powerful bond, and is integral to the effective coordination of highly interdependent work (Eisenberg, 1990; Rubenstein, Barth, & Douds, 1971).

Relational Coordination: Coordinating Work Through High-Quality Connections

The theory of relational coordination states that high-quality relationships—of shared goals, shared knowledge, and mutual respect—support high-quality communication, and vice versa. Together they enable participants to coordinate highly interdependent work. Shared goals motivate participants to move beyond subgoal optimization and to act with regard for the overall work process. Shared knowledge informs participants of how their own tasks and the tasks of others contribute to the overall work process, enabling them to act with regard for that overall work process. Respect for the work of others encourages participants to value the contributions of others and to consider the impact of their actions on others, further reinforcing the inclination to act with regard for the overall work process. This web of relationships reinforces, and is reinforced by, the frequency, timeliness, accuracy, and problem-solving nature of communication, enabling participants to effectively coordinate the work processes in which they are engaged.

Low-quality relationships have the opposite effect, undermining communication and hindering participants' ability to effectively coordinate their work. For example, when participants do not respect or feel respected by others who are engaged in the same work process, they tend to avoid communication, and even eye contact, with each other. Furthermore, participants who do not share a set of superordinate goals for the work process are more likely to engage in blaming rather than problem solving with each other when problems occur. Finally, participants who are not connected to each other through shared knowledge of the work process are less able to engage in timely communication with each other—they do not understand what others are doing well enough to anticipate the urgency of communicating particular information to them.

In sum, the theory of relational coordination argues that high-quality connections—in particular high-quality communication and high-quality relationships—are integral to the effective coordination of highly interdependent work.

ORGANIZATION DESIGN RECONCEPTUALIZED

The theory of relational coordination suggests a new way to understand the role of organization design. The role of organization design is not merely to create the structures through which information can flow. Rather its role is to build high-quality connections—in particular high-quality communication and relationships—through which coordination can effectively occur. Work processes typically span multiple functional boundaries, and people in different functions are often divided by differences in goals, knowledge, and status. Organization design can be reconceptualized as a means to create not merely information flows, but high-quality connections, among these parties.

Figure 18.1
A New Role for Organization Design

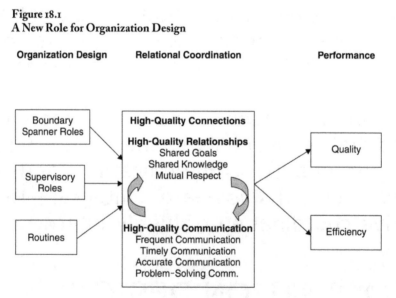

The following sections review boundary spanners, supervisors, and routines, and show how each can be reconceptualized as a means to create high-quality connections that are conducive to the coordination of highly interdependent work. Figure 18.1 illustrates the roles they are expected to play.

Boundary Spanners[1]

Organizational scholars have noted a range of roles that boundary spanners can play, from information processing to relationship management, to the building of high-quality connections.

Information Processing

Boundary spanners have traditionally been understood as playing primarily an information-processing role. The study of boundary spanners derived from an open systems view of organizations (e.g., Katz & Kahn, 1966; von Bertalanffy, 1950), which portrays organizations as having interior segments separated from the external environment by permeable boundaries. Boundary spanners collect, filter, translate, interpret, and disseminate knowledge from the external environment to members of their organization so that the organization is better able to monitor and adapt to changes emanating from the external environment (Katz & Tushman, 1983; Aldrich & Herker, 1977). Boundary spanners filter information from the environment to focus participants' attention around priority issues, and they filter requests for information to prevent participants from becoming overwhelmed (Tushman & Scanlan, 1981a).

Boundary spanners play this information-processing role not only between organizations and their external environments, but also between units within an organization. Ancona and Caldwell (1992) further extended the information-processing role of the boundary spanner to address teams within organizations, suggesting that boundary spanners within the team manage the flow of information between the team and other parties in the organization.

Relationship Management

Some of this work on boundary spanners has gone beyond a purely information-processing perspective to consider the relationship-management role that boundary spanners can play. Aldrich and Herker (1977) proposed that boundary spanners play an external representation role in addition to an information-processing role. In their external representation role, boundary spanners interact with parties external to the organization and attempt to influence them to accommodate the preferences of the boundary spanner's organization. If it is not possible to achieve accommodation from external parties, the boundary spanner either attempts to buffer the host organization from the external party or influence the host organization to accommodate external demands.

Adams (1976) suggested that boundary spanners act as agents of influence to both external and internal parties. Ancona and Caldwell (1992) explored efforts by boundary spanners within teams to mold the impressions of other parties in the organization and to negotiate with them, as well as to manage the flow of information with them. These attempts by the boundary spanner to negotiate and exert influence move beyond a purely information-processing role.

Different personal characteristics are required for carrying out the relational versus the purely informational aspects of the boundary spanner role. Boundary spanner effectiveness has been shown to depend on relational skills such as the ability to quickly read emotional and contextual cues when translating across boundaries (Caldwell & O'Reilly, 1982; Tushman & Scanlan, 1981b). A boundary spanner who is understood as contributing primarily informational benefits would not be required to possess these qualities.

Building High-Quality Connections

While theorists have recognized that boundary spanners manage relationships as well as the flow of information, even suggesting that perhaps these two roles are intimately related, very few theorists have portrayed boundary spanners as builders of high-quality connections. Some steps have been taken in this direction, however. Friedman and Podolny (1992) and Currall and Judge (1995) have shown that one critical role that boundary spanners play in the context of negotiations is to build trust among the parties. Furthermore, Gittell (2002) has shown that boundary spanners facilitate coordination by building high-quality communication and relationships among parties who are engaged in highly interdependent work. These three studies move beyond the traditional information-processing role of boundary spanners, and even their relationship-management role, to consider the contribution that boundary spanners can make in building high-quality connections. The final study in particular suggests that boundary spanners can build high-quality connections to facilitate the coordination of highly interdependent work.

But how do boundary spanners build these high-quality connections to facilitate coordination? Boundary spanner roles can be designed to include contact with every party that is involved in a particular work process, with sufficient time to engage in conversation with each party. The role can also involve moving across spatial boundaries that often divide participants from different functional areas, to move into the separate spaces occupied by different parties, symbolically creating connection among those parties. Through these activities, including both physical movement and conversation, boundary spanners can build shared goals, shared knowledge, and mutual respect with each person involved in the work process, and then from this base seek to build those connections among the participants themselves.

Supervisors

There are also competing views among organizational scholars regarding the role that supervisors play in achieving coordination. Some theorists argue that supervision is particularly irrelevant when work is highly interdependent because in such settings participants should be coordinating directly with each other rather than through a supervisor. These theorists argue for a minimalist, hands-off approach to supervision. Others take a more activist approach, arguing that supervision is about building connections with workers *and among* workers, and that supervisors therefore add the most value when work is highly interdependent.

The Minimalist Approach

Some theorists see the supervisory role as best carried out through minimal intervention in the activities of frontline workers (Hackman

& Oldham, 1980; Mowday, Porter, & Steers, 1982; Walton, 1985; Walton & Hackman, 1986). According to Hackman and Oldham (1980: 209):

When a group is first formed ... it may be necessary to help members get off to a good start by inviting them to participate in some "team-building" activities intended to establish the boundaries and identity of the group and to assist members in coming to grips with their shared authority for managing internal group processes.

Then, as the group gains a sense of its identity and begins to develop its own ways of dealing with task and organizational issues, the manager or consultant can gradually withdraw from prominence in group activities.

The gradual reduction of supervisory involvement is argued to be a win/win proposition for participants and for the organization. Both individual needs for autonomy and organizational needs for performance can be met through the transfer of responsibilities and capabilities from supervisors to participants, reducing the number of supervisors and expanding their spans of control (Walton & Schlesinger, 1979).

Theorists who take this minimalist perspective tend to argue that the evolving nature of work—the increasing interdependence of work, the increasing demand for quality and customization, and increased time constraints—has created the need for self-directed, committed workers. Such workers are argued to have correspondingly less need for supervision (Piore & Sabel, 1984; Zuboff, 1988). A minimalist approach to supervision is seen as a critical component of this team-based form of work organization (Appelbaum & Batt, 1994; Heckscher & Donnellon, 1994: 138; Batt, 1996: 59, 67 ff.; MacDuffie, 1996: 81, 114; Appelbaum & Berg, 1997: 15; Applegate, 1999). Supervisors are still needed, but they should operate from an arm's length. This minimalist approach allows participants to focus more on their lateral relationships and less on their hierarchical relationships, therefore contributing to stronger connections with each other.

Some empirical research lends support to this view. Wall, Kemp, Jackson, and Clegg (1986) found that the elimination of supervisory positions was associated with improved productivity in a manufacturing setting. A meta-analysis concluded that work teams without supervisors performed better than work teams with supervisors (Beekun, 1989).

The Activist Approach

In contrast to the minimalist approach, other organizational scholars have argued for an activist approach on the grounds that effective supervision is both time-consuming and relationship-intensive. According to McGregor (1960: 76):

> Roles cannot be clarified, mutual agreement concerning the responsibilities of a subordinate's job cannot be reached in a few minutes, nor can appropriate targets be established without a good deal of discussion. It is far quicker to hand a subordinate a position description and to inform him of his objectives for the coming period.

This activist approach to supervision involves working alongside of one's direct reports, with ample opportunities for building shared goals and for providing coaching and feedback (Likert, 1961; Tannenbaum, 1968). Even Frederick Winslow Taylor, founder of scientific management, pointed out the benefits of the activist approach to supervision for building connections (1998: 75):

> More than all other causes, the close, intimate cooperation, the constant personal contact between the two sides, will tend to diminish friction and discontent. It is difficult for two people whose interests are the same, and who work side by side in accomplishing the

same object all day long to keep up a quarrel.

This activist approach to supervision is made possible by high levels of supervisory staffing per nonsupervisory participant—that is, small spans of control. Porter and Lawler (1964) found that supervisors with small spans of control were more available for coaching and feedback. Managers with large spans were found to have less opportunity for interacting with individual subordinates and maintaining effective relationships with them (Ford, 1981). They had less time to provide support, encouragement, and recognition to individual subordinates (Goodstadt & Kipnis, 1970). Managers with large spans were more likely to handle problems with subordinates in a more formalized, impersonal manner, using warnings and punishments instead of coaching and feedback (Kipnis & Cosentino, 1969; Kipnis & Lane, 1962). As spans of control increase, managers have been found to make more autocratic decisions (Heller & Yukl, 1969). Narrower spans of control allow more contact and more opportunities for communication between frontline and managerial employees (Porter & Lawler, 1964; Blau, 1968).

Interdependence and the Activist Approach

Contrary to the argument made from the minimalist perspective, the activist approach to supervision may be particularly effective for highly interdependent work. Empirical studies have consistently found that highly interdependent work is associated with smaller supervisory spans (Udy, 1959; Woodward, 1965; Hickson, 1966; Hunt, 1970; Blau, 1972). However, the benefits of smaller supervisory spans do not seem to stem from the greater need for coordination *by supervisors.* Van de Ven, Delbecq, and Koenig (1976) found no significant increase in supervisory coordinating activities associated with more interdependent work. In addition, they found that more highly interdependent work benefits from an increase in coordination among participants themselves.

If highly interdependent work benefits from increased coordination among participants themselves, rather than increased coordination by supervisors, how are supervisors adding value? Woodward (1965) suggested that supervisors add value by the role they play in building connections. She argued that narrow spans lead to a "more intimate and informal" relationship between supervisors and frontline workers, allowing for the development of shared goals. More activist approaches to supervision—working   with subordinates to solve problems (Galbraith, 1977), consulting with subordinates (Jermier & Berkes, 1979), and acting to promote coordination (Lord & Rouzee, 1979)—were found to be particularly valuable when work is highly interdependent.

Supervisors add value to highly interdependent work not only by building connections *with* participants, but also by building connections *among* participants. Gittell (2001) theorized that supervisors can help to build connections among participants in a common work process, characterized by high-quality communication and relationships, thus enabling them to better coordinate their work with each other. Qualitative data in this study suggested that narrow spans of control create the opportunity for more intensive supervisory coaching and feedback to participants, due to the greater availability of supervisory time (Gittell, 2001). Supervisors with narrower spans of control had greater opportunities for working side-by-side with those who they were responsible for supervising. Working side-by-side appeared to reduce distance between supervisors and participants, resulting in stronger connections between them and in greater receptiveness to coaching and feedback.

Activist supervisors can use detailed, well-informed feedback to increase each participant's understanding of how their actions influence other participants, thus building bonds of shared knowledge among participants. In addition, supervisory feedback can reduce the need for forms of performance measurement that tend to be divisive, and that tend to undermine shared goals and shared knowledge among participants in the work process. Rather than *preventing* connections from forming among participants, as suggested by advocates of minimalist supervision, activist supervisors can therefore help to *build* those connections.

Routines

Routines are commonly understood to be an effective coordinating mechanism. But there are competing views of why and how they are effective, and under what conditions.

Routines as a Substitute for Connection

Routines facilitate coordinated action by pre-specifying the tasks to be performed and the sequence in which to perform them. Routines capture the lessons learned from previous experiences, enabling a process to be replicated without reinventing the wheel (Levitt & March, 1986). By using routines to codify best practices, individual capabilities can be transformed into organizational capabilities, and therefore into potential sources of competitive advantage (Nelson & Winter, 1981). Total quality management relies heavily on the use of standardized work to capture and implement previous learning and thereby to create a platform for further improvements (Deming, 1986; Adler & Borys, 1996).

The traditional organization design perspective on routines is that they serve as a *substitute* for connections among participants in the work process (Thompson, 1967; Galbraith, 1973; Van de Ven, Delbecq, & Koenig, 1976). Standards work by eliminating "the need for further communication among the subunits.... To the extent that the job-related situations can be anticipated in advance and rules derived from them, integrated activity is guaranteed without communication" (Galbraith, 1977: 320). Those who hold this view argue that routines work best under low levels of uncertainty, when participants can depend on the same scenario to repeat itself without significant variation.

Routines as a Facilitator of Connection

An alternative perspective on routines, however, is that routines can *facilitate* connections among participants in a work process, rather than serving as a replacement for those connections (Adler & Borys, 1996; Feldman & Rafaeli, 2002). Adler and Borys (1996: 73) suggest that routines can be "designed to afford [participants] an understanding of where their own tasks fit into the whole." Similarly, Feldman and Rafaeli (2002: 321) suggest that routines are sources of connections and shared understanding among participants. Routines generate "understandings about what actions will be taken in a specific instance of a routine, and understandings about why the routine is being performed or the purpose of the routine." By generating connection and shared understanding, routines increase participants' ability to adapt as circumstances change.

Building on these arguments, Gittell (2002) showed how routines can facilitate connection among those who are engaged in highly interdependent work. Routines were shown to improve performance by strengthening connections among participants in the form of high-quality communication and relationships, rather than by reducing the need for them. The implication, consistent with Feldman and Rafaeli (2002) and supported empirically by Gittell (2002), is that routines can be increasingly useful, rather than increasingly irrelevant, as uncertainty increases.

It is not just any kind of routine that can build high-quality connections among participants, however. Routines that build connections need to do more than specify the sequence of tasks to be performed by each participant. Routines that build connections look more like process maps—they clarify the key interdependencies in the work process, thus building shared knowledge among participants. The theory of relational coordination suggests that when participants share knowledge of each other's tasks and how those tasks fit together, they share a powerful bond. Specifically, they share a context for knowing who will be impacted by any given change and therefore for knowing who needs to know what and with what urgency. By building shared knowledge among participants, these kinds of routines enable participants to adapt fluidly to each other—like "poetry in motion"—when circumstances change unexpectedly.

ORGANIZATION DESIGN THROUGH THE LENS OF RELATIONAL COORDINATION

Reconceptualizing organization design through the lens of relational coordination, it appears to be a more vital, less mechanistic field of study than traditionally conceived. The role of organization design is not simply to design structures that facilitate the flow of information. The role of organization design is also to design structures that help to foster high-quality communication and relationships among participants who are engaged in highly interdependent work.

Boundary spanners can build relationships among participants in a given work process—fostering shared goals by linking the subgoals of each participant to the overall goals of the work process, fostering shared knowledge by relating each participant to what is happening in the rest of the work process, and fostering mutual respect by treating each participant with respect. Supervisors can do the same, reinforcing shared goals, building shared knowledge, and modeling mutual respect through supervisory coaching and feedback, and through working side-by-side with their direct reports. In addition, supervisory coaching and feedback can reduce the need for forms of performance measurement that tend to create division, undermine shared goals, and encourage the withholding of information. Lastly, routines in the form of process maps can increase the level of shared knowledge among participants by illustrating where each task fits in the overall work process, and how each participant's task relates to the work of others. The role of organization design is thus potentially more transformative than traditionally conceived, creating new resources through high-quality connections in addition to channeling existing information more effectively.

There are some who would take a more radical perspective and claim that the whole premise behind organization design is flawed. The structures with which organization design has been concerned are increasingly irrelevant, they argue. If connections are to play a vital role in getting work done, they must emerge spontaneously in the workplace. Nohria and Berkeley (1994: 119–120) describe this view:

> Organizational structure is a legacy of the bureaucratic era, one that has decreased relevance in the "immaterial" world of the virtual organization. Although structure does not necessarily disappear per se, this disappearance at the level of ordinary perception is becoming part of the dominant discourse of organization.

Krackhardt (1994: 218) develops the argument further, stating that

> networks of relations [that] span the entire organization [should be] unimpeded by preordained formal structures and fluid enough to adapt to immediate technological demands. These relations can be multiple and complex. But one characteristic they share is that they emerge in the organization, they are not preplanned.

Any attempts to reconceptualize organization design theory, including my own attempt in this chapter, must contend with this argument.

Furthermore, this argument may be even more relevant when high-quality communication and relationships are needed. Even more than in the case of ordinary connections, one might expect that high-quality connections must emerge spontaneously or not at all. The sensitivity and responsiveness to the needs of the other found in high-quality connections must perhaps be motivated from within, by deep-seated personal desires and qualities, rather than by organizational structures such as supervisory or boundary spanning roles, or routines.

And yet it would be problematic for organizations to rely only on the high-quality connections that happen to emerge spontaneously, because high-quality connections are not likely to emerge spontaneously in some cases where they are critically needed—as in the case of coordination. Work processes nearly always include participants from multiple functional areas, whether it is the flight departure process, with pilots, mechanics, cabin cleaners, and gate agents, or the patient care process, with doctors, nurses, social workers, and physical therapists. Previous work suggests that participants who work in different functional areas will tend to suffer from weak connections, due to functionally based differences in work goals (March & Simon, 1958), "thought worlds"

(Dougherty, 1992), and status (Van Maanen & Barley, 1984). To achieve coordination of highly interdependent work, we therefore need high-quality connections where they are unlikely to emerge on their own—and yet perhaps these connections by their very nature are not amenable to being shaped by external forces.

How to resolve this dilemma? In fact, positive organizational scholarship is not incompatible with the premise of organization design. As we have seen throughout this book, positive organizational scholarship focuses not only on extraordinary *behaviors* like high-quality connections. Positive organizational scholarship also focuses on the organizational *conditions* that enable these behaviors to flourish. Consistent with positive organizational scholarship, organization design can be reconceptualized as suggesting a set of principles for putting into place the conditions that enable high-quality connections to flourish.

However, more work remains to flesh out a positive organizational scholarship approach to organization design. Important as they are, boundary spanners, supervisors, and routines are not the only structures that organization design can offer to foster high-quality communication and relationships to facilitate the coordination of highly interdependent work. Many traditional human resource practices—for example, hiring, training, promotion, performance measurement, and conflict resolution—can be reconceptualized in this light. How might these formal practices be reconceptualized in terms of their ability, or lack of ability, to create the conditions that foster high-quality communication and relationships among those who need to coordinate their work? Positive organizational scholarship thus presents significant opportunities for bringing new meaning to classical organizational theories such as organization design, as well as to theories of human resource management.

ACKNOWLEDGMENT

Thanks to participants in the positive organizational scholarship conference at the University of Michigan Business School, December 2001, for helping to spark this perspective on coordination. Thanks in particular to Keith Bahde for a fruitful collaboration on the concept of boundary spanning.

NOTE

[1]   This section draws upon Bahde & Gittell, 2002.

Chapter 19

Finding Positive Meaning in Work

Amy Wrzesniewski

Basically, the reason I keep at it ... is that my wife is from this area, she is very happy to be here, and this is the only firm of its type here that does the kind of law that I have now trained for and worked in over the last seven years of my life. It would be very difficult to break out ... so I find myself basically saying, "Well, as long as I can do this to keep the family together, that's what I'm going to do." ...It's a deal with the devil.... I'm not a happy guy.

Corporate Securities Lawyer
(Bowe, Bowe, & Streeter, 2000: 415)

I don't see myself ever stopping [working] completely.... I like it too much. It's very satisfying. I mean, this is an art form, for one thing. It's a tremendous art.... I did a duck for a guy the other day ... and when he came and picked it up he almost started crying because it looked so nice. He was just so happy ... and that makes me feel good, that he thought I'd done a great job. Self-satisfaction is a big deal in any job. It's a big deal in life.

Taxidermist (Bowe, Bowe, & Streeter, 2000: 95)

Because work dominates our psyches and social lives, we must attempt to understand the forces it generates, shaping society and channeling individual behavior.

Frederick Gamst

As demonstrated by the quotes above, work can be a source of pain, drudgery, and boredom, or a source of joy, energy, and fulfillment, or a complex mix of all of these elements. That work plays *some* significant role in nearly everyone's life is clear. Whether work has a starring role, is a bit player, or is the hero or villain in one's life largely depends on the dynamic interplay between the individual, the organization, and the work itself.

In this chapter, I take up the call issued above by Gamst to explore the reasons work plays such varied roles in people's lives, and offer a proactive perspective on work that creates possibilities for finding deeper meaning in work. As well, I describe the benefits of finding meaning in work for individuals, workgroups, and organizations. My perspective on meaning and work assumes that it is not so much the *kind* of work that matters as it is the *relationship* to the work (e.g., Is it just a job, or something that is inherently important?), which creates possibility for individuals and organizations. A view of the experience of work that carefully considers the ways in which people come to view their work as more meaningful, satisfying, and necessary for the functioning of their organizations and of the wider world is thus complementary to the positive organizational scholarship (POS) perspective on organizational life and its possibilities. However, while the effects of finding deeper meaning in work may intuitively seem unilaterally positive, I explore both the positive outcomes and the surprising potential drawbacks to the pursuit of meaning in work.

A NOTE ON THE MEANING OF WORK

The concept of work meanings is one that is often studied (Colby, Sippola, & Phelps, 2002; Chapter 20 in this volume) but not as often defined. The meaning of work, and, for the purposes of this volume, positive meanings of work, are often left to the imagination of the reader, or to the interpretation of the research respondent. For example, respondents in a recent study on work meanings reported that they saw the following kinds of meaning in their work: contributing to the economic maintenance of one's family, the job as allowing one to have a positive impact on the organization, work as self-expression (among others) (Colby, Sippola, & Phelps, 2002). In this volume, Pratt and Ashforth define meaning as a subjective kind of sense that people make of their work. Other scholars define meaning differently; in the research area of positive psychology, positive meaning is defined as the connection between two different entities or things that create a nonphysical reality accessible to humans (Baumeister & Vohs, 2002).

More specifically, scholars note that meaning is a tool used by individuals for imposing stability on life (Baumeister & Vohs, 2002). As a work life (or any domain of life) unfolds, individuals strive to fulfill needs for purpose, values, efficacy, and self-worth (Baumeister, 1991). While the shape of the elements that satisfy those needs may differ (e.g., making money, helping others, doing religious work), the basic tenet remains that people everywhere need to find some way of interpreting the deeper purpose, or meaning, of what they do. In this chapter, I make the argument that the domain of work is a rich area for inquiry about the different kinds of meanings that get created around work. As well, the kinds of meaning people derive from their work have implications for a POS perspective on work and organizations.

DETERMINANTS OF THE MEANING OF WORK

For most adults, work represents nearly half of waking life (Wrzesniewski, McCauley, Rozin, & Schwartz, 1997). The majority of us must work to support ourselves and our families, making work a necessity. What is striking to scholars of work is that this compulsory domain of life represents such a range of experience, from a distasteful necessity to a source of joy. In their efforts to determine the sources of such varied experience, scholars of work have historically focused their efforts on finding either individual determinants of the experience of work (Dubin, 1956; Lodahl & Kejner, 1965; Roberson, 1990) such as expectations or values, or external characteristics of the job itself (Griffin, 1987; Hackman & Oldham, 1976, 1980), such as work tasks or social interaction at work. A brief tour through the research history of the concept of work meaning is helpful in understanding the approaches that have been taken to understanding how people relate to their work.

In their pursuit of measuring the meaning of work, researchers have created a number of constructs, including work centrality (Dubin, 1956; MOW, 1987), work commitment (Loscocco, 1989), job involvement (Lodahl & Kejner, 1965), work involvement (Kanungo, 1982), intrinsic/extrinsic motivation (Kanungo, 1981; Kanungo & Hartwick, 1987; Roberson, 1990), and work values (Nord, Brief, Atieh, & Doherty, 1990). Work centrality is typically defined in terms of how relatively important work is in comparison with other domains of life, like leisure and family (Dubin, 1956), while work commitment is defined as "the relative importance work has to people's sense of self" (Loscocco, 1989: 370). Kanungo (1982: 342) defines job involvement as attachment to work, while *work* involvement denotes a normative belief about the importance of work in life. While these constructs aim to identify the relative salience of work in life, others have focused on the nature of the importance of work itself.

Herzberg, Mausner, and Snyderman (1959) were the first to identify the intrinsic and extrinsic motivations for working. In their original model, intrinsic motivations for working included opportunities for advancement, achievement, and recognition, while more recent definitions have focused on interesting work, creativity, and fulfillment (Kanungo & Hartwick, 1987). Extrinsic motivations for working include pay, working conditions, and job security. The research that has followed this model of work motivation has supported the notion that different elements of work have the ability to motivate and challenge individuals (Amabile, Hill, Hennessey, & Tighe, 1994).

All of the constructs above share in common their relation either to the importance or salience of work in the context of the rest of life, or to the specific aims, goals, or reasons people have for working. For decades, they have been used to chart the importance of work in life, and the reasons work matters to us. While research in the 1950s showed that most people are likely to agree that they would continue with their work without pay if they had all the money they would need (Morse & Weiss, 1955), this trend decreased in later decades (Vecchio, 1980). However, the most recent evidence suggests that money is losing its power as a central motivator, in part because the general population is realizing, in greater numbers, that above a minimum level necessary for survival, money adds little to their subjective well-being (Seligman, 2002). In an age in which people have come to define themselves and be socially defined by their work (Casey, 1995), understanding alternative sources of meaning and motivation in work becomes a central aim of scholars of work. From a POS perspective (see Chapters 1 and 20), the existence of alternative sources of meaning in work is a natural outgrowth of organizational systems that value human thriving, contribution to the greater good, and a celebration of human agency in the workplace to make improvements to the organization.

The presence of alternative meanings of work in life raises the question of how the meaning of work is shaped, and what effects it has in people's lives. The ongoing debate in the literature over whether the meaning of work is determined internally (i.e., within the individual) or externally (i.e., by the job and wider environment) has yielded results that support both views. According to the latter perspective, the jobs people have exert strong influences on their work commitment (Kohn et al., 1983). In this view, it is the job features that largely determine the nature of our attachment to the job. Such a view is aligned with a job characteristics perspective of the experience of work (Oldham & Hackman, 1981).

In contrast, the first perspective differs from a job-characteristics approach to the experience of work by claiming that individual personalities determine work commitment (Alderfer, 1972; Staw, Bell, & Clausen, 1986). According to this view, individual needs, demographic factors, and social-class background affect commitment to work. Loscocco (1989) and others have found that both external and internal influences affect work commitment. Thus, people experience and make meaning of their work as a result of the interaction of both forces.

Both perspectives on the meaning of work have proven valuable in providing insight into the lived experience of work in organizations. They suggest a dynamic view in which both the individual and the system act together to determine the types of meaning that will be experienced. This is consistent with perspectives on meaning that define the source of all meaning as existing in the interplay between two different entities to create a new reality (Baumeister & Vohs, 2002). However, both perspectives have left space for a third perspective, on *what* constitutes the experience of work—one that is not predetermined by individual attributes or the design of the job, but instead is open to the ways in which people shape their jobs to fit their own unique orientation toward the domain of work.

AN ALTERNATIVE PERSPECTIVE ON THE MEANING OF WORK

This third perspective on the meaning of work constitutes the main focus of this chapter. It is presented with the intention of orienting readers who are new to the fields of POS and positive psychology to a different theory of the meaning of work. The general assumption on which this research is based is that people can derive different kinds of meaning from most any job or occupation. This work is based on recent research on the meaning of work that suggests that people tend to frame their relationship to work in different ways. More specifically, sociologists (Bellah et al., 1985) and psychologists (Baumeister, 1991; Schwartz, 1986, 1994; Wrzesniewski, McCauley, Rozin, & Schwartz, 1997) have argued for a tripartite model of people's orientations to their work. These general orientations help to determine our thoughts, feelings, and behaviors toward work. The orientations offer a window into the ways in which people see their work, and, more importantly, how they craft their jobs (Wrzesniewski & Dutton, 2001) in order to realize their orientations toward the work. As such, work orientation can be thought of as the interplay between the person and the work.

Bellah and his colleagues (1985; see also Schwartz, 1986, 1994) describe three dominant orientations toward work that reflect the experience of work in the United States. In the first work orientation, people view work as a Job, focusing on the material benefits of work to the relative exclusion of other kinds of meaning and fulfillment. The work is simply a means to a financial end that allows people to enjoy their time away from work. Usually, the interests and ambitions of those with Jobs are expressed outside of the domain of work (Wrzesniewski, McCauley, Rozin, & Schwartz, 1997) and involve hobbies and other interests. In contrast, those with Career orientations work for the rewards that accompany advancement through an organizational or occupational structure. For those with Careers, the increased pay, prestige, and status that come with promotion and advancement are a dominant focus in their work. Advancement brings higher self-esteem, increased power, and higher social standing (Bellah et al., 1985: 66). Finally, those with Calling orientations work not for financial rewards or for advancement, but for the fulfillment that doing the work brings. In Callings, the work is an end in itself, and is usually associated with the belief that the work contributes to the greater good and makes the world a better place.

Traditionally, Callings have meant being "called" by God to do morally and socially significant work (Weber, 1958, 1963), but in modern times they have lost their religious connection and retained a focus on doing work that makes a contribution to the wider world (Davidson & Caddell, 1994). It is necessary to note, however, that it is the *individual doing the work* who defines for him- or her-self whether the work does contribute to making the world a better place. For example, a schoolteacher who views the work as a Job and is simply interested in making a good income does not have a Calling, while a garbage collector who sees the work as making the world a cleaner, healthier place could have a Calling.

In a study designed to determine how much of a role work orientations actually played in people's work lives, Wrzesniewski, McCauley, Rozin, and Schwartz (1997) operationalized the Job, Career, and Calling orientations, created measures of each, and surveyed 196 people from a variety of occupations. The measures took two forms: one, a set of three paragraphs that described a prototypical Job, Career, and Calling person; and two, a set of eighteen items that were designed to reflect the thoughts, feelings, and behaviors that were likely to accompany each work orientation. For example, it was expected that those with Job orientations would report that work was largely a way to make a living, and that they were not particularly excited about their work. For those with Career orientations, it was expected that work would be approached with a focus on promotions and advancement. Finally, it was expected that those with Callings would report that work was an end in itself, as opposed to a means to some other end, and that they would continue to work without pay if financially secure. In addition, those with Callings were expected to report that their work contributed to making the world a better place.

In this first study, participants were surprisingly unambiguous in reporting that they experienced their work as Job, Career, or Calling. The sample was nearly evenly divided into thirds, with each third feeling that their work was a Job, Career, or Calling. What was more intriguing was that within the sample, there was a group of twenty-four administrative assistants who worked in the same organization, with similar levels of pay, education, and tenure. In this subsample, as in the full sample, each work orientation was represented by a third of the administrative assistants such that they were nearly evenly divided into the three work orientations. This suggests that even in the same job done in the same organization, there are significant differences in how people make meaning of their work.

Overall, it appears that those with Calling orientations have a stronger and more rewarding relationship to their work, which is associated with spending more time at work, and gaining more enjoyment and satisfaction from it (Wrzesniewski, McCauley, Rozin, & Schwartz, 1997). While this initial study was not longitudinal, thus making it impossible to posit causal relationships (i.e., Does the experience of the work produce the orientation, or does the orientation shape the experience of the work?), later longitudinal research revealed that those with Calling orientations sought out work that fulfilled their need for meaning in this domain (Wrzesniewski, 1999). This finding supports the view that individuals are proactive in seeking out, and, as will be described below, shaping their work so that it has meaning and significance in their lives (Wrzesniewski & Dutton, 2001).

The three work orientations reflect different types of relationships to work. These relationships are likely to vary in their intrinsic and instrumental focus and in their implications for the other domains of life. Those with Jobs are not likely to have a deep connection with their work, as the work primarily represents a means to an end. Those with Careers may be more deeply engaged with their work, as the work is a source of achievement in the rewards, positions, and power it yields. Only for those with Callings is work a wholly enriching and meaningful activity. In our pursuit to understand how people may find deeper meaning in their work, it is this group for whom work is a Calling that is worthy of deeper study.

The findings described above raise the question of how people with Callings come to have them, and how others without Callings may find theirs. One factor that seems to contribute to a Calling orientation is good psychological health. Traits such as optimism (Gillham, Shatte, Reivich, & Seligman, 2001), mastery (Rawsthorne & Elliott, 1999), and conscientiousness (McCrae & Costa, 1999) may be associated with having a Calling. But do people with these traits tend to enter a line of work they view as a Calling, or is any line of work likely to be viewed as a Calling? Staw, Bell, and Clausen (1986) have shown that job attitudes are highly stable over time and over different kinds of jobs (see also Arvey, Bouchard, Segal, & Abraham, 1989, for evidence of a heritable component to job attitudes). Thus, it may be that a Calling orientation is a portable benefit of those who tend to have a generally more positive outlook on life. However, this view of work orientation is rather static, and suggests that those with Callings are predisposed to view any kind of work positively, and are a select group, one that cannot be joined by others who view their work differently.

THE CREATION OF MEANING IN WORK

Earlier, I described research findings that suggest that in all kinds of jobs, people can view the work as a Job, a Career, or a Calling. Thus it is not the design of the work itself that seems to determine the experience of the work. This promising possibility raises the question of how people with Callings may do their work differently in ways that allow them to experience it as a source of joy and meaning in their lives. Recent research on the practice of "job crafting" (Wrzesniewski & Dutton, 2001) by individuals offers insight into how people with different orientations toward their work may actually structure their work differently in ways that help to create or undermine meaning in work.

Job crafting is defined as "the physical and cognitive changes individuals make in the task or relational boundaries of their work. Thus, job crafting is an action, and those who undertake it are job crafters; making job crafting both a verb and a noun" (Wrzesniewski & Dutton, 2001: 179). By crafting their jobs, people are able to change the way they approach the tasks in their work, increase or decrease the number and kinds of tasks they do as part of their job, and change the number and nature of the relationships they have with others they encounter in their work. For example, we can imagine someone who cleans offices for a living who works within the job description, and leaves at the end of the shift, satisfied that the offices are clean, the trash is emptied, and the floors are vacuumed.

However, we can also imagine someone doing the same job who, in addition to tackling all of the tasks in the job description, is also attuned to the state of the offices she cleans. This cleaner, let us call her Maria, has chosen to focus on knowing when people are away on vacations or sick leave, and takes over the care of their office plants while they are gone. In addition, she takes plants that are discarded by members of the organization and nurses them back to health, repotting them and placing them in other offices to brighten up the space.

While this may seem to be a rather small instance of extra-role behavior, it is actually a powerful example of job crafting in action. The attention to and care of the plants represents the addition of other tasks to her job, but changes too the way in which she cleans offices, by requiring her to be aware of which offices have dying plants, which offices could benefit from new plants, and proactively handling these movements of the plants to brighten all of the offices.

In addition to changing the task boundary of her job, Maria is also changing the relational boundary of her job by constructing her relationship with members of the organization as both cleaner and decorator, and procurer of flowers and plants when she realizes that someone is going through a hard time or has been working long hours for many days in a row. By engaging in this different form of relationship with members of the organization, Maria becomes a more integral part of the organizational community, and in turn views her own role as caretaker of the organization's space *and* members. Clearly, the meaning of the work that Maria does is different for her than for the cleaner who stays within tighter task and relational boundaries.

In job crafting, new possibilities open for the meaning of work by allowing for the creation of meaning in any job by the way in which it is constructed by the individual. Through job crafting, one can realize a Calling orientation by reshaping the task and relational boundaries of the job in ways that allow one to view the work as making a bigger contribution to the wider world. Through this proactive perspective on the creation of meaning in work we can see the impact of the third perspective described earlier in this chapter. This perspective suggests the possibilities that arise from viewing the meaning of work as a dynamic interplay between the individual and the work, and opens the relationship between the person and the work to include the organization as well (see Chapter 20).

While the job-crafting perspective concentrates on the things people do to change the boundaries of their jobs, it also offers an organizational lens on the meaning of work. In the example above, Maria is likely to find her actions to be noticed and responded to, whether they be celebrated, punished, or altered in some way. As well, the organizational setting in which she finds herself is more or less likely to invite the possibility of engaging in job crafting (see Chapter 20). Thus, while crafting is most often observed on the individual level, it grows from an organizational context, and expresses itself within a community that will respond to crafting actions in ways that can create more positive possibilities in the work (which is the aim of the POS perspective) or can inhibit such actions from occurring in the future.

WORK AS A CALLING: BENEFITS, COSTS, AND CORRELATES

In this section, the effects of a Calling orientation for the individual, workgroup, and organization are examined. As well, the contrasts between those with Callings and those with Careers in a number of different work domains are considered. By combining research findings on the role of work orientation at each level of organizational life, a more comprehensive picture emerges of the profound effects of different meanings of work.

Individual Effects

For the individual, a Calling orientation toward work has behavioral, attitudinal, and emotional effects that differ from those experienced by people with Jobs or Careers. For example, people with Callings tend to put more time in at work (Wrzesniewski, McCauley, Rozin, & Schwartz, 1997), whether or not this time is compensated. As well, those with Callings report higher job and life satisfaction than those with Jobs or Careers (Wrzesniewski, McCauley, Rozin, & Schwartz, 1997). They also derive more satisfaction from the domain of work than the domain of leisure and hobbies. While this may seem to paint a bleak picture for those with Jobs and Careers, it may only mean that the sources of meaning and satisfaction differ for these groups. People with Jobs and Careers rank the satisfaction they get from their leisure time (i.e., hobbies and friends) as higher than the satisfaction they get from work. The differences between those with Callings and the other two groups are significant on each dimension. Clearly, for those with Callings, work is one's main focus, whereas for those with Jobs and Careers, the deeper satisfactions are found in leisure or in relationships outside of the workplace.

Work Group Effects

The role of work orientation in work group functioning is another area in which work meanings can have profound effects on groups and organizations. In a study designed to assess the role of work orientation in the context of work groups, I sought to examine the general and combinatory effects of work orientation on the group level.[1] A survey that included the measures of work orientation described earlier, in addition to measures of work group functioning, was given to 425 respondents. Each respondent was part of a real work group in an organization, and each group met the criteria for an interdependent team (Hackman, 1990). A total of ninety-four complete work groups were represented in the data, from organizations ranging from travel agencies to investment banking teams.

The picture that emerged from the data supported the notion that work orientation is related to the manner in which individuals approach their work. Individual respondents with Calling orientations toward their work reported higher job satisfaction ($r=0.63$, $p < 0.0001$), confirming findings from earlier studies of work orientation. However, the focus of this study was on the effects of work orientation to work group functioning. In order to assess group-level outcomes, measures of team iden-tification (Bhattacharya, 2001), group process (Taylor & Bowers, 1972), faith and trust in management (Cook & Wall, 1980), conflict, and team commitment (Mowday, Steers, & Porter, 1979) were included. After a check was done to ensure that members of the groups were largely in agreement about these outcome variables (i.e., the variance within groups was less than variance between groups, signifying agreement among group members),[2] the outcome variables were aggregated at the group level.

The results paint a compelling picture. In workgroups in which the proportion of members with Calling orientations is higher, groups report stronger overall identification with the team ($r=0.31$, $p < 0.002$), less conflict ($r = -0.24$, $p < 0.02$), more faith and trust in management ($r=0.34$, $p < 0.001$), more commitment to the team itself ($r=0.47$, $p < 0.0001$), and healthier group process (e.g., more communication, less conflict) ($r=0.42$, $p < 0.0001$). Clearly, having more group members with Callings yields benefits for *all* members of the group. In addition to playing a positive role in group-level outcomes, individual members of these Calling-majority groups report more satisfaction with their coworkers ($r=0.36$, $p < 0.0001$) and with the work itself ($r=0.56$, $p < 0.0001$).

Surprisingly, the results are exactly the opposite for workgroups with a majority of Career-oriented members. These groups report weaker identification with the team ($r = -0.36$, $p < 0.0001$), more conflict ($r=0.30$, $p < 0.003$), less commitment to the team itself ($r = -0.49$, $p < 0.0001$), and more negative group process ($r = -0.51$, $p < 0.0001$). In this case, when members of the team have Careers, their interaction with group members appears to leave much to be desired. The data on satisfaction support this; members of Career-majority groups report less satisfaction with their coworkers ($r = -0.30$, $p < 0.003$) and with the work itself ($r = -.43$, $p < 0.0001$). While the data do not address the performance levels of the groups, it seems likely that groups composed of less happy, more individually focused members would be less likely to exceed performance expectations.

Organizational Effects

The benefits of Calling orientations to organizations are promising. In a study of work orientation in the nursing profession, Wrzesniewski and Landman (2000) attempted to assess performance as an outcome. However, only a subset of participants consented to the release of their performance data; all had Callings, and all were at the ceiling of top performance in the organization. This example is only suggestive, of course, but seems to point to the likelihood that those with Callings may be top performers in their organizations. More evidence comes from the strong relationship between job satisfaction and having a Calling. In a definitive meta-analysis designed to help settle the debate over whether or not job satisfaction and job performance are linked, Judge, Thoresen, Bono, and Patton (2001) determined that the mean true correlation between job satisfaction and performance was 0.30. Thus, one can indirectly make the argument that if Calling orientations are linked to high job satisfaction, and job satisfaction is linked to work performance, then it is likely that the best performers in organizations tend to see their work as a Calling.

IMPLICATIONS AND CONCLUSION

In all, the results presented here combine to suggest a powerful and optimistic set of points about the meaning of work. First, it appears that the way in which people see their work is highly predictive of their own individual thriving, and has positive implications for the groups and organizations of which they find themselves a part. In particular, people with Calling orientations toward their work engage with the domain of work in qualitatively different ways than those who have Jobs or Careers. What is perhaps most exciting about this finding is that it is found across different kinds of jobs and occupations (Wrzesniewski, McCauley, Rozin, & Schwartz, 1997). Thus, from a POS perspective, it raises additional questions for research that are likely to bear fruit for understanding what can make work and organizations more positive life domains. For example, this research raises additional questions about how managers and coworkers can help to create social and organizational contexts in which Callings can be expressed, and in which job crafting in service of finding deeper meaning in work is encouraged. It also suggests that the available frames we have for the meaning of work could be expanded to create the potential for deeper meaning in nearly any job.

One potential area for inquiry is the dynamic interplay between organizational context and individual behavior. In this chapter, I have made the argument that people take proactive positions in creating meaning in their work, and have suggested that organizational contexts can be more or less supportive of these initiatives. Systematic study of the differences between more and less encouraging organizational contexts in the expression of jobcrafting behaviors and the presence of Calling-oriented employees would be a valuable direction for future research. From a POS perspective, the kinds of organizational structures and cultures that celebrate and welcome job crafting in service of finding deeper meaning in work should be identified and studied.

Second, while some research evidence supports the notion that these orientations are traitlike and stable, an alternative is presented here that opens the door to the possibility of deeper positive meaning in work for people doing all kinds of different work. By crafting the task and relational boundaries of their jobs, employees in most any job have the opportunity to recast their job as it is objectively described (Oldham & Hackman, 1981) into work that is freed from any one static set of descriptors. This possibility raises research questions that open new streams of research, including inquiries into *who* engages in crafting and *when* (Zhou & George, 2001), as well as what effects such behavior has on others in the organization. Might an active job crafter spark positive, proactive action among other employees? Or is job crafting a personal endeavor? The group-level data summarized earlier suggest that the approach taken to one's work can have powerful and positive effects on interdependent others.

Finally, the work described in this chapter contributes to an alternative view of individuals and their work. It takes as its starting point the rich tradition of research in job attitudes and work meanings, and builds upon them to suggest how the relationships forged between individuals and their work helps to recast the domain of work in a variety of ways. Ultimately, it celebrates the benefits of proactively finding deeper meaning in work in ways that enable individuals to decide for themselves what role to cast work into on the stage of their lives.

NOTES

[1]	I gratefully acknowledge the research assistance of Jessica Scheidt in compiling and entering these study data.
[2]	All outcome variables were run through a one-way ANOVA analysis. In each case, the F values were significant at the 0.0001 level.

Chapter 20

Fostering Meaningfulness in Working and at Work

Michael G. Pratt and Blake E. Ashforth

One's work is believed to provide one with many things: economic gain, social status, a sense of belonging, and even a sense of purpose or meaning (see ˇ Sverko & Vizek-Vidoviæ, 1995, for a review).[1] Work as a source of meaning has been of particular interest to organizational scholars and practitioners for some time, as it is commonly believed that finding meaning within one's place of work is expected and that "meaningful work" is as important as pay and security—and perhaps more so (O'Brien, 1992). Interest in this area has also been fueled by the assumption that meaningful work influences various job and organizational attitudes, as well as motivation and performance (Roberson, 1990). One of the most common outcomes linked to meaningful work is satisfaction with one's job. Given that nearly half of U.S. workers have recently reported being unhappy with their work (*USA Today,* 2002), research that examines how work and working can be made more meaningful remains timely.

As with other authors in this volume, we see meaningful work (and other forms of positive meaning)[2] as central to positive organizations. Although research on the salutary effects of meaningfulness has been sparse, it does suggest that a sense of meaningfulness—whether from work or other social domains—is associated with (and may even be a defining feature of) psychological and even physical health (e.g., Baumeister, 1991; Dunn, 1996; Ryff & Singer, 1998a, 1998b; Treadgold, 1999). In this chapter, we examine organizational practices that foster workers' experience of "meaningfulness" both in and at work.

Like Isaac Newton, if we can advance understanding about meaningfulness in the workplace, it will be because we have "stood on the shoulders of giants." There has been considerable research on the "meaning of work" that we build upon but, due to space constraints, cannot fully explore. Reviews of this literature (e.g., ˇ Sverko & Vizek-Vidoviæ, 1995) suggest that research has focused primarily on work values (see also Nord, Brief, Atieh, & Doherty, 1990; O'Brien, 1992), work involvement/salience/centrality (see also Harpaz & Fu, 2002; MOW International Research Team, 1987), work orientation (Wrzesniewski, Mc-

Cauley, Rozin, & Schwartz, 1997), as well as the causes and consequences of work alienation and the absence of work (Brief & Nord, 1990; Gill, 1999). As such, this literature has centered on, respectively, what goals one attempts to attain at work; how important work is vis-à-vis other areas of one's life; whether one sees work as a job, career, or calling; and how one copes when work is considered meaningless or when one is not working. Taken together, this research ultimately focuses on individuals' attitudes toward and perceptions of work. Still other research has attempted to embed the meaning of work in how societies and religious belief systems have viewed human labor—such as exploring work as a means of attaining salvation (see Tausky, 1995, for a review).

Our work builds upon, but differs, from these perspectives in three ways: (1) we delineate meaningfulness *in* working and meaningfulness *at* work—a distinction confounded in most treatments of "meaning of work"; (2) we focus on organizational practices that attempt to foster meaningfulness, rather than focusing on the resulting member attitudes;[3] and (3) we accord the individual's identity a mediating role in determining what practices are construed to be meaningful. We begin by defining what we mean by "meaningfulness" and linking this term to the concept of identity. We then develop a typology of organizational practices that infuse meaningfulness. We close with some speculations about the intersection of meaningfulness in working and meaningfulness at work.

MEANING AND MEANINGFULNESS IN THE WORKPLACE

Like Frankl (1962) and many others, we assume that individuals actively desire and seek meaningfulness in their lives and work. By "meaningful," we mean that the work and/or its context are perceived by its practitioners to be, at minimum, purposeful and significant (see also Feldt, Kinnunen, & Mauno, 2000; Hackman & Oldham, 1980; Shamir, 1991; Spreitzer, 1995; Wong, 1998). This perception may derive from the intrinsic qualities of the work itself, the goals, values, and beliefs that the work is thought to serve, or the organizational community within which the work is embedded. It is important to note that in the case of goals, meaningfulness is not necessarily dependent on the goals actually being realized: the pursuit of valued goals such as zero defects and complete customer satisfaction may by itself foster a sense of purpose (Baumeister, 1991; Emmons, 1999).

However, meaningfulness is not a fixed property of a job (e.g., teaching=helping others) or organization (e.g., Rubbermaid=ingenuity), something one finds as if on an Easter egg hunt. Rather, meaningfulness is necessarily subjective. And because individuals—and the social groups within which they are embedded—differ widely, the meaning attached to a particular piece of work and work setting may vary radically not only across individuals but also across historical and physical contexts. We doubt that there are any universal meanings in the sense that everyone sees a given job as meaningful for the same reasons; however, there are likely to be (1) a limited number of meaning archetypes in a given society that individuals draw from, and (2) strong similarities in the *processes* by which meaningfulness is created.

We view the process of meaning creation as a type of sensemaking. Sensemaking has been defined as the attribution of significance to some target or stimulus (e.g., work) by placing it into an existing or emerging cognitive framework (Starbuck & Milliken, 1988). Thus, when one assigns a social or other stimulus to a category, one has "made sense of" the stimulus, giving it meaning. However, assigning meaning does not necessarily make something meaning*ful* in the sense we are using the term.

When something is meaningful, it helps answer the question, "Why am I here?" Thus, we view meaning(fulness)-making as a subset of sensemaking: it is sensemaking in the service of answering a broader existential question about the purpose of one's existence.

Sensemaking in organizational contexts is seldom a solitary exercise: meaningfulness tends to be socially constructed among individuals within work groups, departments, and so on (Weick, 1995). Through social information processing and social comparison processes, individuals tend to resolve the inherent equivocality of stimuli by triangulating on a limited set of meanings. The resulting consensus serves to "validate" the set: social speculation becomes social fact. As attested by research on so-called dirty work occupations (see Ashforth & Kreiner, 1999, for a review), one implication of the motivated and socially embedded desire and search for meaning is that *any* task, job, or organization can be imbued with meaningfulness. The desire spawns the reality.

Viewing meaning creation as a type of sensemaking has at least two implications for our discussion. First, partly because sensemaking is often a social activity, we argue that organizations can influence whether and how members interpret their work as meaningful

(Weick, 1995). As noted, our focus is on the practices that organizations use to facilitate meaning-making in and at work. Second, how one makes sense of the world is inexorably tied to one's identity (Ashforth, 2001; Pratt, 2000b; Weick, 1995). That is, one path to answering "Why am I here?"—and perhaps the major path in Western cultures—is to first answer "Who am I?" Like Guevara and Ord (1996), we argue that questions of "Who am I?" are at the heart of meaning creation. We suggest, therefore, that organizations can facilitate the creation of meaningful work by influencing those factors that positively influence worker identity.

FOSTERING MEANINGFULNESS VIA IDENTITY: "IN" VS. "OF"

Building on insights from identity theory (Stryker & Serpe, 1982) and social identity theory (Tajfel & Turner, 1979), we argue that identity is primarily influenced by what one does (e.g., one's roles) and by one's social groups/memberships. This bifurcation reflects the different foci taken by other authors in this book. Wrzeniewski, for example, discusses "what one does" as the main driver of positive meaning at work. Dutton and Heaphy, by contrast, focus more on the quality of connections one has with others. Guevara and Ord (1996)

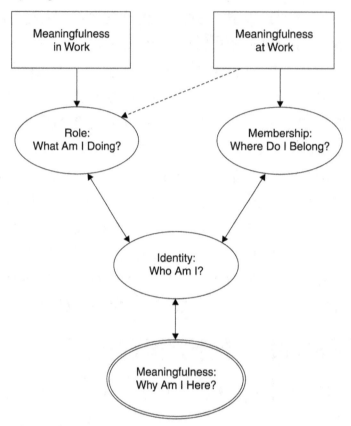

Figure 20.1
An Overview of Creating Meaningfulness in Working and at Work from an
Identity Perspective

suggest a similar division. They argue that identity is influenced by determining where we belong and how we relate to others (both of which are tied to group member-ship), as well as by issues of contribution (which are often bound to what one does). The relationships among roles (What am I doing?), membership (Where do I belong?), identity (Who am I?), and meaningfulness (Why am I here?) are summarized in Figure 20.1.

Three fundamental assumptions underlie "meaningfulness" from an identity perspective. First, because the "path" to meaningfulness is through identity, meaningfulness arises through an integration of identity with roles (e.g., work and tasks) and/or membership. As we discuss below, words such as "fit," "match," and "alignment" are often used to explain how and why members come to see their work and their organizations as meaningful. Second, the reciprocal arrows between the core questions in Figure 20.1 suggest that these various integrations are dynamic and negotiated: they are ongoing and may involve changes in how meaning seekers view their identities, membership, roles, and purpose. As Ryff and Singer (1998a: 8) argue, meaningfulness is "an ongoing, day-by-day, constantly unfolding phenomenon, not an end state that is once-and-for-all resolved." Third, because identities—as well as organizations and roles—are complex entities, integrations between or among "what we do," "where we belong" and "who we are" are rarely, if ever, an all-or-nothing proposition. That is, there will always be "pockets" of alignment and mis-alignments among them (see also Gardner, Csikszentmihalyi, & Damon, 2001). Of course, we do not believe that individuals must function in alignment all of the time. Individuals appear to be capable of working and living with considerable amounts of latent conflict, ambiguity, and ambivalence.

Linking what we do with who we are—and thus fostering meaningfulness—has a long tradition within theories of identity. For example, identity theory argues that who one is coalesces around the roles one plays (Stryker & Serpe, 1982); Markus (1977) contends that identity formation is linked to behaviors such that self-schemata form to help explain and organize domain specific (e.g., work) behavior; Gini (2000) argues that work helps create, express, and confirm one's self-conceptions; and Heise's affect control theory (1977: 164) maintains that situational and self definitions connote certain "fundamental sentiments" that one seeks to experience and thereby confirm through behavior. The upshot is that work, over time, tends to implicate one's sense of self such that behavior, cognition, and affect converge to validate that sense of self (Ashforth, 2001). Creating meaningfulness in working, therefore, involves tapping into desired identities by making the tasks one performs at work intrinsically motivating and purposeful. Although our discussion focuses on organizational practices that confer meaningfulness, it is important to remember that individuals are not passive respondents: individuals help create the meanings that express and confirm their desired sense of self.

Linking identity and meaningfulness with those with whom we surround ourselves also has a long intellectual history. Cooley's notion of a "looking-glass self" (1922), for example, suggests that our perceptions of how others see us influences how we see ourselves. More recently, social identity theory has discussed the importance of group categories and memberships in defining one's identity (see Pratt, 2001, for a review). Creating meaningfulness at work, therefore, involves changing the nature of one's organizational membership. One finds meaning not in what one does, but in whom one surrounds oneself with as part of organizational membership, and/or in the goals, values, and beliefs that the organization espouses.

A TYPOLOGY OF PRACTICES THAT INFUSE MEANINGFULNESS

Taken together, organizational practices can be assessed by the degree to which they help create meaningfulness by either enhancing the roles, tasks, and work that individuals perform, or enhancing the characteristics of group membership and/or attendant goals, values, and beliefs. Partitioning these two sets of practices into high and low categories gives the two-by-two model summarized in Figure 20.2. Practices believed to enrich only tasks are said to be "fostering meaningfulness in working," and those that enrich only membership characteristics are said to be "fostering meaningfulness at work." To this set we add "fostering worker alienation," whereby practices neither enrich work nor membership, and "fostering transcendence," whereby practices enrich both.

Figure 20.2
A Typology of Oraganizational Practices That Attempt to Foster Meaningfulness by Enriching Tasks and Membership

	Focus on Enriching Tasks and Roles	
	Low	High
Low	**Fostering Worker Alienation** *Meaningfulness in and at work comes solely from individual— not organizational—initiatives.*	**Fostering Meaningfulness in Working** *Meaningfulness comes from doing a specific type of work, not from where that work is done.*
High	**Fostering Meaningfulness at Work** *Meaningfulness comes from one's membership in the organization, not from what one does.*	**Fostering Transcendence** *Meaningfulness comes from both doing and being in the organization.*

Focus on Enriching Membership

Technically, only three of the four quadrants involve practices that infuse meaning. Because our focus is on how organizational practices attempt to foster meaningfulness, we do not focus on those that foster alienation. These practices, however, are akin to ones found in organizations described in Marxist treatments of worker alienation (e.g., Braverman, 1974). Such practices may result in workers feeling detached from their products and coworkers. However, it is important to remember that meaningfulness is socially constructed and therefore not simply a function of organizational practices. As noted, meaningfulness can be derived from any job or organization—thus workers in these organizations may not actually feel alienated. However, the onus for meaning-making in such organizations is on the worker and his or her coworkers.

General Practices for Infusing Meaning

The general logic underlying most of the organizational practices described below—especially those involving creating meaningfulness in and at work—is one of fit or alignment. For example, inherent in the discussion of fostering meaningfulness in working is the creation of some sort of personjob fit. Similarly, the logic of person-organization fit and similar constructs (e.g., person-culture, person-organization) often underlies discussions of fostering meaningfulness at work (see Kristof, 1996, for a review of various types of fit). To illustrate, as Kahn (1990) notes, work becomes meaningful when one's "preferred self" can be expressed

Figure 20.3
Organizational Practices That Foster Meaningfulness

through one's work and through one's membership in an organization. And several scholars argue that it is through achieving a type of work-identity integrity—or fit between doing and being—that helps make work more meaningful (Gini, 2000; Pratt, Rock, & Kaufmann, 2001; Wrzesniewski & Dutton, 2001). Finally, Gardner, Csikszentmihalyi, and Damon (2001) suggest that work that we refer to as involving "transcendence" involves the alignment of individuals, roles, and values. References to this fit or alignment logic may be either implicit or explicit in these practices. A nonexhaustive listing of these practices can be found in Figure 20.3.

As shown in Figure 20.3, there are some general practices that are central to creating meaningfulness at work, meaningfulness in working, and transcendence: recruitment, selection, and socialization. To illustrate, organizations typically use *recruitment* and *selection* processes to find individuals who are likely to have a good person-job or person-organization fit (Barber, 1998; Bowen, Ledford, & Nathan, 1991). Organizations may refine and maintain these alignments by engaging in training and, more broadly, *socialization* practices (Bauer, Morrison, & Callister, 1998; Saks & Ashforth, 1997). Socialization practices, especially those focused on getting workers to view the organization as self-referential (also known as identification management practices—Cheney, 1983; Pratt, 2000b) often go beyond a narrow focus on knowledge, skills, and abilities to affect newcomers' workplace identity, and the processes through which newcomers socially construct the meaning of their work and organization (Ashforth, 2001). For example, institutionalized socialization involves a relatively structured program where newcomers are exposed to a developmental sequence of activities under the tutelage of veterans (Jones, 1986). Ricks (1997) chronicles how, in eleven short weeks, the U.S. Marine Corps gradually shapes raw recruits into a disciplined team who regard themselves as elite soldiers—despite the fact that few are "washed out" during basic training.

And finally, to the degree that fostering transcendence involves fostering some sort of alignment among identity, role, and membership, we believe that recruitment, selection, and socialization may be useful in this regard as well.

While some practices can be used in all or most attempts to foster meaningfulness, others are more unique to a particular realm. That said, the lines in Figure 20.3 denote that the boundaries delineating the effects of these practices on creating meaningfulness are sometimes blurry. Given space constraints, we are unable to review all of the practices featured in Figure 20.3 in detail, nor the inter-relationships among them. Rather, we focus on some exemplary organizational practices that attempt to foster meaningfulness at work, meaningfulness in working, and transcendence.

Fostering Meaningfulness at Work

Organizations that focus only on enriching one's organizational membership—and not the work that one does—can be said to foster meaningfulness at work. Fostering meaningfulness at work may actually involve two sets of practices: those that focus on promoting the goals, values, and beliefs of the organization, and those that focus on changing the nature of the relationships among members. As implemented, however, these practices often accomplish both simultaneously: indoctrinating members into a particular set of beliefs often changes how members relate to each other and to nonmembers (Pratt, 2000a, 2000b). As noted in Figure 20.3, such practices include those that build *cultures* (O'Reilly, 1989; Trice & Beyer, 1993)—which may include comprehensive *ideologies* (Hartley, 1983; Pratt, 2000a)—as well as collective level *identities* (Albert & Whetten, 1985).

Fostering meaningfulness at work may also involve the practice of *visionary leadership.* Visionary leadership, often associated with *charismatic* or *transformational* leadership, creates "a general transcendent ideal that represents shared values" (Kirkpatrick & Locke, 1996: 37). While visions may include reference to individual roles (and thus may be indirectly related to creating meaningfulness in working), they are often articulated as idealistic, future-oriented, and organizationally based (and hence membership-based) goals (Conger & Kanungo, 1987). Visions, like cultures, ideologies, and collective identities, make membership within a particular organization special, enriching, and meaningful. They create such meaning by appealing to and resonating with members' identities (Shamir, House, & Arthur, 1993).

Organizations that exemplify creating meaningfulness at work are those that employ practices that build organizational communities. Building communities can—but does not necessarily need to—involve practices that are qualitatively different from those noted above. Designing mutually reinforcing sets of practices that emphasize a sense of caring and "oneness" with the organization may be enough to achieve a sense of community. However, we wish to emphasize two general sets of practices that appear to enhance community building: (1) creating family-like dynamics at work, and (2) emphasizing a mission focused on goals and values beyond simple profit.

Individuals have a need to belong, to be part of a community (Baumeister & Leary, 1995)—particularly in social domains, such as work, where they spend a significant amount of time and where interacting with people is a major part of the experience. Thus, one form of community building focuses on the organization as a collective of mutually caring people—a "family" of sorts, where respect, solidarity, and cohesion are relatively high. Creating family dynamics can occur through two primary means: making work more family-like, and recognizing and supporting members' family lives (Pratt & Rosa, in press). With regard to the former, Frost, Dutton, Worline, and Wilson (2000: 26) describe how organizations create an "emotional ecology where care and human connection are enabled or disabled." Such an ecology involves recognizing that beneath the work roles we occupy lie flesh-and-blood individuals struggling for meaningfulness through personal connection. Leaders may signal a caring orientation through myriad ways, such as by encouraging trust and openness, demonstrating personalized attention and humor, self-disclosing, displaying inclusiveness and compassion, tolerating honest mistakes, providing instrumental and expressive support, and engaging in social rituals—whether celebratory (e.g., role transitions, significant achievements) or commemorative (e.g., sending flowers to the funeral of an organizational member).

Practices may also blur the boundaries between work and family life by recognizing and affirming that members have a life outside of work. This may involve including family members at work functions, allowing members to spend critical time with family members (e.g., family leave, flex time, in-house daycare), and aiding families in need. For example, Brooker (2002) describes how Sandler O'Neill—a firm that lost 40 percent of its employees on September 11, 2001—sent at least one of the remaining partners to each funeral, continued to pay full salary, bonuses, and benefits to the families of the deceased, provided grief counseling, and set up a family center to help with the numbing logistics of the aftermath of the terrorist attacks. As noted earlier, meaningfulness at work can also be promoted through attention to the organizational mission and supporting culture. Missions and cultures that promote community tend to be focused on values that transcend economic survival and the creation of wealth. Good examples of community-building organizations are ones that strive to be socially responsible, such as "green" organizations that attract individuals who want to engage in "environmentally friendly" business tactics (e.g., The Body Shop). Other examples include organizations, such as Southwest Airlines (O'Reilly & Pfeffer, 1995) and JetBlue Airways (Gittell & O'Reilly, 2001), that have strong missions focusing on "service"—as well as fun. As one Southwest employee notes, "There is no deep, dark secret here. It's so simple. It's a cult. It's a religion with us" (O'Reilly & Pfeffer, 1995: 12). Perhaps the most famous example of an organization that attempts to create a community is the Walt Disney Company. This organization combines a strong culture bolstered by intensive selection and socialization practices, along with community outreach programs (Disney VoluntEARS), to help infuse the workplace with meaningfulness (http:// disn ey.go.com/corporate).

In sum, community-building practices create meaningfulness in two ways. First, by blurring boundaries between work and non-work life, communities allow members to invest and express more of who they are while at work, thus facilitating a sense of holism (see the discussion of transcendence below). Second, by including more of the individual in the organization, community-building practices allow members more opportunity for realizing similarity, creating deeper inter-personal bonds, and thus make one's membership more salient in one's life. An important qualification is that community-building efforts must not be covert attempts to create productivity and profit. Unfortunately, many organizations with alienating work environments routinely institute pallid initiatives to foster pseudocommunities (e.g., Ehrenreich, 2001). Not surprisingly, employees tend to view such initiatives with skepticism, which can easily metastasize over time into cynicism. Ironically, then, insincere community building can result in an even more alienating work environment.

Fostering Meaningfulness in Working

As noted in Figure 20.3, organizations may attempt to foster meaningfulness in working in many ways. For example, *job redesign* practices may allow members to more fully engage who they are in what they do by increasing the variety of skills used on the job, allowing members to complete a whole and identifiable piece of work, providing autonomy over what to do and when, and offering feedback to facilitate learning (Hackman & Oldham, 1980). *Employee involvement* practices may effectively empower individuals by sharing information, developing knowledge, rewarding skill acquisition, inviting participation, and so forth (Lawler, Mohrman, & Benson, 2001).[4] Indeed, job redesign and employee involvement may foster "flow experiences" that dissolve barriers between self and work, and allow individuals "the full expression of what is best in us" (Gardner, Csikszentmihalyi, & Damon, 2001: 5).

Of course, practices such as job redesign and employee involvement only lead to meaningfulness when employees are given the opportunities and resources to actually perform their work. Thus, we suggest that *pathgoal leadership* may enhance the aforementioned practices by clarifying links between effort and performance and by removing obstacles to performance (House, 1997). The literatures on workplace hassles and frustration suggest that such performance obstacles can erode the meaningfulness of even the most inspiring of jobs (e.g., Fox & Spector, 1999; Zohar, 1999).

We believe that practices that *best* typify meaningfulness in working are those that *nurture callings.* When one's work is a calling, it is seen as "socially valuable—an end in itself—involving activities that may, but need not be, pleasurable" (Wrzesniewski, McCauley, Rozin, & Schwartz, 1997: 22). Callings have also been associated with expressing one's "authentic self" in what one does. As Furey (1997: 133) argues, when you answer your calling, "you become the person that only you can be." As such, callings involve role, identity, and meaningfulness (see Figure 20.1). As with our discussion of community building, nurturing callings does not necessarily entail qualitative differences from the practices mentioned above; rather, it may involve integrating several practices into a coherent *system* of motivation, leadership, and so on, such that the practices are mutually reinforcing (O'Reilly & Pfeffer, 2000).

In particular, callings arise where one perceives, in the language of job redesign, high *task significance* (Hackman & Oldham, 1980). Whereas the other design dimensions focus on the doing of work, task significance focuses on the perceived purpose of work. However, it is important to note that task significance in callings often translates into a purpose that serves a collective larger than just the organization, such as "society." As Wrzesniewski (2002: 232) notes, "Those with callings often feel that their work makes the world a better place."

Accordingly, organizations that can articulate how work serves a valued purpose can foster a sense of calling. As noted, meaningfulness at work practices may also promote meaningfulness in work. In particular, espousing edifying goals, values, and beliefs—as through such means described earlier as visionary leadership and culture-building—may help members frame what they do as a special part of who they are as an organization. As Emmons (1999) argues, seemingly small tasks can have tremendous personal meaning if they are framed as connecting to something larger. Wrzesniewski (2002: 233) offers two examples from the recruitment literature: "The teaching profession has drawn in applicants with employment ads stating, 'Your spreadsheets won't ever grow up to be doctors and lawyers.' The New York Police Department also cues the calling element of its mission with the motto, 'It's not just a job.'"

In a related vein, Davidson and Caddell (1994) found that individuals who worked with people rather than things were more likely to view their work as a calling. Witness this testament from a noted physician:

> Medicine is a service profession and traditionally requires of its members 24-hour service to people who are ill and frequently distraught, irrational, and hostile. It is this requirement of service given willingly and skillfully at all times and to all people that separates our profession from occupations that require an investment in education and apprenticeship equal to that of doctors. (Stead, 2001: 198–199)

Working with people may be most strongly linked to callings when it involves employing a wide variety of skills in contexts where the significance of one's work (e.g., helping people) is salient.

Davidson and Caddell (1994) also found that people with internalized religious frameworks were more likely to see their work as a calling than as a career. Thus, allowing the expression of spiritual concerns at work may facilitate task significance and thereby callings. Ashforth and Pratt (2002) discuss a range of work organizations that accommodate spirituality, from those that passively enable idiosyncratic expressions of spirituality to those that actively direct a corporate spirituality. For example, Tom's of Maine invites diverse spiritual leaders to speak to employees, and ServiceMaster's founder "dedicated his business to serving the Lord" (Gunther, 2001: 64).

To summarize, whereas building communities appears to work "horizontally" by forging connections between organizational members and within oneself, nurturing callings appears to work more "vertically." Enhancing the societal significance of one's tasks, working with (and helping) others, and being in touch with one's spiritual yearnings connects what one does and who one is with something that extends beyond any particular organization (see discussion of transcendence below). However, a cautionary note is warranted in nurturing callings. As suggested by Gouldner's (1957) distinction between cosmopolitans and locals, practices that focus on work as a calling may implicitly downplay the importance of context. Thus, graduate medical education centers train physicians not to work in a specific hospital, but to work in a wide variety of settings (various hospitals, private clinics, in the field, etc.). As such, organizations more interested in retaining their workers may be wary of employing practices that nurture callings without supplementing them with other practices designed to increase members' connection with the organization (e.g., building communities).

Fostering Transcendence

Drawing on the workplace spirituality literature, Ashforth and Pratt (2002) used the term *transcendence* to describe three loosely coupled phenomena: (1) a connection to something greater than oneself, such as a cause or other people (i.e., transcendence of self through attachment), (2) an integration of the various aspects of oneself, such as identities and traits, into a roughly coherent system (i.e., transcendence of fragmentation through holism and harmony), and (3) self-development, a realization of one's aspirations and potential (i.e., transcendence of the status quo and of limits through growth). Similar themes can be found in Gardner, Csikszentmihalyi, and Damon's (2001) description of "good work." They argue that work is most meaningful when it is a calling, when work values and practices are clear, when one's contribution to society is known, and when work reflects one's identity. Thus, we argue that organizations that foster transcendence provide strong linkages between who we are, what we do, and why we are here in this context, while simultaneously connecting workers to something greater than themselves, their tasks, or perhaps even the organization for which they work.

Unlike fostering meaningfulness at work and meaningfulness in working, extant research provides few examples of transcendent practices, and fewer of exemplary organizations. However, we suggest a few elements that may be critical to fostering transcendence; namely, facilitating particular thoughts (providing a cosmology) and feelings (promoting psychological safety), while at the same time implementing these practices so that one's actions and words align (enacting with integrity).

Providing a Cosmology

A *cosmology* is a comprehensive system of beliefs that connects and explains "who one is (identity) and who belongs (membership), what matters (values) and what is to be done (purpose), how and why things hang together ... to constitute 'reality' and 'truth' (ideology), [and] how one is embedded in that reality and connects to what matters and what is to be done (transcendence)" (Ashforth & Vaidyanath, 2002: 361). Cosmologies are akin to "visions on steroids," as they not only provide a roadmap for where the organization and its members are going, but also attempt to embed this journey in a larger, more ordered picture of the universe (Weick, 1993). They transcend the individual and the organization. Cosmologies may also be similar to the creation of "ideological fortresses," where traditional boundaries between work, family, friendships, and religion are dissolved and reordered in such a way that these life domains support, rather than compete, with each other (Pratt, 2000a). In the vernacular, cosmologies foster transcendence by helping individuals to find their place within the "grand scheme of things."

Promoting Psychological Safety

Transcendence as holism, harmony, and growth involves a willingness to leave one's old self-configuration for a new and uncertain one. And transcendence as connection to something greater involves a major change in how one frames events. Thus, the pursuit of transcendence requires a certain courage and even faith that the uncertain journey will be rewarded. Moreover, the transcendent ends of work—the ultimate purpose(s) for which the job and organization were created—may provide a beacon, but given equifinality and individual differences, the specific means for attaining the ends are often left unspecified. And cosmologies—as belief structures—are aimed primarily at what one thinks rather than what one feels or does.

Accordingly, for members to *experience* transcendence, they must *feel* safe to venture forth. Kahn (1990) argues that the presence of *psychological safety*—in conjunction with complex and creative work and the resources available to perform such work—is critical for experienced meaningfulness in and at work. Psychological safety involves "feeling able to show and employ one's self without fear of negative consequences, status, or career" (p. 709). Similarly, Fredrickson's broaden-and-build theory (see Chapter 11) maintains that psychological safety promotes positive emotions, which in turn broaden one's modes of thought and action and thereby builds personal and social resources. For example, joy "creates the urge to play, push the limits, and be creative." Psychological safety enables individuals to engage in "creative individualism" (Schein, 1970): to engage in trial and error, to find personal connection, and to both unlearn and relearn new behaviors (Edmondson, 1999; Pratt & Barnett, 1997). Thus, we argue that psychological safety provides a necessary lubricant for the personal change implied by transcendence.

Enacting with Integrity

For cosmologies to be believed—and thus to be effective—workers must trust that they are in place to promote self-growth and not just organizational growth. *Integrity* exists when members perceive congruence between leaders' words and deeds (also known as behavioral integrity; Simons, 2002). Enacting with integrity serves two purposes in the creation of transcendence. First, it provides role models. Grand statements about "truth" and "reality" are often difficult to translate into behaviors. But such links are necessary if cosmologies are to amount to more than pretty words displayed in corporate advertisements. When leaders act with integrity, they personify the cosmology and ground it in concrete actions, making the cosmology a "living" document. Leaders become visible exemplars of the cosmology, facilitating the learning of the cosmology by members. Indeed, members are more likely to identify with leaders who enact with integrity, thereby shaping their own self-conceptions.

Second, enacting with integrity builds trust in the system and among individuals. In this age of the disposable worker, individuals tend to act as "intuitive auditors" (Kramer, 1996), vigilant for—and sensitive to—signs of insincerity and duplicity. If cosmologies are simply paid lip service, it is likely that workers' innate suspicions will be confirmed and they will become jaded and alienated. Additionally, because trust and safety often coincide, enacting with integrity might facilitate the feelings of psychological safety discussed above (Edmondson, 1999). Thus, as with community building, it is critical for organizational leaders to enact the cosmology with integrity.

The three means of fostering transcendence reinforce each other. Psychological safety promotes action, enactment gives action form, and cosmologies give action purpose. Moreover, enacting with integrity affirms and reinforces a sense of trust and psychological safety within the organization, thereby validating the cosmology and protecting it from cynicism.

CONCLUSION

We have argued that organizations can facilitate meaningfulness both in and at work by enriching what we do and the physical and social context in which we do it. We conclude by discussing some implications of these attempts.

First, we should note that attempts to create meaningfulness in working might sometimes be at odds with creating meaningfulness at work. For example, the type of leadership necessary to implement these respective practices might be very different. We argued that visionary leadership is integral to creating meaning at work; however, more "path-goal" leadership that allows individuals to fully engage in tasks with little disruption might best serve some forms of creating meaningfulness in working. In addition, practices that enhance meaningfulness in working may detract somewhat from the meaningfulness at work by making individuals less willing to disengage from their tasks to participate in organizational community activities. Similarly, practices that enhance meaningfulness at work may at times distract individuals from their particular roles.

Second, creating meaningfulness at work may be generally more effective than creating meaningfulness in working. As we have noted, the meaningfulness-at-work practices may indirectly render the work itself more meaningful; and meaningfulness in working may involve a disengagement from the organization, as it is the task itself—not where it is done—that is of ultimate importance. Thus, if trade-offs between the two sets of practices are required, organizations may opt for those that make the workplace more meaningful.

Third, it is not clear that attempts to create "more meaningfulness" are always a good thing. For example, organizations might implement different initiatives in different parts of the organization. For instance, fostering meaningfulness in working in professional departments (e.g., legal) and upper levels of management—but fostering worker alienation in other areas (e.g., Hodson, 2001)—may cause resentment and conflict within organizations. It is also not clear that fostering transcendence is always better than just fostering meaningfulness in or at work. What is considered "transcendent" is a matter of opinion: meaningfulness is in the eye of the beholder. Also, transcendence may not be necessary. For individuals who seek meaningfulness outside of work and the workplace, such practices may have little impact. Thus, attempts to achieve transcendence may ultimately alienate some workers (Ashforth & Pratt, 2002).

Fourth, we viewed fostering transcendence as practices that are high on creating meaningfulness in working and meaningfulness at work. However, it is not clear whether transcendence is a simple aggregation of these practices or whether it involves some unique fusion or gestalt arising from the coexistence of these practices. It is also possible that promoting transcendence involves something qualitatively different. While we have offered a preliminary—and incomplete—view of what those practices should attain, further research is needed to discover the unique nature of the practices.

Fifth, although we have linked meaningfulness strongly to identity, there appears to be an *identity paradox* inherent in some of these practices. Furey (1997), for example, suggests that callings involve destroying one's existing identity while at the same time discovering and strengthening one's true self. Similarly, in transcendence, fulfillment of one's sense of self is both heightened and diminished by connecting to "truths" that are bigger than one's self and one's organization. Thus, while meaningfulness may derive from identity, the process of finding meaning may simultaneously alter that identity.

Finally, we reiterate the importance of integrity in this process. While we have said little about the motivation underlying the adoption of these practices, we believe that such motivation is critical. Whereas some organizations may consciously adopt them to enrich members' lives, others might mindlessly adopt them from others as a means of securing legitimacy with key stakeholders. Others may have even more sinister motives. Consequently, leaders and managers in these organizations might consciously or unconsciously transform these practices from those that encourage meaningfulness to ones that promote manipulation. We caution that such a manipulation is likely to backfire and lead to disillusionment, alienation, and turnover. Creating meaningfulness is not only a means of increasing performance—it is also an end in itself.

ACKNOWLEDGMENT

We are indebted to Erik Dane and Jane Dutton for their very helpful comments on an earlier draft of the paper.

NOTES

[1] We deliberately sidestep the thorny issue of what "work" means. In general, we view it as the activities one engages in when employed (whether salaried or nonsalaried) in an organization. However, we realize that definitions of work are quite varied in the literature (see England & Harpaz, 1990).

[2] By "positive meaning," we are referring to the fact that such meaning is beneficial in some way to the individual. We are not assuming that these meanings always lead to positive states, such as positive affect.

[3] We use the term "organizations" as a shorthand reference to organizational elites, such as managers and leaders, who have the power to implement these official or unofficial policies or practices. We do not wish to anthropomorphize the organization.

[4] Total quality management (TQM) practices sometimes adopt or subsume elements of employee involvement and job re-

design. However, it is important to note that "pure" TQM practices often eschew many traditional involvement practices (see Hackman & Wageman, 1995, and Lawler, 1994, for a more complete discussion), and often have different goals than fulfilling the needs of employees.

Chapter 21

Positive Organizational Network Analysis and Energizing Relationships

Wayne Baker, Rob Cross, and Melissa Wooten

Scientific innovations arise, argued Donald Campbell (1969), where two fields overlap like the scales of a fish. This chapter applies his fish-scale theory by overlapping positive organizational scholarship (POS) and organizational network analysis (ONA) to produce what we call positive organizational network analysis (PONA). Our approach combines POS's focus on resiliency and extraordinary performance with ONA's theories of social structure and analytical methods. By doing so, we hope to make contributions to both POS and ONA. First, our chapter suggests that POS can be expanded beyond its predominately psychological focus to include a *sociological* perspective. In particular, network analytic techniques permit scholars to move beyond individual- or dyadic-level views of positive organizational phenomenon and examine the structural context in which they exist. For example, how does a person's pattern of positive connections to others in an organization produce positive organizational phenomenon? Do positive aspects of organizational life tend to cluster in subgroups? Does the network structure of positive ties influence individual performance?

Second, our chapter suggests that a POS perspective can enrich network research. To date, social network theorists have focused on structural properties of networks and paid comparatively less attention to the kinds of relationships that bind a network together (Adler & Kwon, 2002; Monge & Contractor, 2000). Early on, the social network paradigm addressed both instrumental and expressive ties, as evidenced in sociometry, small-group research, and anthropology (Wasserman & Faust 1994: 10–13). For example, Jacob Moreno's first studies in what became sociometry mapped "liking" and "disliking" relationships among 500 girls in the New York State School for Girls, among 2,000 students in a New York public school, and other communities (*New York Times* 1933: L17). Since then, research on networks and important organizational outcomes has tended to emphasize instrumental ties, such as task-related communication, information flow, work flow, or material or monetary resources (e.g., Allen, 1977; Baker, 2000; Baum, 2002; Burt, 1992; Hansen, 1999; Uzzi, 1997). To be sure, researchers have continued to explore socioemotional and expressive relationships, such as friendship (Kilduff, 1992; Lincoln & Miller, 1979; Krackhardt, 1992), personal or career support (Ibarra, 1992; Higgins & Kram, 2001), and trust (Tsai & Ghoshal, 1998; Uzzi, 1997). However, such studies are often not linked to individual performance outcomes in organizations. In this chapter we set out to establish the link between positive relationships and individual performance, demonstrating how a POS perspective can enhance the explanatory power of network models.

We begin by reviewing the social network literature, tabulating evidence of the prevalence of data on positive ties in network studies. Next, we introduce findings from a series of research studies that examine the social structure and performance outcomes of "energizing relationships" (defined below) in organizational settings (Cross & Baker, 2003). Here we demonstrate how POS scholars can employ both visual and quantitative social network techniques to further understand the social network context of positive organizational phenomenon. Next, we offer quantitative evidence of the link between position in a network of positive ties and individual performance, controlling for traditional network and information-processing predictors of performance. By doing so, we demonstrate one way in which network research can be extended to account for positive dimensions of relationships. We conclude the chapter with suggestions for future research in this area.

POSITIVE TIES IN SOCIAL AND ORGANIZATIONAL NETWORK STUDIES

In our review of past work, we looked for evidence of "positive" ties in social network studies.[1] A tie between two people is "positive" if it conveys positive affect, such as liking or love, socioemotional support, material support, mentoring, and so forth. Positive ties vary in type, as well as strength or quality. Strength, for example, can range from mild liking to what Dutton and Heaphy call "High Quality Connections" (HQCs) (see Chapter 17). We also looked for evidence of "positive" outcomes stemming from positive networks, such as empowerment, high individual or organizational performance, improved well-being, and so forth. To assess the prevalence of

positive ties, quality of tie, and positive outcomes in network studies, we systematically
reviewed all articles published in *Social Networks* since its first issue, covering the years
1978 to 2001. We chose *Social Networks*
because it is "the premier journal for the
study of social networks" (from the website
for INSNA, the International Network for Social Network Analysis).[2] Articles on networks appear in journals throughout the social and behavioral sciences, as well as in
engineering, economics, and marketing.
However, since *Social Networks* is dedicated
exclusively to the study of networks and it
is the main venue for articles on new developments in the field, we feel that it is the
best selection for the purposes of our literature review.

We content-analyzed all articles published
in *Social Networks* from 1978 to 2001, focusing on empirical studies of network data. We
first considered all articles whether or not
the studies were about networks in organizations. Of the 425 articles published in these
years, 39 percent (166) were empirical analyses of network data. Of these, 42 percent
(69 of 166) contained data on positive ties.
But only 16 of the 69 articles examined positive outcomes as well as positive ties (about
10 percent of all empirical articles). A

roughly similar pattern emerges when we examine empirical studies of organizational networks. Sixty-five articles were published in *Social Networks* about organizations. Of these, 32 percent (21 of 65) contained data on positive ties. But only 6 articles examined positive ties and positive outcomes, about 9 percent of all articles about networks in organizations.

Our review indicates a surprising prevalence of network studies with data on positive ties. Does this prevalence suggest that POS is alive and well in the social network tradition? Data on positive ties are necessary but not sufficient for PONA. A study's purpose also must be considered. For example, if the purpose of a study is to reveal how actors exploit network structure for personal and private gain, the study would not qualify as PONA even if it included data on positive ties. To qualify as PONA, a network study must include data on positive ties and their quality, *and* address the subject matter of POS: "the dynamics in organizations that lead to the development of human strength, foster resiliency in individuals, make possible healing and restoration, and cultivate extraordinary individual and organizational performance" (Cameron, Dutton, & Quinn, n.d.). When we use these criteria, we find very few articles in *Social Networks* that would qualify as PONA.

ENERGIZING RELATIONSHIPS IN ORGANIZATIONAL NETWORKS

In our series of empirical network studies, we focused on one type of positive relational tie—"energizingrelationships"—inorganizations. Specifically, we assessed the extent to which interpersonal relationships generated or depleted a subjective feeling of energy, examining this type of tie within several large distributed groups.[3] Scholars have posited how energy accrues in conversation. Quinn and Dutton (2002) define energy as "a type of positive affective arousal, which people can experience as emotion—short responses to specific events—or mood—longer lasting affective states that need not be a response to a specific event." Their definition draws on work in psychology and sociology, including the concepts of energetic arousal (Thayer, 1989), emotional energy (Collins, 1993), subjective energy (Marks, 1977), positive affect (Watson, Clark, & Tellegen, 1988), vitality (Ryan & Frederick, 1977), and zest (Miller & Striver, 1997). We simply extend this perspective on a sociological front by applying network analytic techniques to the socioemotional experience of energizing relationships.

We analyzed energizing relationships with network techniques in seven different organizations: a strategy consulting firm, a financial services company, a petrochemical company, a government agency, two software companies, and a technology company (Cross, Baker, & Parker, 2002). In each, we used social network surveys and interviews to collect data on different types of relationships, including relationships that created the subjective perception of energy. Our survey item for "energizing relationships"[4] was: "When you typically interact with this person how does it affect your energy level?" We used a five-point Likert scale, with 1 indicating "strongly de-energizing" and 5 indicating "strongly energizing." A value of 4 or 5 is an energizing relationship, a value of 1 or 2 is a de-energizing relationship, and a value of 3 is considered neutral—neither energizing nor de-energizing. We also asked a network question about "information flow." Our survey item here was: "Please indicate which people listed below that you typically turn to for information or knowledge on work-related topics." Because people also use impersonal information sources, we asked about use of internal and external databases, personal computer files, and paper files. Control variables include tenure in the organization, gender, and hierarchical level (see Cross & Baker, 2003, for details).

We also conducted semi-structured interviews with sixty-three people drawn from each of the organizational settings. (We call these interviewees "informants" to distinguish from the "respondents" to our network surveys.) In an open-ended interview format, we asked each informant to describe "energizing relationships" and how these affect the informant. After several open-ended probes, we then placed the "energy" network diagram (examples below) in front of the informant and asked him or her to reflect on relationships the informant had nominated as energizing in the survey. We asked each informant to recount in as much detail as possible specific interactions with these people, focusing on the subjective experience of being energized in these relationships. Throughout, informants were asked to ground recollections in specific behaviors, names, and dates to guard against memory errors (Dougherty, 1992).

Almost all informants described both physical and psychological aspects of energizing relationships. For example, informants said they felt stimulated and they themselves expressed this stimulation with various physical cues, such as voice inflection, eye contact, and gestures. Some physical descriptor of energizing relationships emerged in each of the sixty-three interviews when we asked an informant to describe what he or she meant when claiming to be energized in an interaction. For example, one executive said:

> I am just "there" more. Physically I feel more up, more aroused, more intense and attuned to what is going on. And I guess this comes through in voice inflection, body language. All those things kind of reflect how you feel and can be contagious to others too.

Informants consistently described cognitive and motivational characteristics of energizing relationships. Fifty-nine of the informants described being more cognitively engaged in and attentive to dialogue with others in these energizing relationships. They reported a subjective belief that they attended to and processed information more rapidly and more thoroughly. They also felt they retrieved ideas from memory and/or made connections to other ideas more quickly in a way that generated new insights. This allowed them to learn and engage in the "give and take" of a good conversation or "scaffolding" in a meeting or problem-solving session. For example, one informant told us:

> They are quick relationships mentally. I am sure I literally think better and faster. I think I remember more and make more

connections and that is what is so energizing. To see things newly or differently and still be able to contribute back to the conversation in a way that opens up even more ideas or perspectives.

From a motivational perspective, all informants described being enthused or drawn into the issues of a problem-solving session or conversation. Informants were willing to commit themselves to the interaction. These conversations could be about business concerns, career issues, or personal topics, but they were distinguished by the way in which they generated enthusiasm. This motivation often carried over into a willingness to devote discretionary time to an issue after the interaction (e.g., willingly staying late or thinking about a problem during the commute home). For instance, this person described the motivation created by energizing relationships:

> I think when it really happens, when energy is really created, it's more than the intellectual thing. To me it's more than bantering back and forth no matter how interesting the ideas might be. It's when I let go of all the things that say "I've seen this before" or "You're not going to fool me with that one." Rather than looking for the problems and pitfalls, you start to get caught up in the possibilities and this is

both energizing and, I think, opens many new doors to possibilities *because you are looking for them, hoping for them* [emphasis from interviewee].

WHAT A NETWORK PERSPECTIVE OFFERS POS

Bringing network theory and methods to study positive organizational phenomena enables POS scholars to observe and measure the "invisible" network of positive relationships in an organizational setting. Network visualization aids interpretation. To illustrate, consider the contrasting network diagrams in Figures 21.1 and 21.2. These diagrams were generated by a computerized visualization method that places well-connected "nodes" in the center of the plot and less-connected or isolated nodes in the periphery. Lines between nodes represent energizing relationships (Figure 21.1) or de-energizing relationships (Figure 21.2). Figure 21.1 is the visualized network of energizing ties among leaders and staff in a government agency. This agency had been reorganized in response to the terrorist attacks on September 11, 2001, with new executives brought in to rebuild the organization around a new set of priorities. As shown in Figure 21.1, the three executive leaders are central in the energizing network

Figure 21.1
Network of Energizing Relationships Among Leaders and Staff in a Reorganized
Government Agency

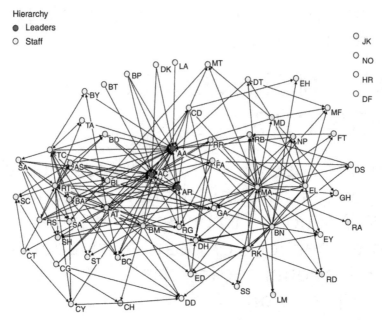

From Cross, Baker, & Parker, 2002.

diagram. Indeed, many staff employees reported that relationships with these new leaders elevated the employees' energy levels. Further, they reported that these leaders were successful in capturing their commitment to the new set of organizational priorities.

In contrast, consider the network of de-energizing relationships in a petrochemical company (Figure 21.2). Many engineers reported that relationships with supervisors decreased their energy levels. Visual inspection of Figure 21.2 reveals a large number of de-energizing supervisors located in the center of the network diagram, indicating their central role in depleting energy in the organization. Our interviews revealed considerable resentment among workers regarding what they call "micro-management." We learned that the supervisors were following standard procedures and were not aware of their de-energizing influence on others. The network diagrams became a tool for the group to engage in a constructive discussion about their procedures, roles, and relationships, and to redesign their policies, procedures, and organization.[5]

Network analytic techniques also inform POS via quantitative methods, allowing researchers to precisely describe a social system and analyze the link between network patterns and outcomes. To illustrate, we focus here on three of seven organizations we studied (Cross & Baker 2003): (1) 125 consultants and managers in a major office of a global strategy-consulting firm ("strategy consultants"), (2) 86 statisticians in a major credit card organization ("statisticians"), and (3) 101 engineers within a major petrochemical organization ("engineers"). We focus on these settings for two reasons. First, we were able to obtain reliable performance information on the people in each of these networks.[6] Second, these groups are similar because their work is knowledge intensive, but different fundamentally on the extent to which output is a product of social construc-

148

tion (Berger & Luckman, 1966). For example, strategy consultants construct almost limitless realities to which their clients must react. In contrast, statisticians are constrained by the rules of mathematics and statistics; engineers are constrained by physical realities. Thus, we can examine whether the hypothesized link between centrality in the energizing network and performance varies by the nature of the work done. For example, we expect that the relationship of performance and centrality in the energizing network would be stronger for strategy consultants than for either statisticians or engineers.

Figure 21.2
Network of De-Energizing Relationships Among Supervisors and Engineers in a Petrochemical Organization

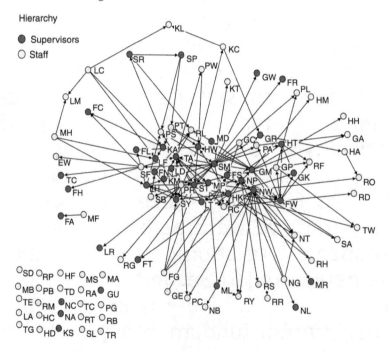

Since energizing ties have never been measured before, even basic statistics are interesting. Basic statistics reveal the frequency, distribution, and location of positive organizational phenomena (in our case, energizing ties in an organization). Consider the frequency distributions of energizing ties and information ties in the three settings (Table 21.1). A key finding, for example, is that energizing relationships are as common as information ties, suggesting that energizing relationships are pervasive features of organizational life.

Table 21.1 presents summary statistics of key structural variables for the "energizing network" (3 or 4 on the Likert scale; see above), the "de-energizing network" (1 or 2 on the Likert scale; see above), and the information network. There are many ways to measure actor (or point) centrality in social networks (Wasserman & Faust, 1994: chap.5). Here, we focus on measures that reveal theoretically appropriate features of energizing networks. "Indegree" is a simple measure of actor centrality that indicates the number of "choices" received by a person in a social network. (In a network diagram, "incoming" arrows illustrate indegree.) A person with high indegree in an energizing network would be chosen by many others as a person with whom they have energizing relationships; a person with low indegree in the same network would be chosen by few others. For example, the statistician with the highest indegree has a score of 27, indicating that 27 of the 125 statisticians reported having energizing relationships with this person. The statistician with the lowest indegree had a score of 0, indicating that no other statistician reported having energizing ties with this person. A person with high indegree in the de-energizing network would be named by many others as a person with whom relationships are de-energizing. For example, the consultant with the highest indegree has a score of 16, indicating that 16 of the 125 consultants reported having de-energizing relationships with this person. The consultant with the lowest indegree had a score of 0, indicating that no consultant reported having de-energizing ties with this person.

Table 21.1: Descriptive Statistics on Energy, De-Energy, and Information Networks in Three Settings

Variable	Strategy Consultants	Engineers	Statisticians
Energizing network			
Indegree (average)	8.5	4.39	6.27
Minimum indegree	0	0	0
Maximum indegree	33	23	27

Variable	Strategy Consultants	Engineers	Statisticians
Graph centralization (degree)	19.90%	18.80%	24.70%
De-energizing network			
Indegree (average)	1.72	0.32	2.43
Minimum indegree	0	0	0
Maximum indegree	16	3	14
Graph centralization (degree)	11.60%	2.70%	13.80%
Information network			
Indegree (average)	5.41	8.23	8.07
Minimum indegree	0	1	0
Maximum indegree	29	27	27
Graph centralization (degree)	19.20%	19.00%	22.50%

From Cross & Baker, 2002.

Table 21.1 also shows measures of graph centralization. Graph centralization combines the measures of actor centrality in a network, indicating the extent to which one actor is highly central and others are not. It is an indicator of the overall structure of an entire network, showing the extent to which a network is centralized (dominated by a highly central actor, such as the hub of a hub-and-spoke graph) or de-centralized (all actors have the same centrality, such as a circle or fully connected graph). This measure varies between 0 and 100 percent, where higher numbers indicate greater network centralization. In the context of energy, a highly centralized energizing network would mean that one actor accounts for most of the energizing ties; a highly centralized de-energizing network would mean that one actor accounts for most of the de-energizing ties. The centralization statistics in Table 21.1 show that positive ties, in this case energizing relationships, are not concentrated in the hands of a few people.

In sum, these basic statistics show that positive organizational phenomena (like energizing relationships) appear throughout an organization, but they are distributed unevenly. (1) The average number of energizing ties is always higher than the average number of de-energizing ties. (2) The average number of de-energizing ties is always lower than energizing ties or information ties. (3) At least one actor is isolated in each of the three types of networks (minimum indegree is 0 in each network). (4) At least one actor in each of the three types of networks accounts for a large number of ties (examine scores for maximum indegree). However, (5) no graph is dominated by a single actor (graph centralization never exceeds 25 percent). Hence, energizing ties, de-energizing ties, and information-seeking ties are distributed throughout these organizational settings, rather than concentrated in one or a few highly central actors, but they are unevenly distributed—there is a considerable range of centrality, with some people much more central and some people much more peripheral.[7]

WHAT POS OFFERS TO ONA

POS opens the door for network analysts to look at features of organizational life that have not been examined before. Our chapter is further support of Cameron, Dutton, and Quinn's argument that "POS uncovers new sources and forms of dynamic capabilities that build on human generative processes" (see Chapter 1). Energizing relationships have always existed in organizational settings, but the lens of social network analysis has not been used to observe or measure these positive ties. Our chapter demonstrates the value of observing and measuring networks of energizing relationships and suggests that other types of positive ties could be measured in future network studies.

Our fusion of POS and ONA also supports the emerging view of contemporary organizations as dynamic, flexible, and fluid social networks. The traditional structural perspective suggests that people accrue power and influence by occupying particular positions in a relatively stable network (e.g., Burt, 1992, 2000; Granovetter, 1973). For example, a person who links otherwise disconnected parts of a network has multiple sources of information, tends to get more and better information, and is better able to spot and act on emergent opportunities. Yet this view, to some degree, assumes stability in the social fabric of an organization. This seems less the case today as work itself is transformed from stable, long-term employment in large organizations to project-specific, flexible, and short-term jobs (e.g., Castells, 2000: 216–302). In addition, significant organizational changes, such as de-layering, re-engineering, and team-based designs, to name just a few, have decreased organizational network stability and the relationships that are a product of position in formal organizational structure. Together, work-force mobility and continual internal restructurings produce organizational networks that are more dynamic and less static and durable than those analyzed in foundational organizational network studies. Therefore, the structural source of power and influence may be shifting from position in a stable network to an ability to attract, engage, and energize others in the network.

The results from our quantitative analysis support this dynamic view of organizational networks. In addition to measuring energizing relationships, we measured information flow among members of the organizational network. We also measured each person's usage of impersonal information sources such as files and databases. We expected that performance ratings would be correlated with network positions usually thought to confer advantages—positions rich in structural holes[8] (Burt, 1992, 2000)—as well as the use of impersonal sources of information. We found, however, that the use of impersonal sources of information and positions rich in structural holes only influenced performance for the statisticians and engineers once we factored in the effect of position within the energy network. In other words, in organizational settings that tend to be constrained by rules or a physical reality, the ability to acquire information via a structural-hole position does seem to promote performance beyond energizing behavior. In all three settings, performance was predicted by people's position within the energizing network. Specifically, individuals who energized others were better performers—even after controlling for information processing variables, structural holes, and other variables (see Table 21.2). These findings imply that the ability to energize others—to develop a network of energizing relationships—may be more important than occupying certain positions in an information or communication network.

Table 21.2 OLS Regression Models of the Relationship Between Energy and Performance

Variable	Strategy Consultants	Engineers	Statisticians
Controls			
Tenure	0.114	-0.124	0.072
Gender	0.031	0.05	-0.045
Hierarchy	-0.004	0.031	0.097
Information acquisition variables			
Internal database usage	-0.121	-0.106	0.144
External database usage	-0.137	0.05	0.004
Personal computer files usage	0.095	0.189	0.084
Paper files usage	-0.118	-0.311**	0.144
Structural hole information network (constraint measure)	-0.123	-0.214*	-0.195*

Variable	Strategy Consultants	Engineers	Statisticians
Energizing network variable			
Number of people energized by ego (indegree in energizing network)	0.380***	0.246*	0.387***
Adjusted R-Square	0.109	0.243	0.268
N	125	101	86

***p < 0.001, **p < 0.01, *p < 0.05, ^ < 0.10. Beta coefficients are standardized. From Cross & Baker, 2002.

CONCLUSION

This chapter combines positive organizational scholarship and organizational network analysis to produce what we call positive organizational network analysis. This approach links POS's focus on resiliency and extraordinary performance with ONA's theories and methods. One of our contributions to POS is to demonstrate that POS can be expanded profitably beyond its psychological focus to include a *sociological* perspective on organizational phenomena. This contribution suggests that it may be possible to successfully combine POS with other organizational theories and perspectives, such as institutional theory, organizational ecology, diffusion theory, and resource dependence. One of our contributions to ONA is to show that the POS perspective can open new territory for social network analysts—the analysis of energizing relationships and other types of positive ties that have not been examined before. The full toolbox of social network analysis (e.g., Wasserman & Faust, 1994) could be applied to study and understand positive organizational phenomena.

We hope our initial work on PONA will stimulate future research. First, our conception of energizing networks holds potential for theorizing about positive dimensions of relationships and networks. Rather than considering network structure as a constraint and network position as power (e.g., Brass and Burkhardt, 1992; Burt, 1992; Krackhardt, 1990), we suggest that patterns in energizing networks can be generative and enabling. Energizing networks are not merely affect or liking—our informants provided evidence that they were energized on tasks they did not care for and with people they did not like. Rather, the relationships themselves were perceived to generate energy. We hope that future network research will explore organizational processes (e.g., diffusion) and organizational outcomes (e.g., group-level performance, individual satisfaction, and organizational commitment) of energizing networks.

Second, empirical work will also be important to disentangle the role of individual behaviors and traits, relational characteristics, and contextual factors such as network structure and task design in promoting energy. Future research should undertake egocentric network and more standard attribute data-collection processes to further understand the contributing role of networks, attributes and context. Combined with hierarchical linear modeling (Raudenbush & Bryk, 2002; Wellman & Frank, 2001) as an analytic approach, this will allow researchers to measure precisely how the individual, relational, and contextual factors contribute to energy in organizational settings.

Third, another avenue of inquiry lies with the downsides of energy. We do not mean negative relations, though those are clearly important subjects of study (e.g., Labianca, Brass, & Gray, 1998; Sparrow, Liden, Wayne, & Kraimer, 2001). Rather, it is important to understand the potential downsides of energizing relations themselves. For example, do they introduce biases into organizational learning and the diffusion of knowledge? Our data show that, when choice exists, people seek energizers, even when de-energizers have the necessary expertise and knowledge. In contrast, we found that people attend to, process, and so deeply learn in energizing relationships. People acquire information and learn from others (Allen, 1977; Lave & Wenger, 1991; Orr, 1996). Demographic similarity is a strong predictor of interaction patterns (McPherson, Smith-Lovin, & Cook, 2001). People might get locked into certain sources of information or ways of thinking about a problem due to well-intended but less than effective energizers. At a network level, we might find that energizers account for path dependence in groups. Those central in energizing networks might disproportionately dictate what information a group attends to and processes.

ACKNOWLEDGMENT

We thank Tom Bateman, Jane Dutton, Ryan Quinn, Gretchen Spreitzer, and Ellen Whitener for helpful comments on versions of this chapter.

NOTES

[1]   A social network is defined as a specified set of actors and their relationships. Social network analysis applies mathematics to understand the patterns of relationships among actors and the implications of these relationships. In contrast to most approaches in the social sciences, network analysts view actors "as interdependent

rather than independent, autonomous units" (Wasserman & Faust 1994: 4). The "actor" and the "relational tie" are the fundamental building blocks of the social network approach (Wasserman & Faust, 1994: 17–18).

[2] *Social Networks* "is an inter-disciplinary and international quarterly that provides a common forum for representatives of anthropology, sociology, history, social psychology, political science, human geography, biology, economics, communications science and other disciplines who share an interest in the structure of social relations and associations" (INSNA website).

[3] Our colleague Steve Borgatti has also conducted network analyses on energy in unpublished work.

[4] As is typical in network research, each independent network variable was measured using a single network question. We constructed question items to be specific and to elicit typical or long-term patterns of interaction rather than one-time events (Freeman, Romney, & Freeman, 1987). Further, our interviews suggest both a common interpretation of the item and consistency to the construct.

[5]   Network diagrams also offer advantages for sample selection. It is well known that the choice of informants in qualitative research can be biased by snowball sampling, by using the formal organizational chart, or by a researcher's beliefs and preferences. Network diagrams provide a means of selecting informants systematically, identifying both central and peripheral members of a group for informant interviews.

[6]   In each setting, performance is the annual human resource rating of each person. Generally, this is a composite figure based on aggregating project evaluations and some objective data collected throughout the year. They are not identical because each organization might be more concerned with different components of the full annual evaluation. However, these evaluations are consistent in process, wording, and scale; each is a general appraisal of a person's performance and not a self-assessment.

[7]   We can assess the extent to which the three types of networks are correlated, using QAP-correlation (a nonparametric measure similar to the Pearson product-moment correlation). The energy and information networks are significantly corre-

lated (p < 0.001) in each setting (consultants=0.37, statisticians=0.40, engineers=0.40). The de-energy and information networks, however, are not significantly correlated (p > 0.05). These patterns suggest a preference for energizing ties: people tend to seek out energizers when they search for information. Our qualitative interview data support this interpretation.

[8] Structural holes is an indicator of the extent to which a person's relationships provide them access to information in different subgroups within a network. For example, a person who links otherwise disconnected parts of a network has "structural holes" in his/her network. Such people are claimed to enjoy performance benefits because they hear about and so are able to take action on new opportunities earlier than others. People who bridge different groups often learn about new information earlier than others.

Chapter 22

Empowerment and Cascading Vitality

Martha S. Feldman and Anne M. Khademian

In 2001 the city of Grand Rapids, Michigan, began a process to develop the first master plan for the city in nearly four decades. Rather than delegate the responsibility to a handful of city planners, the structure and growth of the new planning process and the content of the plan were determined through broad inclusion of individuals, neighborhood organizations, and citywide representatives. The impetus for the new process grew from city management efforts to enhance the agency of city employees by encouraging them to find better ways to accomplish the goals of government. For the city planner who facilitated the new master plan process, the opportunity to pursue planning in a more creative way fostered a new understanding of the planning task, a more inclusive approach to participation, an understanding of the benefits of alternative sources of information for the quality of public efforts, and more knowledge about the environment within which the plan was crafted. Ultimately, the planner's own empowerment allowed her to support a process that empowered the public as participants in the planning process and enhanced the capacity of the city to plan, and the ability of the government to reconnect with the people of the city.

This chapter presents a model of cascading vitality that focuses on the internal empowerment of public employees as the source of positive energy that flows to, and empowers, members of the public. Vitality is an important concept in positive organizational scholarship. Vitality is physical or mental vigor that creates the capacity to live, grow, and develop. Vital individuals are "energetic and fully functioning" (Ryan & Bernstein, 2002). They exude positive physical and intellectual energy that can be applied to find innovative ways to live and contribute. Individual vitality, or energy, "is a feeling that one is eager to act and capable of action," and it is a positive feeling individuals will try to sustain or enhance (Quinn & Dutton, 2002; Collins, 1993). We view vital organizations in a similar light. Vital organizations exude positive energy that nurtures and supports the growth and development of the people within the organization and fuels the collective work of the organization. "[C]reativity and innovation thrive" in vital organizations (Vicenzi & Adkins,

2000: 105), and an organization "eager to act and capable of action" will seek ways to sustain and enhance high energy to accomplish the work of the organization.

The model we present explains the relationship between empowered employees, such as the city planner in the above example, and the creation of processes broadly inclusive of members of the public. Inclusion for defining and addressing public problems increases the democratic capacity of the people and the communities served. In this way, the organizational vitality extends beyond the boundaries of the organization and creates vitality in the external environment. Scholars working to document democratic practices and to theorize about the historical manifestations of democracy cite direct public engagement as essential to the development of social capital, the identification of a community, and ultimately the ways in which individuals understand their liberty and their role in governance (Sandel, 1997; Putnam, 2000; Box, 1998; Markus, 2002). Here, we suggest how this inclusive result is rooted, in part, in the organizational effort to enhance the agency of individual public employees. Enabling employees to approach the task of the organization and to utilize and engage information and people in creative and alternative ways, we suggest, is empowering, and nurtures individual vitality, which can expand and create organizational resources and enhance organizational vitality—or the capacity to grow, flex, and develop. This vitality can cascade outside the organization through employees to empower the public, and we argue could be key for building and sustaining inclusive processes with the capacity for civic engagement in addressing public problems. The ultimate result is the enhancement of democracy. In this sense, the organization becomes a source of vitality in the effort effectively to address public problems.

Many organizations, both public and private, make efforts to engage and improve the communities in which they are located. We suggest that one way to achieve this goal is through the empowerment of employees. We show how enhancing the agency of employees can empower the members of the public they deal with in their work, thus enabling organizations to strengthen the communities in which they operate. Our focus in this chapter is the public sector, in which the services provided are public services and increasing the vitality of the community and people who live in it is central to the tasks of the organization. We leave to future research the examples and modifications that may need to be made to embrace private-sector organizations.

In the next section we nest our interest in employee and public empowerment within two distinct literatures, and show the way our model connects and builds upon them. We then present and develop the model of cascading vitality and propose a set of questions for future research in positive organizational scholarship.

TWO LITERATURES ON EMPOWERMENT

Civic participation is integral to the enactment of democratic politics. It provides the public an opportunity for direct input into the policies and programs that affect their lives. It provides a venue for the development of community that scholars suggest is currently in short supply (Putnam, 1995; Sandel, 1996). A significant body of research investigates public empowerment through civic participation. Throughout this literature, public empowerment is examined on a spectrum from empowerment as access to government and government decisionmaking, to empowerment reflected in the increased knowledge and sophistication of public participants, to the developing capacity of the public to organize and address a variety of issues in an effective manner. The understanding of empowerment is diverse in this literature, and so too are the mechanisms examined for implementing civic participation. The major approaches are depicted in Figure 22.1 and briefly described below.

One approach looks at policies that mandate the creation of public venues or forms of participation as a part of policy implementation. These assessments of civic participation examine the legislative vehicles for inclusion, as well as the empowerment consequences of these policies for citizenship and community capacity to address public problems (Parr & Lampe, 1996; Ingram & Smith, 1993; Berry, Portney, & Thompson 1993). A second approach to civic participation looks at efforts by managers as leaders to empower members of the public by incorporating the public directly in the implementation process. Managers, for example, might create forums or councils for public participation in identifying solutions to a particular public problem (Reich, 1988a). In this approach to public involvement, managers are viewed as having a role in fostering democratic processes outside of the organization (Feldman & Khademian, 2002; Rabe, 1994; Weber, 1998) and even a responsibility for helping the wheels of government find solutions to problems that might not be solvable through legislative debate (Reich, 1988b; Behn, 1998). A third approach to the study of civic participation looks at access to information and technol-

ogy as exemplified in the e-government movement. The emphasis here is on empowerment
through public convenience and accessibility to
information and participation opportunities
(OECD, 2001; Abramson & Means, 2001). One
topic this literature on civic participation has
not explored is the role that empowered employees within a public organization might have in
facilitating civic participation.

Figure 22.1
Means of Encouraging Civic Participation

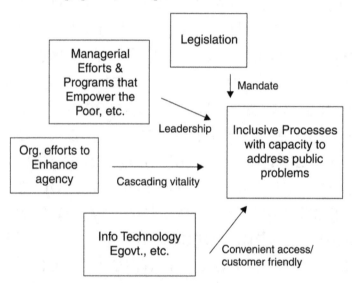

Employee empowerment is the focus of a
second literature that examines the impact
empowerment has for the individuals, and the
consequences of that empowerment for organizational creativity, flexibility, learning, and
ultimately performance. Employee empowerment has been an important topic in management in recent years (Conger & Kanungo, 1988;

Spreitzer, 1995), but it has many roots (O'Connor, 2001; Prasad & Eylon, 2001). Much of the argument connecting employee empowerment to organizational performance has roots in studies of participatory management written four decades ago (Argyris, 1957; Likert, 1961) and in the writing about industrial democracy (Follett, 1924, 1940; Tead, 1945). The early empowerment literature dealt with the democratic implications of empowerment and considered industrial democracy as a means of supporting the connection between capitalism and democracy within an organization and forestalling moves toward socialism and communism (Follet, 1924, 1940; Tead, 1918, 1951). From this perspective, empowerment builds on and helps to develop democratic values that unite the good of the private and the public domains (O'Connor, 2001; Prasad, 2001).

Today, employee empowerment is viewed as an essential element in the management of change, or the ability of an organization to adjust to internal and external factors and to hone and improve upon the services or products of the organization (Jarrar & Zairi, 2002; Jones & Thompson, 1999; Kanter, 1983; Peccei & Rosenthal, 2001; Kim, 2002). Reformers in the public and private sectors argue that employee empowerment is essential for breaking through bureaucratic tendons that constrain the capacity of organizations to innovate and change (Barzelay, 1992; Peters & Waterman, 1982). Empowered employees able to participate in defining the work of an organization and in its governance are viewed as a fundamental dimension of organizations able to learn or grow from mistakes and past experiences (Dixon, 1998; Senge, 1990). Empowered employees are also viewed as an essential feature of decentralized systems that build control around results, rather than inputs, written rules, and processes (Ingraham, Thompson, & Sanders, 1998; Thompson, 1991).

This literature, however, has not explored the potential for such empowerment to cascade outside the organization to foster inclusive public processes. In this chapter, we explore one way in which the ideas in these literatures could be connected. The connection we propose involves a dynamic in which both supervisors and employees expand their power by sharing it and empowering others. We suggest the possibility of a cascade of vitality that moves from empowered employees to empowered members of the public. Thus, we claim that employees can learn to empower by being empowered.

THE MODEL

In this section we present a model of the connection between employee empowerment and public empowerment. The model is depicted graphically in Figure 22.2. The fundamental movement in the model is the cascade from empowerment to capacity to inclusive processes. Efforts by managers in public organizations to enhance the agency of employees provide the starting point of the model. Individual employee empowerment becomes capacity through expanding resources. Managers can empower their employees to think more broadly about how tasks are defined, what people need to be involved with in addressing an issue, and what information is relevant to it, and to act on these thoughts. The new understandings, new connections, and new information that result are resources that increase the capacity of the employees and the organization. The increased capacity can be used to empower members of the public by creating inclusive processes that enable them to participate in creating the policies and programs that affect their lives. The employee empowerment provides an example of how power expands when shared, and how the expansion of power creates energy and momentum for approaching the work of the organization. Having learned this lesson it makes sense that some employees would replicate the example among people with whom they interact and have the ability to empower. It is a feeling that one is eager to act and capable of action. This cascading vitality builds on itself when the inclusive processes lead to new understandings, new connections, and new information and thus contributes to the expanded capacity of the employees and the organizations they work for.

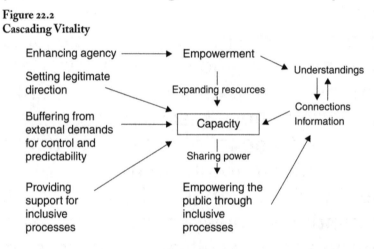

Figure 22.2
Cascading Vitality

Managers are important to this dynamic potential in several ways. As mentioned above, they can show that power increases by sharing it. Some employees will already know this, but managers provide a focal point and the example set by their behavior is an effective way to disseminate an idea. Managers can also affect the energy in the system. First, they can put energy into the system by sharing their power in a manner that enhances the agency of their employees. Second, they can help keep energy in the system by providing a buffer to external demands and criticisms. Empowering the public goes beyond simply listening to ideas to acting and encouraging the public to act on those ideas. Less control and less predictability are inevitable results. Managers can act as a buffer for the system of cascading vitality by nurturing vitality within the organization and preventing external demands for more control and pre-dictability from impacting the system and creat-ing leaks that drain energy. Finally, managers can help employees figure out how to use the new capacity. They do this both by setting di-rection and also by making available information about inclusive processes, in the form of train-ing and examples.

The following example from Charlotte, North Carolina, illustrates the cascade from empower-ment to inclusive processes as well as the role for management that we propose in the model. For years, employees sent out bills to absentee landlords when the city had mowed their grass. As a manager described the situation:

> What aggravates you about that job is you're going to send the same landlord the same bill during the growing season every year because they're never going to cut the grass ... the same bill which usually then winds up in your accounts receivable,

doesn't get paid, you carry it for four months, you try and get it on the tax bill eventually. You've shuffled an enormous amount of paper on the same people.

Then, along comes a manager who says it's okay to think about why you are doing this task and it's okay to "leave your desk" and talk with other people who are trying to achieve the same goals. Here's what he says happens:

> You get all the way back to—we started out trying to make a contribution to the aesthetics or the appearance of the environmental quality of the neighborhood. Well, if you get everybody from the person who's out doing the inspection to the person who's sending the bill together, which even in a big organization is only four or five people, ...give them some smart consulting assistance, they will devise an entirely new strategy of how to improve the appearance of the neighborhood.... [S]o far, that particular little team has 47 recommendations ... and they're working their way through strategies.... [T]hey have already assembled a group of landlords. They've assembled a group of target neighborhoods who have the problem. The neighborhoods and the landlords have devised some strategies around employing neighborhood people to take care of the lots. We think we're going

to get this whole problem out of city hall entirely within a year. (videotaped interview with Borgsdorf, September 27, 1997)

CASCADING VITALITY

In the following sections, we discuss the major features of this model. We explore how the concepts in the model need to be understood and enacted in order to achieve the result of empowering the public through inclusive processes. We draw on existing literature to develop the features of the model.

Empowerment

Earlier we discussed how the idea of empowerment has been used in the literature. Here we discuss one way of thinking about what empowerment is and how it is created. Empowerment involves the generation, distribution, and use of power. We think of power as something that is created by and enhanced (or diminished) within the context of relationships (Kanter, 1979; Lappe & DuBois, 1994; Weber, 1946). Managers in an organization have power because they have formal authority to make decisions and take actions that influence others and distribute organizational resources. When managers share that formal authority by presenting employees with opportunities to leave

their desk, they are redefining the relationships between employees and managers by
redefining the flow and supply of power.
Rather than power that flows from a single
source at the top of a hierarchy, shared
power relationships generate more power
in that employees have new capacity to act
or produce an effect within the organization.

Empowerment is transformative, in part,
because it involves the process of altering
and building relationships that share and
create power. This process provides the
dynamic potential of the cascading vitality
model. Mary Parker Follett characterized
this transformation as moving from "power-
over" to "power-with" relationships (1940),
as have others (Kreisberg, 1992). The
"power with" conception does not involve
giving away power (Boje & Rosile, 2001).
It is not a zero-sum conception of power
(Kanter, 1979). The people with formal authority use it in a way that generates power
by sharing it with others (Feldman &
Khademian, 2000). As James Kouzes and
Barry Posner (1995) suggest, leaders can
"take the power that flows to them and
connect it to others, becoming power gener-
ators from which their constituents draw
energy" (p.185).

Expanding Resources

An essential feature of this model is the claim that empowering employees in the manner discussed above results in expanding resources available to the organization and the individuals in it. This claim rests on an understanding that resources are not inert but are critically affected by the context in which they are created and used. Scholars have shown that context affects both the availability and the meaning of resources (Feldman, 2002; Leblebici, Salancik, Copay, & King, 1991; Lichtenstein & Brush, 2001; Sewell, 1992). As organizations move into and create different contexts, they require and use different resources.

Anthropologists and sociologists have shown that cultural schemas are a particularly important feature of context:

> To take perhaps the most obvious case, an immense stack of Hudson Bay blankets would be nothing more than a means of keeping a large number of people warm were it not for the cultural schemas that constituted the Kwakiutl potlatch; but given these schemas, the blankets, given away in a potlatch became a means of demonstrating the

power of the chief and, consequently of acquiring prestige, marriage alliances, military power, and labor services (Boas 1966; Sahlins 1989). (Sewell 1992: 11–12)

Cultural schemas alter the relevance or salience of resources and consequently alter their availability for use and what they can be used for. Empowering employees affects their cultural schemas or understandings of what they are supposed to be doing and how they are supposed to be doing it. We focus particularly on the "soft" resources of connections and information. Research has shown that soft resources may be the most salient in change processes (Lichtenstein & Brush, 2001). This may be because they are the most mutable.

Our model identifies three aspects of work that expand resources and that are affected when employees are empowered in the manner identified in the previous section. First, empowered employees are able to develop new understandings of the work of the organization and their individual role in that effort. These new understandings lead to new ways of approaching work and the ability to engage in job-crafting, which Wrzesniewski and Dutton (2001) have shown to affect work meaning and work identity. Their work is not just to process forms or papers, for example, but also to figure out why the forms need to be processed and to find alternative ways to accomplish the same goal if possible. Though some scholars make a clear distinction between cultural schemas and the resources affected by them (e.g., Sewell, 1992), we think that the distinction is not so clear. If a resource is "anything that can serve as a source of power in social interactions" (Sewell 1992: 9), then we think that understandings that allow employees to take new actions are resources.

Less controversially, these understandings affect two other aspects of the work that are clearly resources: the connections employees make with other people and the information they have access to. Employees who are empowered to "leave their desks" are able to make new connections with people who do work that is relevant to theirs. If accomplishing the goals will be better served by connecting with others outside of their unit but within the same organization, across other organizations, or with members of the public, they have the freedom to make these connections. Moreover, they can act on these connections in a way that's constructive. They are also able to utilize new sources and types of information in the pursuit of their work. New information comes from three sources: managers, new understandings, and new connections. Sharing power involves greater transparency and, thus, managers empowering their employees provide more access to information. New understandings of the work mean that employees look for information that is relevant to new ways of seeing what they are doing. New connections mean that employees put themselves in a position to access different sources of information and information interpreted through different lenses.

Capacity

In our model of cascading vitality, these understandings, connections, and information are all resources that empowered employees can utilize to develop organizational capacity. Our understanding of capacity draws on two distinct literatures. First, organizational capacity is of central concern among scholars who examine the role of nonprofit organizations in the delivery of public services. The primary interest in capacity in this literature is concern for the quality of government programs as well as the degree to which such organizations are held accountable as government contractors. This literature defines capacity as a set of organizational characteristics that demonstrate vision and strategic thinking, leadership, human resources, skills, financial systems, and operation structures for the day-to-day operations of an organization and its ability to grow and flex in the future (McKinsey and Co., 2001; Fredericksen & London, 2000; Bryson, 1995).

Another important literature examines capacity at a community level. This literature ranges in its definition of capacity. At one end of the spectrum is an understanding of capacity as a community with access to government information through electronic systems and other opportunities, and at the other is an understanding of capacity as a public engaged in the identification, development, implementation, and evaluation of public policy approaches (OECD, 2001). This latter, more engaged understanding of community capacity is clearly recognized in the literature as the most difficult to accomplish and sustain (Stone, Henig, Jones, & Pierannunzi, 2001; Reardon, 1998; Khademian, 2002; LaBonte, 1999; Markus, 2002). Community capacity is recognized as a continuous process that evolves as hierarchies and traditional boundary-forming structures are relaxed (or even removed) so that individuals can recognize the value of a wide range of experiences and expertise, and begin to trust one another and recognize common bonds and connections (LaBonte, 1999; Reardon, 1998; Lappe & Dubois, 1994).

We view capacity as the ability of an organization to utilize understandings, connections, and information effectively to take on the broad objectives of the organization. Like the effective empowerment of employees, this requires both an ability to approach the work of the organization in a continuously creative manner, and the opportunity. While the capacity dimensions presented by the literature on nonprofits are essential for both dimensions, many of the characteristics of community capacity seem essential for our approach to organizational capacity. The ability of an organization to think and act collectively is contingent upon the breaching of boundaries and hierarchies with power-sharing relationships that not only create opportunities for action, but also facilitate the growth of trust. Most critically, this interconnected and collective effort nurtures the vitality cascade that begins with the individual empowerment of employees, and flows out to public participation. Capacity within the organization is ultimately an ability to apply this energy to address the challenges of the organization or the community, and to do so in a way that utilizes the new resources created through the empowerment process.

Sharing Power

In this model, we suggest that employees who experience empowerment and the consequent enhancement of resources learn the model of empowerment, and in turn can use that model to continue generating resources as a means continuously to find ways to address the challenges of their work. They do so by finding ways to enhance the agency of members of the public by engaging them and giving them the ability (opportunity, resources, and skills) to think broadly and creatively about public problems, the people who might be involved in addressing those problems, and the source and type of information that might be brought to bear. Because they have experienced the liberating effects of "leaving the desk," they have a greater capability to enable members of the public to take on new roles in the policy process.

Essential to this part of the model is the attraction of sharing power. We argue that some employees who understand that their supervisors enhance their agency by sharing their power will imitate this behavior and enhance their own agency by sharing their power. This is a probabilistic rather than a deterministic argument. Some employees will not understand the powersharing dynamic; others will not choose to expand their power. Still others will have understood the dynamic long before it is modeled by their supervisors. But role-modeling is important not only because it shows others how to do things, but also because it can make it safe to do them. The latter effect may be especially strong when the model is the supervisor. The claim here is that when people are shown how to share power and given permission to do so, some percentage of them will find the opportunity attractive and will act on it.

Empowering the Public Through Inclusive Processes

There are, of course, many ways that people could act on the opportunity to share their power. We suggest that one way vitality can be used is toward the development of inclusive processes or the empowerment of the public. The most available group of people that public-sector employees can empower is the public with whom they interact. Scholars have noted that people who work for the public sector tend to be motivated by their ability to serve the public effectively (Bozeman, 1993). Inclusive processes in which the public servants are responsive to the public by partnering with them is one way in which employees can share their power. Inclusive processes are increasingly required by the demands for responsiveness (Vigoda, 2002) and the need to take into consideration diverse perspectives (Bryson, Cunningham, & Lokkesmoe, 2002). Moreover, inclusive processes are intrinsically attractive because they enable public employees to make their work more meaningful.

There are many ways in which the public can be included, and both "public participation" and "civic engagement" are two other terms that are used to discuss processes that are inclusive of the public. The International Association for Public Participation (IAP2) defines a spectrum of activities that include informing the public, consulting with them, involving them, collaborating with them, and empowering them (IAP2, 2000). Government organizations and government employees play a vital role in both initiating and sustaining inclusive processes (Vigoda, 2002). As representatives of the common interest, one challenge of these processes is to guide participation toward the common good rather than toward narrow self-interest (Thacher, 2001). One way government organizations and government employees can play this vital role is to facilitate a collective understanding, or "collective cognition," of the need to take on a public issue, and the desire or drive to do something about it (Stone, Henig, Jones, & Pierannunzi, 2001).

We provide here just one of many possible examples that show how empowered employees can empower the public through inclusion. We began this chapter with an example of a planner from the city of Grand Rapids, Michigan. The planner in charge of the process worked closely with the Master Plan Committee, a committee of citizens broadly representative of the city population that was appointed by the mayor. The power-sharing relationship between the committee and the planner was key to the empowerment (Feldman & Khademian, 2002). She could have constructed a relationship in which the committee provided input to her decisions, but instead she thought of herself as working *for* the committee and providing expertise for their decisions. Consultants worked for the planner and helped her execute the directives of the committee. A series of community forums provided broad input from the public. Community forums were held in multiple locations around the city in order to make it easy for people in the neighborhoods to participate. Community organizations were used extensively to encourage neighborhood participation. Forums were also advertised broadly in both citywide and neighborhood newspapers. A website was developed and kept up-to-date. Information was available in both English and Spanish. Members of the Master Plan Committee, members of the Grand Rapids planning staff, and the consultants attended and facilitated the forums. Overall, the process involved over 200 meetings and over 2,500 participants

(Feldman, fieldnotes, September 12, 2002). Interviews with community organizers, representatives of business, and environmental activists all suggest that the Grand Rapids planning process achieved a level of participation on the part of the public and responsiveness on the part of the city administration that overcame general cynicism about the sincerity of the empowerment rhetoric.

As indicated in Figure 22.2, processes that share power with the public are also capable of creating resources in much the same way that sharing power within organizations does. For instance, the planning effort in Grand Rapids has also produced its own dynamic cascade, as it has energized elements in the community, created new connections among them, and provided information broadly. The city administration also used the planning process as an opportunity to make further connections with the community. At every meeting, there were representatives of the Community Oriented Government team, a team charged with making connections between neighborhoods and city services. These people kept track of issues that came up in the discussion that could not be addressed by the master plan process and made sure that these issues were taken back to the appropriate departments and addressed.

Managerial Contributions

On the left side of Figure 22.2 are the contributions that management makes to this system of cascading vitality. They include enhancing agency, which we have already discussed in its relation to empowerment and setting the cascade in motion. Managers also make useful contributions in setting direction so that the power created is used in a manner that is consistent with the service mission. They buffer the system from external demands for control and predictability that can prevent employees from making changes and consequently drain energy from the system. Finally, they can provide support for inclusive processes. We describe each of these briefly below.

A key dimension of leaving the desk is the provision of legitimate direction for the responsible and accountable application of power that is generated in the empowerment process. Fear that sharing power with employees or members of the public entails losing control is one reason for avoiding empowering relationships. We argue that people with formal authority can continue to exercise control as they empower others (Boje & Rosile, 2001; Follett, 1940; Feldman & Khademian, 2000). They exercise control over things other than the direct actions of their subordinates. For instance, they exercise control over the kind of training opportunities that are available to their employees and the type of accounts that people are asked to make of their actions (Feldman & Khademian, 2000). Managers, we suggest, generate power and energy in the establishment of relationships among employees, across organizational boundaries, and with the public.

Another crucial part of the management contribution involves keeping energy from being drained out of the system. If employees are going to be leaving their desks and trying new ways of accomplishing their work, they are going to make mistakes. Moreover, if they are going to empower the public through inclusive processes, they are going to have less control over both the timing and the ultimate output of their work. Managers have to be able to protect and buffer their employees from the demand for work that is narrowly controlled from above. The demands for predictable and predictably defensible work are understandable, but seem likely to drain motivation from the system.

A third contribution that we identify is oriented to increasing the energy associated with inclusive processes as a particular way of empowering the public. Managers can provide specific support for engaging in inclusive processes. They can, for instance, help their employees learn about inclusive processes through traditional training practices and provide consulting support that makes available expertise specifically about the role of the public and how to engage the public more fully.

We suggest that managers, through these contributions, play an important part in maintaining and building the energy in the model. Just as they can buffer and protect the system of cascading vitality, they can provide guidance for the application of vital energy to public problems through the types of relationships they create and support, and the resources, skill, and information they provide to employees attempting to leave the desk.

CONCLUSION AND FUTURE RESEARCH QUESTIONS

A large literature created by consultants for organizations promotes many of the ideas we discuss in our model of cascading vitality. We agree with many authors in this literature who argue that leaders who share power can create energy within their organizations that will rival competitors and ultimately make organizations more competitive. In this chapter we extend these ideas to another domain of positive attention, the strengthening of the people and communities served by the organization. We are interested in the creation of vitality in public organizations that can cascade to members of the public and nurture the development of democratic processes. We present a model that outlines the dynamic relationships that we think are responsible for these outcomes. We draw on existing literature as well as on our interviews and observations of the dynamic cascade in operation. Whereas the consulting literature provides energy and enthusiasm for this approach to management, we hope to contribute to positive organizational scholarship by presenting a model as a basis for understanding the dynamic and for asking further research questions. We conclude with a few questions that the model helps us think about.

We have proposed thinking about the model as a system of energy. This raises questions about dynamics. Does the system need to import energy, is it self-sustaining, or does it export energy? If all three dynamics are possible, in what ways are they related to one another? Are power-sharing relationships the key source of energy, or are there other energy-generating techniques? Once generated, what are the most effective ways to channel the energy? Are there ways to channel the energy that are more likely to produce new cascades of energy? How does the system distinguish between negative and positive energy, or energy that stresses and wears upon individuals versus energy that lifts and invigorates (Ryan & Bernstein, 2002)?

This is an open system. Interactions with the political environment (or in the case of private-sector organizations, the market environment) and the public are both important to this system. Often, scholars view these environments as sources of energy loss for a public policy system, and ultimately a source of dysfunction (Warwick, 1975; Moe, 1989). We view these environments as potential sources of energy in part because they are sources of meaningfulness in work and meaningfulness at work (see Chapter 20). How can these environments be utilized to support or participate in the vitality cascade?

This is a system that has no boundaries. Participants reach across organizational and jurisdictional boundaries to craft processes that engage, address, and work to improve upon public issues, but there is never a point at which the job is done and one should stop. As with the external environment, this could be a source of energy depletion. Can this aspect of the system also become a source of invigoration?

Finally, this is a system that enables and requires flexibility. At the same time, one is likely to learn ways that "work" and likely will want to replicate and institutionalize them. This poses a fundamental dilemma. How does one institutionalize flexibility? Is this a model that can be institutionalized, or is it a model of positive deviance (see Chapter 14) that is most likely to succeed in a crisis or temporary situation?

Our model contributes to positive organizational scholarship by showing the dynamic potential in the relationship between individual, organization, and community and the role that organizational empowerment can have in creating and feeding these relationships. The model presents dynamic links between internal management efforts and democratic processes. Pratt and Ashforth (see Chapter 20) have shown that job redesign, employee involvement, and nurturing callings are all ways to make work more meaningful. Our model shows that these three are connected as employee involvement leads to job redesign, which enables employees to pursue their job as a calling. Inclusive processes allow employees to pursue the calling of creating democratic processes and expanding empowerment. Probing these links enables us to contribute to a better understanding of inclusive public processes that effectively address public problems, and also to understand the organizational dimensions of vitality that plant the seeds for such processes.

ACKNOWLEDGMENT

The research in this paper was supported in part by the Center for Local, State and Urban Policy at the University of Michigan.

CONCLUSION

Chapter 23

Developing a Discipline of Positive Organizational Scholarship

Kim S. Cameron, Jane E. Dutton, Robert E. Quinn, and Amy Wrzesniewski

The chapters in this book have introduced a wealth of insights and developments born of the new and emerging discipline called positive organizational scholarship (POS). Collectively the chapters chart exciting and relatively un-mapped territory in the study of behavior, processes, structures, and dynamics in organizations. The objective of this final chapter is to summarize and integrate some themes and insights found in the book. One liability of edited books is that the threads that bind the chapters together, and the overall value of the aggregation of the topics, are lost without an attempt at integration. It is not difficult to get excited about individual chapters in this volume and the specific contributions made by each, but it is also important to highlight the excitement and the positive energy that is associated with the overall discipline of POS. This final chapter aspires to help illuminate some exciting paths that, hopefully, will be traversed by other scholars in the future.

Baumeister, Bratslavsky, Finkenauer, and Vohs (2001) demonstrated the pervasiveness and impact of negative events, behaviors, and outcomes in human behavior. Negative or "bad" occurrences, for example, appear to have greater impact on individual emotions and behavior than positive or "good" occurrences. Thus, because negative phenomena capture the most attention and, according to Baumeister and colleagues, account for the most variance in predicting outcomes, it is not surprising that most research in psychology and organizational studies has been problem focused.

On the other hand, positive phenomena are associated with what individuals and organizations aspire to be when they are at their very best. These are the phenomena that separate humans from other creatures. Even household pets learn the meaning of "bad" and "good," but states of virtuousness, transcendence, and high-quality connections, for example, are uniquely human. They represent states of flourishing, ennoblement, and vitality. What makes life meaningful and abundant is more closely connected to positive phenomena than to negative phenomena. Endeavoring to understand these positive human processes and dynamics within organizations requires that new phenomena are examined, new explanatory theories are developed, and new ways of seeing are created. POS aims to contribute to these outcomes.

The chapters in this volume demonstrate the importance of positive phenomena and their enablers in organizations. The authors, however, have taken somewhat different approaches to examining this new territory. Some work builds on a definitional foundation—carefully circumscribing concepts and grounding them in scholarly literature. Concepts such as resilience, transcendence, meaningfulness, cascading vitality, virtuousness, callings, courageous principled action, and positive deviance are examples. Other work explores relationships among various positive dynamics in organizations—including positive emotions and individual behavior, highquality connections and performance, social networks and positive energy, virtuousness and profitability, appreciative questioning and organizational change, empowerment and cascading vitality, and meaningfulness and work outcomes. Still other work investigates extraordinarily positive outcomes such as transcendent behavior, meaningfulness in and at work, organizational resilience, positive energy in individuals and systems, learning and new knowledge creation, avoiding highly probable errors, and lifegiving relationships.

We have organized these chapters into three parts, each representing a major domain of POS. The chapters within each part illustrate, demarcate, and elaborate these domains, and the brief introduction to each part highlights the range of generative ideas and research questions associated with the section's theme. This chapter, however, looks across parts to highlight key insights that find synergy across the various authors' perspectives. The purpose is to convey an invitation to other scholars to engage in their own investigations of the exciting and energizing phenomena embedded in the discipline of positive organizational scholarship.

GENERATIVE INSIGHTS

One theme that emerges from the chapters is that individuals, organizations, and societies benefit from institutionalized virtuousness. Virtuousness is an orientation toward human fulfillment and social betterment, characterized by ennobling human behaviors. Social stability, reciprocity, and commerce all are shaped by the collective expression of virtuousness in forms such as character strengths, gratitude, transcendence, courage, forgiveness, compassion, and authenticity. Chapters highlight the positive relationships between virtuousness and individual and organizational functioning—for example, meaningfulness at work, personal improvement among employees, and organizational effectiveness—as a result of its self-reinforcing effects and its associations with high-quality connections. Virtuousness also serves as an inoculation agent against negative, damaging, and weakening occurrences in organizations. Authors' explanations for why virtuousness in and enabled by organizations is such an important enabler of positive outcomes include its capability to provide various kinds of resources, create buffering effects, capitalize on competing values found in organizational forms, provide meaning amid uncertainty, foster new knowledge creation, and enable positive feedback processes that contribute to positive deviance inside and outside organizations (Park & Peterson, Chapter 3; Cameron, Chapter 4; Emmons, Chapter 6; Worline & Quinn, Chapter 10; Lee, Caza, Edmondson, & Thomke, Chapter 13; Spreitzer & Sonenshein, Chapter 14; Feldman & Khademian, Chapter 22).

A second theme relates to the power of appreciating strengths in approaching individual and organizational change. The positive attributes, past successes, and strengths of individuals and organizations serve as more effective targets of change and improvement than do problems, weaknesses, or underdeveloped qualities (Clifton & Harter, Chapter 8). Various authors explain how and why building and accentuating strengths is advantageous over attempts to shore up human weakness. Almost all living systems are subject to the heliotropic effect—an inclination toward the positive and away from the negative—so focusing on achievements, assets, potentials, innovations, strengths, elevated thoughts, opportunities, benchmarks, high point moments, lived values, traditions, strategic competencies, memorable stories, and expressions of wisdom (Cooperrider & Sekerka, Chapter 15) leads to a fusion of individual and organizational strengths. This, in turn, leads to the activation of positive energy and, subsequently, to positive organizational performance. Of course, an emphasis on the positive does not preclude the value of the negative (Bagozzi, Chapter 12). This is illustrated by the finding that high-performing teams and long-lasting relationships have a ratio of five positive interactions to every one negative interaction (Losada, 1999; Gottman, 1994). The ratio is not five to zero, and the negative interactions serve as foil against which to interpret and activate the strengths in the positive. In addition, organizational and individual strengths are sometimes evidenced by mere normality—an absence of mistakes and crises—when deterioration or weakness is the predicted condition. When organizations should fail but don't, when they bounce back but shouldn't, when they remain flexible and agile but ought to become rigid, the presence of resilience—for example, maintaining the status quo—is also an extraordinarily positive strength (Weick, Chapter 5; Sutcliffe & Vogus, Chapter 7; Bateman & Porath, Chapter 9).

A third integrative theme relates to the self-reinforcing nature of positive emotions, positive energy, and positive human connections. For example, positive emotions not only serve as a cause and consequence of positive outcomes in individuals and organizations, but also create positive, self-reinforcing spirals that broaden thought-action repertoires—that is, individuals and organizations develop more human resources, intellectual resources, social resources, and psychological resources (Fredrickson, Chapter 11). High-quality connections are life-giving rather than life-depleting. Their positive energy is easily discerned by those involved in them, they enhance emotional carrying capacity and tensility (the ability to bend under pressure), and they are important contributors to processes of learning, identity creation, and growth (Dutton & Heaphy, Chapter 17). They create the transfer of vital resources between individuals and organizations.

The most generative relationships are infused with physiological significance, so that actual physiological and organizational functioning are enhanced. They are infused with emotional significance in that they highlight how the connection relates to experienced vitality and engagement. They are infused with existential significance emphasizing that different connections facilitate the crafting of different identities and meanings. They are infused with material significance in exposing people to difference amounts and qualities of information and resources, which endow individuals with differing amounts of power, choice points for action, and coordination capacity (Gittell, Chapter 18). Positive emotions, positive energy, and positive human connections lead, in other words, to mutually reinforcing upward spirals of meaningful experience and extraordinary performance.

Fourth, a variety of authors point out that rather than being neutral entities, organizational conditions can enable or disable positive dynamics, primarily through a sense of meaningfulness. Organizational forms and organizing processes determine the micro-contexts in which people function, the meaning that people make of their own experience, the information and opportunities available for people to excel, and the resources that facilitate or hinder positive individual and organizational performance. For example, organizations can make resources available that are motivating and enabling; they can provide empowerment and freedom for individuals to perform at their best; they can structure communication patterns and human connections that enable the execution of coordination in highly dependent tasks; they can provide examples of authentic leadership; and they can institutionalize positive networks that affect both internal and external constituencies' performance. In particular, these mechanisms can infuse meaning into work and into work organizations (Luthans & Avolio, Chapter 16; Wrzesniewski, Chapter 19; Baker, Cross, & Wooten, Chapter 21). Meaningfulness may occur by clarifying goals, purpose, and values and by connecting those factors to the core values of employees—an integration of doing and being (Pratt & Ashforth, Chapter 20). Doing good along with doing well, recognizing and supporting the salience of employee family and personal life, and exemplifying integrity and virtuousness in organizational policies, routines, and culture are among the belief system factors associated with meaningfulness in organizations.

Organizational design, then, can be seen as a positive source of connection and coordination, not merely a structure for achieving task objectives.

In sum, positive organizational scholarship brings together ideas that have not been previously integrated—for example, empowerment on the inside of organizations changes the capacities and dynamics that enable empowerment on the outside. POS makes that which may have been interpreted as detrimental to performance be seen as potentially helpful—for example, contradictions, skepticism, ambivalence, complexity, and advanced publicizing of intentions all are frequently interpreted as antithetical to high reliability, yet they can help organizations maintain positivity and resiliency in the face of tragedy and trauma. POS also enriches our understanding of the dynamics and effects of common phenomena that may not have been considered in a positive light—for example, social networks can collect and distribute not only information and resources but also positive energy. New variables, processes, and relationships that have seldom been considered are uncovered and explained (e.g., positive energy, positive emotions, high-quality connections, virtuousness, vitality, and meaningfulness).

PUZZLES AND UNANSWERED QUESTIONS

One key objective of this volume is to invite organizational scholars to engage in further examination of these and other relevant phenomena related to POS. A number of key questions remain unexamined, and much is yet to be learned. We highlight six categories of questions that emerge from the work in this volume

Level of Analysis

A variety of questions relate to the level of analysis at which phenomena occur and the extent to which relationships at one level of analysis can be observed at another level. Specifically, do individual dynamics reproduce themselves in organizations, and vice versa? Why or why not? Relationships between individual expressions of virtuousness and individual performance and health have been demonstrated, for example, but do these same dynamics occur in organizations?

Expressions of gratitude by individuals affect others' attitudes and behaviors, but how much does this generalize to organizations? Positive individual emotions lead to positive individual outcomes, but does positive emotionality have the same effects in organizations? Do high-quality connections among individuals have the same kinds of effects in organizations as they do in the lives of the individuals involved? Do interpretations of meaningfulness in work produce a sense of meaningfulness of work in the organization? Does empowerment inside an organization lead to empowerment in the network of constituent organizations or the broader social environment? Demonstrating relationships at one level of analysis does not necessarily mean that they will be present in another, and understanding what is *organizational* is an important challenge for POS researchers.

Measurement

The variables and concepts associated with POS have often been ignored or relegated to religion or philosophy. They have been left out of equations in disciplines such as economics and sociology. Few instruments, methods, or reliable indicators have been developed to assess positive phenomena. Specifically, how are positive concepts and variables best identified, measured, and explained? What are the key indicators? How does the process of inquiry shape the results? For example, self-report instrumentation may not be appropriate for measuring concepts such as positive energy, humility, or virtuousness. Key indicators have not been identified for organizational phenomena such as resilience, transcendence, authentic leadership, virtuousness, or even positive deviance. Since POS focuses on what factors help people experience or express more of the whole self in the workplace, what are the dimensions of the whole self? A need exists to locate and measure the existence of extraordinarily positive states, processes, structures, and behavior. What are the markers? Moreover, the manner in which investigations occur may have impact on the phenomena being observed. Asking appreciative questions or seeking for positive dynamics may actually produce them or may alter the interpretations people place on their experiences. Questions relating to what is measured as well as how it is measured are clearly in need of investigation.

Causal Associations

Questions relating to causal directionality have a central place in POS. That is, what are the causal relationships (directionality) associated with various positive phenomena? Do positive emotions produce creativity and learning, or does the causal directionality go in the opposite direction? Do high-quality connections lead to rapid learning, or vice versa? Which comes first, virtuousness or high performance in organizations? Typical questions related to which causal variables are most important are also important in studying positive phenomena. For example, how important is authentic leadership in high-performing organizations? What specific aspects of highquality connections and social networks produce positive outcomes? What features of organizations and of environments shape the construction of positive meaning about work, self, and the organization? Also, why does improvement occur more with a focus on strengths than on weaknesses? To what extent must a balance be present in positive outcomes between strengths and weaknesses? Can weaknesses be ignored?

Supplementing these usual causal questions, however, is an even more complex causality issue that arises when studying positive phenomena. Because some positive phenomena tend to produce mutually reinforcing, positive spirals, the typical causal relationship questions may not be relevant in studying positive dynamics. Differentiating among independent and dependent variables may be less germane in POS because both factors can serve to enhance and reinforce the other. For example, positive emotions foster enduring individual resources and reserves that foster organizational thriving. This, in turn, fosters positive emotions or an elevating spiral of positivity.

Separating predictors from effects—or identifying which is which—under conditions of mutual reinforcement and contagion presents special research challenges to POS investigators as they uncover extraordinarily positive organizational dynamics.

Enablement

In addition to questions of causal association, issues relating to the mere enablement of positivity also are salient. Certain factors appear to enable positive outcomes, and uncovering why and how this happens is an important issue for POS scholars. For example, what are the attributes of the structures, processes, cultures, leadership behaviors, and/or resources that are most conducive to, or resistant of, positive dynamics in organizations? What kinds of organizational arrangements are conducive to high-quality connections, positive energy development, or resilience? What factors create conditions where organizations avoid highly probable errors or disasters? How can organizations best buffer themselves from negative encroachments from the environment? What organizational conditions facilitate the development of emotional competence and authentic leadership, or bring forth the best in people? Studies of enablement are not the same as searching for a "best practices" approach to organizational behavior. Highlighting best practice avoids systems-level thinking that explains the processes and dynamics by which organizations become sites for growth and health. Cameron and Quinn (1999) argued that organizations often fail to get results from implementing the best practices because these organizations import a set of discrete, unconnected pieces of practice without attending to the underlying philosophy or system in which such practices need to be embedded in order to take root and change the organization. Likewise, POS does not merely advocate a research agenda meant to surface best practices, but rather advocates studying the processes and mechanisms that allow for and encourage excellence, growth, and health.

Time

Issues related to the temporal dimension of positive phenomena also invite scholarly research. Illustrative questions are: How long does it take for positive dynamics to unfold, to be demonstrated, and to produce effects? What are the temporal relationships between virtuousness and profitability? How long does heedful interrelating or respectful interaction need to occur to produce positive outcomes? What is the half life of organizational resilience? When does deterioration occur and at what rate? How quickly do positive emotions produce broadening and building outcomes? What is the duration of high-quality connections and of their relationships to positive energy? As POS scholars focus more and more on self-reinforcing positive spirals, issues of time frame and phase development will arise, and these issues represent fruitful areas for future investigation.

New Concepts and New Relationships

Most new areas of investigation are labeled as new because of original theoretical explanations but also because of new variables and new phenomena that are uncovered or highlighted. In POS, there is an orientation toward identifying what previously unexamined factors may help explain positive phenomena. For example, concepts have been examined in this volume relating to positive energy, transcendent behavior, organizational virtuousness, resilience, strengths, courageous principled action, positive deviance, high-quality connections, authentic leadership, meaningfulness, cascading vitality, and positive network ties. Most of these concepts have been newly introduced in this volume or have been rarely examined. POS invites and encourages scholars to increase the number of relevant positive phenomena that can be investigated. What aspects of individual and organizational phenomena have not been taken into account in explaining performance? What environmental, organizational, or individual factors might affect positive organizational and individual outcomes? What concepts from other disciplines might help inform POS? What might be the unexamined effects, causal mechanisms, or manifestations of concepts central to, say, medicine, biomechanics, psychology, or computer science? How might systems dynamics or complexity theory explain self-reinforcing positive spirals among POS concepts? The point is that most empirical organizational studies account for small percentages of the variance in explaining organizational outcomes. POS hopes to encourage the examination of previously underrepresented positive phenomena in organizational scholarship.

In sum, positive organizational scholarship aspires to increase the breadth of phenomena being described and explained in organizational studies by expanding the kinds of variables being examined and by developing richer theories of the dynamics of positivity. Understanding positive dynamics that have heretofore been neglected or underexamined is the desired outcome. A host of research issues are embedded in this aspiration, of course, several of which are highlighted in this volume. They include: the extent to which relationships at one level of analysis—say among individuals—can be extrapolated to another level of analysis (say, organizations); the key indicators and measurement devices to be used in POS research; the causal associations among variables and the relevance of dependent or independent variables given self-reinforcing positive dynamics; identifying enabling factors that enhance or restrict the development of positive processes and outcomes; the time frames that must be considered when identifying positive dynamics and their development; and what new variables and theoretical relationships must be uncovered or developed to explain the positive dynamics in systems.

CONCLUSION

We began this chapter by referring to a review of the psychological literature by Baumeister, Bratslavsky, Finkenauer, and Vohs (2001), concluding that "bad" or negative factors have greater impact on human beings than "good" or positive factors. A single traumatic episode, a single incident of negative feedback, or a single loss, for example, has stronger effects on people than a single happy episode, a single incident of positive feedback, or a single win. Multiple positive events are required to overcome the effects of a single negative event, and a single negative event can undo the effects of multiple positive events. On the other hand, individuals are inherently attracted to that which is inspiring, positive, and uplifting. All human systems *desire* to experience that which is good. The aspiration for fulfillment is ubiquitous, yet it has gone largely unnoticed in organizational studies and has seldom been studied scientifically. Baumeister and colleagues' finding that a dearth of research exists on the effects of the positive and good in psychology is equally typical in organizational studies. Seldom have investigations examined the factors that may lead to self-reinforcing positive cycles and to extraordinarily positive outcomes.

The discipline of positive organizational scholarship is an invitation to investigate, in rigorous, systematic, and enlivening ways, the phenomena that are associated with flourishing, vitality, virtue, meaning, and life-giving dynamics. The fact that the human race, and organizations in particular, thrive and flourish amid difficult, threatening, ambiguous, and turbulent conditions is testimony to the power of positive phenomena in mitigating and overcoming the more impactful negative factors. Too little is known about these positive processes and their interrelationships, and we encourage others to join in this new and exciting adventure.

References

Chapter 1

Batson, C.D. (1991). *The altruism question: Toward a social-psychological answer.* Hillsdale, NJ: Larence Erlbaum.

_____(1994). Why act for the public good? Four answers. *Personality and Social Psychology Bulletin,* 20:603–610.

Bolino, M.C., Turnley, W.H., & Bloodgood, J.M. (2002). Citizenship behavior and the creation of social capital in organizations. *Academy of Management Review,* 27:505–522.

Cooperrider, D.L., & Whitney, D. (2000). A positive revolution in change: Appreciative inquiry. In Cooperrider, D.L., Sorenson, P.F., Whitney, D., & Yeager, T.F. (Eds.), *Appreciative inquiry* (pp.3–28). Champaign, IL: Stipes.

Cowen, E.L. (1977). Baby steps toward primary prevention. *American Journal of Community Psychology,* 5:1–22.

_____(1980). The wooing of primary prevention. *American Journal of Community Psychology,* 8:258–284.

_____(1986). Primary prevention in mental health: Ten years of retrospect and ten years of prospect. In Kessler, M., & Goldston, S.E. (Eds.), *A decade of progress in primary prevention* (pp.3–45). Hanover, NH: University Press of New England.

_____(1994). The enhancement of psychological wellness: Challenges and opportunities. *American Journal of Community Psychology,* 22:149–179.

_____(1999). In sickness and in health: Primary prevention's vows revisited. In Cicchetti, D., & Toth, S.L. (Eds.), *Rochester symposium on developmental psychopathology:Developmental approaches to prevention and intervention,* vol.10 (pp.1–24). Rochester: University of Rochester Press.

Cowen, E.L., Gardner, E.A., & Zax, M. (Eds.) (1973). *Emergent approaches to mental health problems: An overview and directions for future work.* New York: Appleton-Century Crofts.

Cowen, E.L., & Kilmer, R.P. (2002). Positive psychology: Some plusses and some open issues. *Journal of Community Psychology,* 30:449–460.

Durlak, J.A., & Wells, A.M. (1997). Primary prevention programs for children and adolescents: A meta-analytic review. *American Journal of Community Psychology,* 25:115–152.

George, J.M. (1991). State or trait: Effects of positive mood on prosocial behaviors at work. *Journal of Applied Psychology,* 76:299–307.

Jahoda, M. (1958). *Current concepts of positive mental health.* New York: Basic Books.

Krebs, D.L. (1975). Empathy and altruism. *Journal of Personality and Social Psychology,* 32:1134–1146.

Margolis, J.D., & Walsh, J.P. (2002). Misery loves companies: Whither social initiatives by business? Working paper, University of Michigan Business School.

Organ, D.W. (1988). *Organizational citizenship behavior: The good soldier syndrome.* Lexington, MA: Lexington Books.

Podsakoff, P.M., MacKenzie, S.B., Paine, J.B., & Bachrach, D.G. (2000). Organizational citizenship behaviors: A critical review of the theoretical and empirical literature and suggestions for future research. *Journal of Management,* 26:513–563.

Seligman, M.E.P. (2002). *Authentic happiness: Using the new positive psychology to realize your potential for lasting fulfillment.* New York: Free Press.

Snyder, C.R., & Lopez, S.J. (2002). *Handbook of positive psychology.* New York: Oxford University Press.

Srivastava, S., & Cooperrider, D.L. (1999). *Appreciative management and leadership: The power of positive thought and action in organization.* San Francisco: Jossey Bass.

Whetten, D.A., Rands, G., & Godfrey, P. (2001). What are the responsibilities of business to society? In Pettigrew, A., Thomas, H., & Whittington, R. (Eds.), *Handbook of Strategy and Management* (pp.373–408). Thousand Oaks, CA: Sage.

Zax, M., & Cowen, E.L. (1976). *Abnormal psychology: Changing conceptions.* New York: Holt, Rinehart, & Winston.

Chapter 2

Alloy, L.B., & Abramson, L.Y. (1979). Judgment of contingency in depressed and nondepressed college students: Sadder but wiser? *Journal of Experimental Psychology: General,* 108:441–487.

American Psychiatric Association (1994). *Diagnostic and statistical manual of mental disorders.* 4th ed. Washington, DC: APA.

Aspinwall, L.G., & Staudinger, U.M. (Eds.) (in press). *A psychology of human strengths: Perspectives on an emerging field.* Washington, DC: American Psychological Association.

Bacigalupe, G. (2001). Is positive psychology only white psychology? *American Psychologist,* 56:82–83.

Baltes, P.B., & Staudinger, U.M. (1993). The search for a psychology of wisdom. *Current Directions in Psychological Science,* 2:75–80.

Brokaw, T. (1998). *The greatest generation.* New York: Random House.

Buckingham, M., & Clifton, D.O. (2001). *Now, discover your strengths.* New York: Free Press.

Buss, D.M. (1994). *The evolution of desire: Strategies of human mating.* New York: Basic Books.

Chang, E.C. (Ed.) (2001). *Optimism and pessimism: Implications for theory, research, and practice.* Washington, DC: American Psychological Association.

Chang, E.C., D'Zurilla, T.J., & Maydeu-Olivares, A. (1994). Assessing the dimensionality of optimism and pessimism using a multimeasure approach. *Cognitive Therapy and Research,* 18:143–160.

Cowen, E.L., & Kilmer, R.P. (2002). "Positive psychology": Some plusses and some open issues. *Journal of Community Psychology,* 30:440–460.

Crowne, D.P., & Marlowe, D. (1964). *The approval motive: Studies in evaluative dependence.* New York: Wiley.

Csikszentmihalyi, M. (1990). *Flow: The psychology of optimal experience.* New York: HarperCollins.

Danner, D.D., Snowdon, D.A., & Friesen, W.V. (2001). Positive emotions in early life and longevity: Findings from the nun study. *Journal of Personality and Social Psychology,* 80:804–813.

Diener, E. (1984). Subjective well-being. *Psychological Bulletin,* 95:542–575.

Diener, E., & Seligman, M.E.P. (2002). Very happy people. *Psychological Science,* 13:80–83.

Easterbrook, G. (2001). I'm OK, you're OK. *The New Republic,* March 5, pp.20–23.

Fredrickson, B.L. (1998). What good are positive emotions? *Review of General Psychology,* 2:300–319.

Gardner, H. (1983). *Frames of mind: The theory of multiple intelligences.* New York: Basic Books.

Gillham, J.E. (Ed.) (2000). *The science of optimism and hope: Research essays in honor of Martin E.P. Seligman.* Radnor, PA: Templeton Foundation Press.

Greenberg, M., Domitrovich, C., & Bumbarger, B. (1999). *Preventing mental disorders in*

224

school-age children. Washington, DC: Center for Mental Health Services, U.S. Department of Health and Human Services.

Harker, L.A., & Keltner, D. (2001). Expressions of positive emotion in women's college yearbook pictures and their relationship to personality and life outcomes across adulthood. *Journal of Personality and Social Psychology,* 80:112–124.

Jahoda, M. (1958). *Current concepts of positive mental health.* New York: Basic Books.

James, W. (1890). *Principles of psychology.* 2 vols. New York: Holt.

Jamieson, K.H. (2000). *Everything you think you know about politics ... and why you're wrong.* New York: Basic Books.

Keltner, D., & Haidt, J. (in press). Approaching awe, a moral, spiritual, and aesthetic emotion. *Cognition and Emotion.*

Keyes, C.L.M., & Haidt, J. (Eds.) (in press). *Flourishing: The positive person and the good life.* Washington, DC: American Psychological Association.

Kraepelin, E. (1899). *Psychiatrie: Ein lehrbuch fur studirende und Aerzte.* Leipzig: Verlag von Johann Ambrosius Barth.

Lazarus, R.A. (in press). Does the positive psychology movement have legs? *Psychological Inquiry.*

Masten, A. (2001). Ordinary magic: Resilience processes in development. *American Psychologist,* 56:227–238.

Myers, D.G., & Diener, E. (1995). Who is happy? *Psychological Science,* 6:10–19.

Nathan, P.E., & Gorman, J.M. (1998). *A guide to treatments that work.* New York: Oxford.

Park, N., & Peterson, C.M. (in press). Virtues in organizations. In Cameron, K.S., Dutton, J.E., & Quinn, R.E. (Eds.), *Positive organizational scholarship.* San Francisco: Berrett-Koehler.

Peterson, C. (2000). The future of optimism. *American Psychologist,* 55:44–55.

Peterson, C., & Bossio, L.M. (1991). *Health and optimism.* New York: Free Press.

226

Peterson, C., & Seligman, M.E.P. (1984). Causal explanations as a risk factor for depression: Theory and evidence. *Psychological Review,* 91:347–374.

_____(2002). Values in Action (VIA) classification of strengths. Available at http://psych.upenn.edu/seligman/taxonomy.htm.

_____(in press). Character strengths before and after September 11. *Psychological Science.*

Peterson, C., & Vaidya, R.S. (in press). Optimism as virtue and vice. In Chang, E.C., & Sanna, L.J. (Eds.),*Personality, strategies, and adjustment: Beyond virtue and vice.* Washington, DC: American Psychological Association.

Redelmeier, D.A., & Singh, S.M. (2001). Survival in Academy Award–winning actors and actresses. *Annals of Internal Medicine,* 134: 955–962.

Reisman, J.M. (1991). *A history of clinical psychology.* 2nd ed. New York: Hemisphere.

Rokeach, M. (1973). *The nature of human values.* New York: Free Press.

Ryff, C. (1989). Happiness is everything, or is it? Explorations on the meaning of psychological well-being. *Journal of Personality and Social Psychology,* 57:1069–1081.

Saleebey, D. (Ed.) (1992). *The strengths perspective in social work practice.* New York: Longman.

Scheier, M.F., & Carver, C.S. (1985). Optimism, coping, and health: Assessment and implications of generalized outcome expectancies. *Health Psychology,* 4:219–247.

Schwartz, S.H. (1994). Are there universal aspects in the structure and contents of human values? *Journal of Social Issues,* 50(4):19–45.

Segerstrom, S.C., Taylor, S.E., Kemeny, M.E., & Fahey, J.L. (1998). Optimism is associated with mood, coping, and immune change in response to stress. *Journal of Personality and Social Psychology,* 74:1646–1655.

Seligman, M.E.P. (1991). *Learned optimism.* New York: Knopf.

_____(1994). *What you can change and what you can't.* New York: Knopf.

_____(1998a). Positive psychology network concept paper. Available at http://psych.upenn.edu/seligman/ppgrant.htm.

_____(1998b). Positive social science. *The APA Monitor Online,* 29(4). Available at http://www.apa.org/monitor/apr98/pres.html.

_____(1999). The president's address. *American Psychologist,* 54:559–562.

_____(2002). *Authentic happiness.* New York: Free Press.

Seligman, M.E.P., & Csikszentmihalyi, M. (2000). Positive psychology: An introduction. *American Psychologist,* 55:5–14.

Seligman, M.E.P., & Peterson, C. (in press). Positive clinical psychology. In Aspinwall, L.G., & Staudinger, U.M. (Eds.), *A psychology of human strengths: Perspectives on an emerging field* pp.305–318)). Washington, DC: American Psychological Association.

Seligman, M.E.P., Reivich, K., Jaycox, L., & Gillham, J. (1995). *The optimistic child.* Boston: Houghton Mifflin.

Snyder, C.R. (1994). *The psychology of hope: You can get there from here.* New York: Free Press.

Snyder, C.R., & Lopez, S. (Eds.) (2001). *Handbook of positive psychology.* New York: Oxford University Press.

Sternberg, R.J. (1998). A balance theory of wisdom. *Review of General Psychology,* 2:347–365.

Taylor, E.I. (2001). Positive psychology versus humanistic psychology: A reply to Prof. Seligman. *Journal of Humanistic Psychology,* 41:13–29.

Vaillant, G.E. (2002). *Aging well.* Boston: Little, Brown.

Walsh. R. (2001). Positive psychology: East and west. *American Psychologist,* 56:83–84.

Watson, D., Clark, L.A., & Carey, G. (1988). Positive and negative affectivity and their relation to anxiety and depressive disorders. *Journal of Abnormal Psychology,* 97:346–353.

Wilson, E.O. (1975). *Sociobiology: The new synthesis.* Cambridge: Harvard University Press.

World Health Organization (1990). *International classification of diseases and related health problems.* 10th rev. Geneva: WHO.

Wrzesniewski, A., McCauley, C.R., Rozin, P., & Schwartz, B. (1997). Jobs, careers, and callings: People's relations to their work. *Journal of Research in Personality,* 31:21–33.

Yearley, L.H. (1990). *Mencius and Aquinas: Theories of virtue and conceptions of courage.* Albany: State University of New York Press.

Zullow, H., Oettingen, G., Peterson, C., & Seligman, M.E.P. (1988). Explanatory style and pessimism in the historical record: CAVing LBJ, presidential candidates, and East versus West Berlin. *American Psychologist,* 43:673–682.

Chapter 3

Anderman, E.M., Maehr, M.L. (1994). Motivation and schooling in the middle grades. *Review of Educational Research,* 64:287–309.

Baumrind, D. (1971). Current patterns of parental authority. *Developmental Psychology Monographs,* 4(1, Part 2).

_____(1978). Parental disciplinary patterns and social comparison in children. *Youth and Society,* 9:239–276.

Bok, S. (1995). *Common values.* Columbia: University of Missouri Press.

Buckingham, M., & Clifton, D.O. (2001). *Now, discover your strengths.* New York: Free Press.

Buckingham, M., & Coffman, C. (1999). *First, break all the rules.* New York: Simon & Schuster.

Collaborative for Academic, Social, and Emotional Learning (CASEL) (2002). *Safe and sound: An education leader's guide to evidence-based social and emotional learning programs.* Chicago: CASEL.

Collins, J. (2001). *Good to great.* New York: HarperCollins.

Collins, J.C., & Porras, J.I. (1997). *Built to last.* New York: HarperCollins.

Comte-Sponville, A. (2001). *A small treatise on the great virtues.* Trans. C. Temerson. New York: Metropolitan Books.

Confucius (1992). *Analects.* Trans. D. Hinton. Washington, DC: Counterpoint.

Cowen, E.L. (1997). Schools and the enhancement of children's wellness: Some opportunities and some limiting factors. In Gullota, T.P., Weissberg, R.P., Hampton, R.L., Ryan, B.A., & Adams, G.R. (Eds.), *Healthy children 2010: Establishing preventive services* (pp.87–123). Thousand Oaks, CA: Sage.

Dahlsgaard, K., Peterson, C., & Seligman, M.E.P. (2002). *Virtues converge across culture and history.* Unpublished manuscript, University of Pennsylvania.

Elias, M.J., & Weissberg, R.P. (2000). Wellness in the schools: The grandfather of primary prevention tells a story. In Cicchetti, D., Rappaport, J.R., Sandler, I., & Weissberg, R.P. (Eds.), *The promotion of wellness in children and adolescents* (pp.243–269). Washington, DC: CWLA Press.

233

Elias, M.J., Zins, J., Weissberg, R.P., Frey, K., Greenberg, M., Haynes, N., Kessler, R., Schwab-Stone, M., & Shriver, T. (1997). *Promoting social and emotional learning: Guidelines for educators.* Alexandria, VA: Association for Supervision and Curriculum Development.

Felner, R.D. (2000). Educational reform as ecologically-based prevention and promotion: The project on high performance learning communities. In Cicchetti, D., Rappaport, J.R., Sandler, I., & Weissberg, R.P. (Eds.), *The promotion of wellness in children and adolescents* (pp.271–308). Washington, DC: CWLA Press.

Felner, R.D., Felner, T.Y., & Silverman, M.M. (2000). Prevention in mental health and social intervention: Conceptual and methodological issues in the evolution of the science and practice of prevention. In Rappaport, J., & Seidman, E., *Handbook of Community Psychology* (pp.9–42). New York: Kluwer Academic/Plenum.

Haberman, D.L. (1998). Confucianism: The way of the sages. In Stevenson, L., & Haberman, D.L. (Eds.), *Ten theories of human nature,* 3rd ed. (pp.25–44). New York: Oxford University Press.

Hawkins, J.D., & Lam T. (1987). Teacher practices, social development, and delinquency. In Burchard, J.D., & Burchard, S.N. (Eds.), *Prevention of delinquent behavior* (pp.241–274). Newbury Park, CA: Sage.

Hunter, L., & Elias, M.J. (1998). Violence in the high schools: Issues, controversies, policies, and prevention programs. In Roberts, A. (Ed.), *Juvenile justice: Policies, programs, and services,* 2nd ed. (pp.71–94). Chicago: Nelson-Hall.

Jahoda, M. (1958). *Current concepts of positive mental health.* New York: Basic Books.

Jamieson, K.H. (2000). *Civic engagement conference.* Available at www.positive-psych ology.org/ppcivicengage.htm.

Lyon, R. (1999). *Literacy in America.* Symposium at the University of Rhode Island, Kingston, RI, February.

Maehr, M.L. (1991). The "psychological environment" of the school: A focus for school leadership. In Maehr, M.L., & Ames, C. (Eds.), *Advances in educational administration,* vol.2, *School leadership* (pp.51–81). Greenwich, CT: JAI Press.

Maehr, M.L., Ames, R., & Braskamp, L.A. (1988). *Instructional leadership evaluation and development program (I LEAD).* Champaign, IL: MetriTech.

Maehr, M.L., & Braskamp, L.A. (1986). *The motivation factor: A theory of personal investment.* Lexington, MA: D.C. Heath.

Maehr, M.L., & Midgley, C. (1996). *Transforming school cultures.* Boulder, CO: Westview Press.

Maehr, M.L., Midgley, C., & Urdan, T. (1992). School leader as motivator. *Educational Administration Quarterly,* 18:412–431.

Midgley, C., Anderman, E., & Hicks, L. (1995). Differences between elementary and middle school teachers and students: A goal theory approach. *Journal of Early Adolescence,* 15:90–113.

Myers, D.G., & Diener, E. (1995). Who is happy? *Psychological Science,* 6:10–19.

Pepler, D.J., & Slaby, R. (1994). Theoretical and developmental perspectives on youth and violence. In Eron, L., Gentry, J., & Schlegel, P. (Eds.), *Reason to hope: A psychosocial perspective on violence and youth* (pp.27–58). Washington, DC: American Psychological Association.

Peters, T.J., & Waterman, R.H. (1982). *In search of excellence: Lessons from America's best-run companies.* New York: Warner.

Peterson, C. (2003). Classification of positive traits in youth. In Lerner, R.M., Jacobs, F., & Wertlieb, D. (Eds.), *Promoting positive child, adolescent, and family development: A handbook of program and policy innovations,* vol.4 (pp.227–255). Thousand Oaks, CA: Sage.

Peterson, C., & Seligman, M.E.P. (2003). *The VIA classification of strengths and virtues.* Washington, DC: American Psychological Association.

_____(in press). Character strengths before and after September 11. *Psychological Science.*

Roeser, R.W., & Eccles, J.S. (1998). Adolescents' perceptions of middle school: Relation to longitudinal changes in academic and psychological adjustment. *Journal of Research on Adolescence,* 8:123–158.

Schneider, S.F. (2000). The importance of being Emory: Issues in training for the enhancement of psychological wellness. In Cicchetti, D., Rappaport, J.R., Sandler, I., & Weissberg, R.P. (Eds.), *The promotion of wellness in children and adolescents* (pp.439–476). Washington, DC: CWLA Press.

Seligman, M.E.P. (2002). *Authentic happiness.* New York: Free Press.

Seligman, M.E.P., & Csikszentmihalyi, M. (2000). Positive psychology: An introduction. *American Psychologist,* 55:5–14.

Shaw, R.B. (1997). *Trust in the balance.* San Francisco: Jossey-Bass.

Starr, C.G. (1985). *The ancient Romans.* New York: Oxford University Press.

Weissberg, R.P., Barton, H., & Shriver, T.P. (1997). The social competence promotion program for young adolescents. In Albee, G.W., & Gullotta, T.P. (Eds.), *Primary prevention works* (pp.268–290). Thousand Oaks, CA: Sage.

Chapter 4

Adler, P.S., & Kwon, S. (2002). Social capital: Prospects for a new concept. *Academy of Management Review,* 27:17–40.

Aristotle. *Metaphysics XII,* 7:3–4.

Asch, S.E. (1952). *Social psychology.* Englewood Cliffs, NJ: Prentice Hall.

Baker, W. (2000). *Achieving success through social capital.* San Francisco: Jossey-Bass.

Barge, J.K. & Oliver, C. (2003). Working with appreciation in managerial practice. *Academy of Management Review,* 28: 124–141.

Bateman, T.S., & Organ, D.W. (1983). Job satisfaction and the good soldier: The relationship between affect and employee "citizenship." *Academy of Management Journal,* 26:587–595.

Batson, C.D. (1991). *The altruism question: Toward a social-psychological answer.* Hillsdale, NJ: Lawrence Erlbaum.

_____(1994). Why act for the public good? Four answers. *Personality and Social Psychology Bulletin,* 20:603–610.

Batson, C.D., Klein, T.R., Highberger, L., & Shaw, L.L. (1995). Immorality from empathy-induced altruism: When compassion and justice conflict. *Journal of Personality and Social Psychology,* 68:1042–1054.

Baucus, M.S. & Beck-Dudley, C.L. (in press). Designing ethical organizations: Avoiding the long-term negative effects of rewards and punishments. *American Behavioral Scientist.* .

Baumeister, R.F., & Exline, J.J. (1999). Virtue, personality, and social relations: Self-control as the moral muscle. *Journal of Personality,* 67:1165–1194.

Baumeister, R.F., & Exline, J.J. (2000). Self-control, morality, and human strength. *Journal of Social and Clinical Psychology,* 67:1165–1194.

Bennett, A. (1991). Downsizing doesn't necessarily bring an upswing in corporate profitability. *Wall Street Journal,* June 6, pp.B1, B4.

Berkowitz, L. (1972). Social norms, feelings, and other factors affecting helping and altruism. In Berkowitz, L. (Ed.), *Advances in Experimental Social Psychology,* 6:63–108. New York: Academic Press.

Blau, P. (1964). *Exchange and power in social life.* New York: Wiley.

Blum, L. (1980). Compassion. In Rorty, A.O. (Ed), *Explaining emotions* (pp.507–517). Berkeley: University of California Press.

Bolino, M.C., Trunley, W.H., & Bloodgood, J.M. (2002). Citizenship behavior and the creation of social capital in organizations. *Academy of Management Review,* 27:505–522.

Bollier, D. (1996). *Aiming higher: Twenty-five stories of how companies prosper by combining sound management and social vision.* New York: Amacom.

Cameron, K.S. (1986). A study of organizational effectiveness and its predictors. *Management Science,* 32:87–112.

_____(1994). Strategies for successful organizational downsizing. *Human Resource Management Journal,* 33:189–211.

_____(1995). Downsizing, quality, and performance. In Cole, R.E. (Ed.), *The death and life of the American quality movement.* New York: Oxford University Press.

_____(1998). Strategic organizational downsizing: An extreme case. *Research in Organizational Behavior,* 20:185–229.

_____(2001). Leadership through organizational forgiveness. Available at www.bus.umich.edu/leading.

Cameron, K.S., & Caza, A. (2002). Organizational and leadership virtues and the role of forgiveness. *Journal of Leadership and Organizational Studies,* 9:33–48.

Cameron, K.S., Caza, A., & Bright, D. (2002a). Exploring organizational virtues and organizational performance. Working paper, University of Michigan Business School.

_____(2002b). Positive deviance, organizational virtuousness, and performance.

Working paper, University of Michigan Business School.

Cameron, K.S., Freeman, S.J., & Mishra, A.K. (1993). Downsizing and redesigning organizations. In Huber, G.P., & Glick, W.H. (Eds.), *Organizational change and redesign.* New York: Oxford University Press.

Cameron, K.S., Kim, M.U., & Whetten, D.A. (1987). Organizational effects of decline and turbulence. *Administrative Science Quarterly,* 32:222–240.

Cascio, W.F., Young, C.E., & Morris, J.R. (1997). Financial consequences of employment change decisions in major U.S. corporations. *Academy of Management Journal,* 40:1175–1189.

Cassell, E.J. (2002). Compassion. In Snyder, C.R., & Lopez, S.J. (Eds.), *Handbook of positive psychology* (pp.434–445). New York: Oxford University Press.

Cawley, M.J., Martin, J.E., & Johnson, J.A. (2000). A virtues approach to personality. *Personality and Individual Differences,* 28:997–1013.

Chapman, J.W., & Galston, W.A. (1992). *Virtue.* New York: New York University Press.

Cialdini, R.B. (2000). *Influence: The science of persuasion.* New York: Allyn Bacon.

Cialdini, R.B., Schaller, M., Houlihan, D., Arps, K., Fultz, J., & Beaman, A.L. (1987). Empathy-based helping: Is it selflessly or selfishly motivated? *Journal of Personality and Social Psychology,* 52:749–758.

Cole, R.E. (1993). Learning from learning theory: Implications for quality improvements of turnover, use of contingent workers, and job rotation policies. *Quality Management Journal,* 1:9–25.

Coleman, J.S. (1998). Social capital in the creation of human capital. *American Journal of Sociology,* 94 (Supplement):S95–S120.

Comte-Sponville, A. (2001). *A small treatise of the great virtues.* Trans. C. Temerson. New York: Metropolitan Books.

Cooperrider, D.L. (2000). Positive image, positive action: The affirmative basis of organizing. In Cooperrider, D.L., Sorensen, P.F., Whitney, D., & Yaeger, T.F. (Eds.),

Appreciateive inquiry (pp.29–53). Champaign, IL; Stipes.

Cooperrider, D.L., & Srivastva, S. (1987). Appreciative inquiry in organizational life. *Research in Organizational Change and Development,* 1:129–169.

Csikszentmihalyi, M. (1990). *Flow: The psychology of optimal experience.* New York: Harper Perennial.

Curry, L.A., Snyder, C.R., Cook, D.L., Ruby, B.C., & Rehm, M. (1997). The role of hope in academic and sport achievement. *Journal of Personality and Social Psychology,* 73:1257–1267.

Dent, N. (1984). *The moral psychology of the virtues.* New York: Cambridge University Press.

Dienstbier, R.A., & Zillig, L.M.P. (2002). Toughness. In Snyder, C.R., & Lopez, S.J. (Eds.), *Handbook of positive psychology* (pp.515–527). New York: Oxford University Press.

Doherty, W.J. (1995). *Soul searching: Why psychotherapy must promote moral responsibility.* New York: Basic Books.

Dutton, J.E., Frost, P.J., Worline, M.C., Lilius, J.M., & Kanov, J.M. (2002). Leading in times of trauma. *Harvard Business Review,* January, pp.54–61.

Dutton, J.E., Worline, M.C., Frost, P.J., & Lilius, J. (2002). The organizing of compassion. Working paper, University of Michigan Business School.

Eisenberg, E.M. (1990). Jamming: Transcendence through organizing. *Communication Research,* 17:139–164.

Elliott, T.R., Witty, T.E., Herrick, S., & Hoffman, J.T. (1991). Negotiating reality after physical loss: Hope, depression, and disability. *Journal of Personality and Social Psychology,* 61:608–613.

Emmons, R.A. (1999). *The psychology of ultimate concerns: Motivation and spirituality in personality.* New York: Guilford Press.

Emmons, R.A., & Crumpler. (2000). Gratitude as a human strength: Appraising the evidence. *Journal of Social and Clinical Psychology,* 19:56–69.

Enright, R.D., & Human Development Study Group. (1994). Piaget on the moral development of forgiveness: Identity and reciprocity. *Human Development,* 37:63–80.

Fineman, S. (1996). Emotion and organizing. In Clegg, S.R., Hardy, C., & Nord, W.R. (Eds.), *The handbook of organizational studies* (pp.543–564). London: Sage.

Fitzgibbons, R.P. (1986). The cognitive and emotive uses of forgiveness in the treatment of anger. *Psychotherapy,* 23:629–633.

Fredrickson, B.L. (1998). What good are positive emotions? *Review of General Psychology,* 2:300–319.

_____(2001). The role of positive emotions in positive psychology: The broadenand-build theory of positive emotions. *American Psychologist,* 56:218–226.

_____(2002). Positive emotions. In Snyder, C.R., & Lopez, S.J. (Eds.), *Handbook of positive psychology* (pp.120–132). New York: Oxford University Press.

Fredrickson, B.L., & Branigan, C. (2001). Positive emotions broaden the scope of attention and thought-action repertoires: Evidence for the broaden-andbuild theory. Working paper, University of Michigan Department of Psychology.

Fredrickson, B.L., & Joiner, T. (in press). Positive emotions trigger upward spirals toward emotional well-being. *Psychological Science.*

Fredrickson, B.L., Mancuso, R.A., Branigan, C., & Tugade, M.M. (2000). The undoing effect of positive emotions. *Motivation and Emotion,* 24:237–258.

Fry, L.W., Keim, G.D., & Meiners, R.E. (1982). Corporate contributions: Altruistic or for-profit? *Academy of Management Journal,* 25:94–106.

George, J.M. (1991). State or trait: Effects of positive mood on prosocial behaviors at work. *Journal of Applied Psychology,* 76:229–307.

_____(1995). Leader positive mood and group performance: The case of customer service.

Journal of Applied Social Psychology,
25:778–794.

Gergen, K.J. (1999a). Affect and organization
in postmodern society. In Srivastava, S., &
Cooperrider, D.L. (Eds.), *Appreciative
management and leadership* (pp.153–174).
Euclid, OH: Williams Custom Publishing.

_____(1999b). *An invitation to social
constructionism.* London: Sage.

Gittell, J.H. (2000). Organizing work to support
relational coordination. *International Journal
of Human Resource Management,* 11:517–539.

_____(2001). Supervisory span, relational
coordination, and flight departure performance:
A reassessment of post-bureaucracy theory.
Organization Science, 12:467–482.

Gittell, J.H., & Cameron, K.S. (2002).
Compassionate leadership, relationships, and
resilience: Airline responses to the crisis of
2001. Presented at the Academy of
Management Meetings, Denver, CO, 2002.

Harker, L.A., & Keltner, D. (2001). Expressions
of positive emotion in women's college
yearbook pictures and their relationship to

personality and life outcomes across adulthood. *Journal of Personality and Social Psychology,* 80:112–124.

Harter, S. (2002). Authenticity. In Snyder, C.R., & Lopez, S.J. (Eds.), *Handbook of positive psychology* (pp.382–394). New York: Oxford University Press.

Harter, J.K., Schmidt, F.L., & Hayes, T.L. (2002). Business-unit-level relationship between employee satisfaction, employee engagement, and business outcomes: A meta-analysis. *Journal of Applied Psychology,* 87(2): 268–279.

Hatch, M.J. (1999). Exploring the empty spaces of organizing: How improvisational jazz helps redescribe organizational structure. *Organizational Studies,* 20:75–100.

Henkoff, R. (1994). Getting beyond downsizing. *Fortune,* January, pp.58–64.

Hope, D. (1987). The healing paradox of forgiveness. *Psychotherapy,* 24:240–244.

Koys, D.J. (2001). The effects of employee satisfaction, organizational citizenship behavior, and turnover on organizational effectiveness. *Personnel Psychology,* 54:101–114.

Krebs, D. (1987). The challenge of altruism in biology and psychology. In Crawford, C., Smith, M., & Krebs, D. (Eds.), *Sociobiology and Psychology.* Hillsdale, NJ: Lawrence Erlbaum.

Leana, C.R., & Van Buren, H.J. (1999). Organizational social capital and employment practices. *Academy of Management Review,* 24:538–555.

Leavitt, H.J. (1996). The old days, hot groups, and managers' lib. *Administrative Science Quarterly,* 41:288–300.

Lerner, H.G. (1993). *The dance of deception.* New York: HarperCollins.

Luthans, F. (2002). Positive organizational behavior: Developing and managing psychological strengths for performance improvement. *Academy of Management Executive,* 16:57–75.

MacIntyre, A. (1984). *After virtue: A study in moral theory.* 2nd ed. Notre Dame, IN: University of Notre Dame Press.

Maslow, A. (1971). *The farthest reaches of human nature.* New York: Viking.

Masten, A.S., Hubbard, J.J., Gest, S.D., Tellegen, A., Garmezy, N., & Ramirez, M. (1999). Competence in the context of adversity: Pathways to reliance and maladaptation from childhood to late adolescence. *Development and Psychopathology,* 11:143–169.

Masten, A.S., & Reed, M.G.J. (2002). Resilience in development. In Snyder, C.R., & Lopez, S.J. (Eds.), *Handbook of positive psychology* (pp.74–88). New York: Oxford University Press.

McCullough, M.E. (2000). Forgiveness as human strength: Theory, measurement, and links to well-being. *Journal of Social and Clinical Psychology,* 19:43–55.

McCullough, M.E., Pargament, K.I., & Thoreson, C. (2000). *Forgiveness: Theory, research, and practice.* New York: Guilford.

McCullough, M.E., & Snyder, C.R. (2001). Classical sources of human strength: Revisiting an old home and building a new one. *Journal of Social and Clinical Psychology,* 19:1–10.

McKinley, W., Sanchez, C.M., & Schick, A.G. (1995). Organizational downsizing: Constraining, cloning, and learning. *Academy of Management Executive,* 9:32–44.

McNeeley, B.L., & Meglino, B.M. (1994). The role of dispositional and situational antecedents in prosocial organizational behavior: An examination of the intended beneficiaries of prosocial behavior. *Journal of Applied Psychology,* 79:836–844.

Mishra, A.K. (1992). Organizational responses to crisis: The role of mutual trust and top management teams. Unpublished doctoral diss., University of Michigan Business School.

Mishra, A.K., & Mishra, K.E. (1994). The role of mutual trust in effective downsizing strategies. *Human Resource Management Journal,* 33:261–279.

Moore, C., and Richardson, J.J. (1988). The politics and practice of corporate responsibility is Great Britain. *Research in Corporate Social Performance and Policy,* 10:267–290.

Morris, J.R., Cascio, W.F., & Young, C.E. (1999). Downsizing after all these years: Questions and answers about who did it, how many did it, and who benefited from it. *Organizational Dynamics,* Winter: 78–87.

Nahapiet, J., & Ghoshal, S. (1998). Social capital, intellectual capital, and the organizational advantage. *Academy of Management Review,* 23:242–266.

Nussbaum, M.C. (1996). Compassion: The basic social emotion. *Social Philosophy and Policy,* 13:27–58.

Pearlstein, S. (1994). Corporate cutbacks yet to pay off. *Washington Post,* January 4, p. B6.

Peterson, C. (1991). *Health and optimism.* New York: Free Press.

_____(2000). The future of optimism. *American Psychologist,* 55:44–55.

_____(2003). Classification of positive traits in youth. In Lerner, R.M., Jacobs, F., and Wertlieb, D. (Eds.), *Promoting Positive Child, Adolescent, and Family Development* (pp.227–255). Thousand Oaks, CA: Sage.

Peterson, C., & Bossio, L.M. (1991). *Health and optimism.* New York: Free Press.

Peterson, C., & Seligman, M.E.P. (2002). Values in Action (VIA) classification of strengths. Available at http://psych.upenn .edu/seligman/taxonomy.htm.

Piliavin, J.A., & Charng, H. (1990). Altruism: A review of recent theory and research. *Annual Review of Sociology,* 16:27–65.

Podsakoff, P.M., MacKensie, S.B., Paine, J.B., & Bachrach, D.G. (2000). Organizational citizenship behaviors: A critical review of the theoretical and empirical literature and suggestions for future research. *Journal of Management,* 26:513–563.

Putnam, R.D. (2000). *Bowling alone: The collapse and revival of American community.* New York: Simon & Schuster.

Quinn, R.W. (2002). Flow in organizations and flow as organizing: The optimal experience of energy and tension at work. Working paper, University of Michigan School of Business.

Quinn, R.W., & Dutton, J.E. (2002). Coordination as energy-in-conversation: A process theory of organizing. Working paper, University of Michigan Business School.

Rigby, D. (2002). Look before you lay off. *Harvard Business Review,* April, pp.20–21.

Roberts, R.C. (1988). Therapies and the grammar of virtue. In Bell, R.H. (Ed.), *The grammar of the heart: New essays in moral philosophy and theology* (pp.149–170). San Francisco: Harper & Row.

Rousseau, D.M. (1995). *Psychological contracts in organizations: Understanding written and unwritten agreement.* Beverly Hills, CA: Sage.

Ryff, C.D., & Singer, B. (1998). The contours of positive human health. *Psychological Inquiry,* 9:1–28.

Sanchez, C.M. (2000). Motives for corporate philanthropy in El Salvador: Altruism and political legitimacy. *Journal of Business Ethics,* 27:363–375.

Sandage, S.J., & Hill, P.C. (2001). The virtues of positive psychology: The rapprochement and challenges of the affirmative postmodern perspective. *Journal*

for the Theory of Social Behavior,
31:241–260.

Schwartz, J. (2002). Dean's lecture series.
University of Michigan Business School,
January 30.

Seligman, M.E.P. (1991). *Learned optimism.*
New York: Knopf.

_____(2002a). *Authentic happiness.* New
York: Free Press.

_____(2002b). Positive psychology, positive
prevention, and positive therapy. In Snyder,
C.R., and Lopez, S.J. (Eds.), *Handbook of
positive psychology* (pp.3–9). New York:
Oxford University Press.

Seligman, M.E.P., & Csikszentmihalyi, M.
(2000). Positive psychology: An introduction.
American Psychologist, 55:5–14.

Seligman, M.E.P., Schulman, P., DeRubeis,
R.J., & Hollon, S.D. (1999) The prevention
of depression and anxiety. *Prevention and
Treatment,* 2. Available at http://journals.ap
a.org/prevention.

Sethi, R., & Nicholson, C.Y. (2001). Structural and contextual correlates of charged behavior in product development teams. *Journal of Product Innovation Management,* 18:154–168.

Snyder, C.R. (1994). *The psychology of hope.* New York: Free Press._____(2000). The past and possible futures of hope. *Journal of Social and Clinical Psychology,* 19:11–28.

Snyder, C.R. & Higgons, R.L. (1997). Reality negotiation: Governing one's self and being governed by others. General Psychology Review,1:336–350.

Snyder, C.R., & Lopez, S.J. (2002). *Handbook of positive psychology.* New York: Oxford University Press.

Snyder, C.R., Rand, K.L., & Sigmon, D.R. (2002). Hope theory: A member of the positive psychology family. In Snyder, C.R., & Lopez, S.J. (Eds.), *Handbook of positive psychology* (pp.257–276). New York: Oxford University Press.

Solomon, R.C. (1998). The moral psychology of business: Care and compassion in the corporation. *Business Ethics Quarterly,* 8:515–533.

Staw, B.M., Sandelands, L., & Dutton, J.E. (1981). Threat-rigidity effects in organizational behavior: A multilevel analysis. *Administrative Science Quarterly,* 26:501–524.

Sternberg, J.J. (1998). A balanced theory of wisdom. *Review of General Psychology,* 2:347–365.

Turner, N., Barling, J., & Zacharatos, A. (2002). Positive psychology at work. In Snyder, C.R., & Lopez, S.J. (Eds.), *Handbook of positive psychology* (pp.715–730). New York: Oxford University Press.

Tutu, D. (1999). *No future without forgiveness.* New York: Doubleday.

Walz, S.M., & Niehoff, B.P. (2000). Organizational citizenship behaviors: Their relationship to organizational effectiveness. *Journal of Hospitality and Tourism Research,* 24:301–319.

Weick, K.E., Sutcliffe, K.M., & Obstfeld, D. (1999). Organizing for high reliability:

Processes of collective mindfulness. *Research in Organizational Behavior,* 21:81–123.

Weiner, N.O. (1993). *The harmony of the soul: Mental health and moral virtue reconsidered.* Albany: State University of New York Press.

Weiser, J., & Zadek, S. (2000). *Conversations with disbelievers: Persuading companies to address social challenges.* Ford Foundation.

Wildavsky, A. (1991). *Searching for safety.* New Brunswick: Transaction Books.

Witvliet, C.V.O., Ludwig, T.E., & Vander Laan, K.L. (2002). Granting forgiveness or harboring grudges: Implications for emotion, physiology, and health. *Psychological Sciences,* 12: 117–123.

Worline, M.C., Dutton, J.E., Frost, P.J., Kanov, J., & Maitlis, S. (2002). Creating fertile soil: The organizing dynamics of resilience. Working paper, University of Michigan Business School.

Worthington, E.L. (1998). *Dimensions of forgiveness: Psychological research and theoretical perspectives.* Philadelphia: Templeton Foundation Press.

Chapter 5

Asch, S.E. (1952). *Social psychology.* Englewood Cliffs, N J: Prentice-Hall.

Benner, P., Hooper-Kyriakidis, P., & Stannard, D. (1999). *Clinical wisdom and interventions in critical care.* Philadelphia: Saunders.

Campbell, D.T. (1990). Asch's moral epistemology for socially shared knowledge. In Rock, I. (Ed.), *The legacy of Solomon Asch: Essays in cognition and social psychology* (pp.39–52). Hillsdale, NJ: Erlbaum.

Gleason, P. (1991). LCES: A Key to Safety in the Wildland Fire Environment. *Fire Management Notes,* 52(4):9.

Gordon, S., Benner, P., & Noddings, N. (Eds.) (1996). *Caregiving.* Philadelphia: University of Pennsylvania Press.

Hadot, P. (1995). *Philosophy as a way of life.* Oxford, UK: Blackwell.

Katz, D., & Kahn, R.L. (1978). *The social psychology of organizations.* 2nd ed. New York: Wiley.

Kohn, L.T., Corrigan, J.M., & Donaldson, M.S. (Eds.) (2000). *To err is human: Building a safer health system.* Washington, DC: National Academy of Science.

Kuhn, A., & Beam, R.D. (1982). *The logic of organization.* San Francisco: Jossey-Bass.

Lagadec, P. (1993). *Preventing chaos in a crisis.* New York: McGraw-Hill.

Landau, M., & Chisholm, D. (1995). The arrogance of optimism: Notes on failure avoidance management. *Journal of Contingencies and Crisis Management,* 3:67–80.

Maclean, J.N. (1999). *Fire on the mountain.* New York: William Morrow.

Maclean, N. (1992). *Young men and fire.* Chicago: University of Chicago Press.

March, J.G., Sproull, L.S., & Tamuz, M. (1991). Learning from samples of one or fewer. *Organization Science,* 2:1–13.

Maslow, A. (1970). *Motivation and personality.* New York: Harper & Row.

Meacham, J.A. (1990). The loss of wisdom. In Sternberg, R.J. (Ed.), *Wisdom* (pp.181–211). New York: Cambridge.

Meshkati, N. (1991). Human factors in large-scale technological systems' accidents: Three Mile Island, Bhopal, Chernobyl. *Industrial Crisis Quarterly,* 5:131–154.

Mintzberg, H. (1973). *The nature of managerial work.* New York: Harper & Row.

Morita, S. (1998). *Morita therapy and the true nature of anxiety-based disorders (shinkeishitsu).* Albany: State University of New York Press.

Paget, M. (1988). *The unity of mistakes: A phenomenological interpretation of medical work.* Philadelphia: Temple University Press.

Paget, M.A. (1993). *A complex sorrow.* Philadelphia: Temple University Press.

Rasmussen, J. (2000). The concept of human error: Is it useful for the design of safe systems in healthcare? In Vincent, C., & De Mol, B. (Eds.), *Safety in medicine* (pp.31–48). Amsterdam: Pergamon.

Reason, J. (1997). *Managing the risks of organizational accidents.* Aldershot, UK: Ashgate.

Roberts, K.H., & Moore, W.H. (1993). Bligh Reef dead ahead: Grounding of the Exxon Valdez. In Roberts, K. (Ed.), *New challenges to understanding organizations* (pp.231–247). New York: Macmillan.

Scott, W.R. (1998). *Organizations: Rational, natural, and open systems.* 4th ed. Upper Saddle River, N J: Prentice-Hall.

Sharpe, V.A., & Faden, A.I. (1998). *Medical harm.* Cambridge: Cambridge University Press.

Shrivastava, P. (1987). *Bhopal: Anatomy of a crisis.* Cambridge, MA: Ballinger.

Snook, S. (2000). *Friendly fire.* Princeton: Princeton University.

Starbuck, W.H., & Milliken, F.J. (1988). Executives' perceptual filters: What they notice and how they make sense. In Hambrick, D.C. (Ed.), *The executive effect: Concepts and methods for studying top managers* (pp.35–65). Greenwich, CT: JAI.

Suzuki, S. (2002). *Not always so.* New York: HarperCollins.

Vaughan, D. (1996). *The Challenger launch decision: Risky technology, culture, and deviance at NASA.* Chicago: University of Chicago Press.

Weick, K.E. (1979). *The social psychology of organizing.* 2nd ed. Reading, MA: Addison-Wesley.

_____(1987). Organizational culture as a source of high reliability. *California Management Review,* 29:112–127.

_____(1990). The vulnerable system: Analysis of the Tenerife air disaster. *Journal of Management,* 16:571–593.

_____(1993). The collapse of sensemaking in organizations: The Mann Gulch disaster. *Administrative Science Quarterly,* 38:628–652.

_____(1995). *Sensemaking in organizations.* Thousand Oaks, CA: Sage.

_____(1998). Wildfire and wisdom. *Wildfire,* 7(1):14–19.

Weick, K.E., & Roberts, K.H. (1993). Collective mind in organizations: Heedful interrelating on flight decks. *Administrative Science Quarterly,* 38:357– 381.

Weick, K.E., & Sutcliffe, K.M. (2001). *Managing the unexpected.* San Francisco: Jossey-Bass.

_____(in press). Hospitals as cultures of entrapment: A reanalysis of the Bristol Royal Infirmary. *California Management Review.*

Westrum, R. (1982). Social intelligence about hidden events. *Knowledge,* 3(3): 381–400.

Chapter 6

Adler, M.G. (2002). Conceptualizing and measuring appreciation: The development of a positive psychology construct. Unpublished doctoral dissertation, Rutgers University.

Aquinas, T. (1981). *Summa theologica.* Westminster, MD: Christian Classics.

Aquino, K., Tripp, T.M., & Bies, R.J. (2001). How employees respond to personal offense: The effects of blame attribution, victim status, and offender status on revenge and reconciliation in the workplace. *Journal of Applied Psychology,* 86:52–29.

Baron, R.A. (1984). Reducing organizational conflict: An incompatible response approach. *Journal of Applied Psychology,* 69:272–279.

Bertocci, P.A., & Millard, R.M. (1963). *Personality and the good: Psychological and ethical perspectives.* New York: David McKay.

Carlson, M., Charlin, V., & Miller, N. (1988). Positive mood and helping behavior: A test of six hypotheses. *Journal of Personality and Social Psychology,* 55:211–229.

Carman, J.B., & Streng, F.J. (Eds.) (1989). *Spoken and unspoken thanks: Some comparative soundings.* Cambridge, MA: Harvard University Center for the Study of World Religions.

Cherniss, C., & Goleman, D. (Eds.) (2001). *The emotionally intelligent workplace: How to select for, measure, and improve emotional intelligence in individuals, groups, and organizations.* San Francisco: Jossey-Bass.

Clark, H.B., Northrop, J.T., & Barkshire, C.T. (1988). The effects of contingent thank-you notes on case managers' visiting residential clients. *Education and Treatment of Children,* 11:45–51.

Emmons, R.A., & Crumpler, C.A. (2000). Gratitude as human strength: Appraising the evidence. *Journal of Social and Clinical Psychology,* 19:56–69.

Emmons, R.A., & Hill, J. (2001). *Words of gratitude for mind, body, and soul.* Radnor, PA: Templeton Foundation Press.

Emmons, R.A., & McCullough, M.E. (2003). Counting blessings versus burdens: Experimental studies of gratitude and subjective well-being in daily life. *Journal of Personality and Social Psychology, 84,* 377–389.

Emmons, R.A., & Shelton, C.S. (2002). Gratitude and the science of positive psychology. In Snyder, C.R., & Lopez, S.J. (Eds.), *Handbook of positive psychology* (pp.459–471). New York: Oxford University Press.

Fredrickson, B.L. (2001). The role of positive emotions in positive psychology: The broaden-and-build theory of positive emotions. *American Psychologist,* 56:218–226.

George, J.M. (1995). Leader positive mood and group performance: The case of customer service. *Journal of Applied Social Psychology,* 25:778–794.

Haidt, J. (in press). The moral emotions. In Davidson, R.J., Scherer, K.R., & Goldsmith, H.H. (Eds.), *Handbook of affective sciences.* New York: Oxford University Press.

Harpham, E. (in press). Gratitude in the history of ideas. In Emmons, R.A., & Mc-Cullough, M.E. (Eds.), *The psychology of gratitude.* New York: Oxford University Press.

Hatfield, E., Cacioppo, J.T., & Rapson, R.L. (1993). Emotional contagion. *Current Directions in Psychological Science,* 2:96–99.

Hume, D. (1968). *A treatise of human nature.* New York: Oxford University Press. Original work published in 1740.

Kaczmarski, K.M., & Cooperrider, D.L. (1997). Constructionist leadership in the global relational age. *Organization and Environment,* 10:235–258.

269

Kant, I. (1963). *Lectures on ethics.* New York: Harper and Row. Original work published in 1797.

Lundqvist, L.O., & Dimberg, U. (1995). Facial expressions are contagious. *Journal of Psychophysiology,* 9:203–211.

McCraty, R., & Childre, D. (in press). The grateful heart: The psychophysiology of appreciation. In Emmons, R.A., & McCullough, M.E. (Eds.), *The psychology of gratitude.* New York: Oxford University Press.

McCullough, M.E., Emmons, R.A., & Tsang, J. (2002). The grateful disposition: A conceptual and empirical topography. *Journal of Personality and Social Psychology,* 82:112–127.

McCullough, M.E., Kirkpatrick, S., Emmons, R.A., & Larson, D. (2001). Is gratitude a moral affect? *Psychological Bulletin,* 127:249–266.

Nouwen, H.J.M. (1992). *The return of the prodigal son: A meditation on fathers, brothers, and sons.* New York: Doubleday.

Roberts, R.C. (in press). The blessings of gratitude. In Emmons, R.A., & McCullough,

M.E. (Eds.), *The psychology of gratitude.* New York: Oxford University Press.

Seabright, M.A., & Schminke, M. (2002). Immoral imagination and revenge in organizations. *Journal of Business Ethics,* 38:19–31.

Shelton, C.S. (2000). *Achieving moral health.* New York: Crossroad.

Simmel, G. (1950). *The sociology of Georg Simmel.* Glencoe, IL: Free Press.

Simmons, A.J. (1979). *Moral principles and political obligations.* Princeton: Princeton University Press.

Smith, A. (1976). *The theory of moral sentiments.* 6th ed. Oxford: Clarendon Press. Original work published in 1790.

Solomon, R.C., & Flores, F. (2001). *Building trust in business, politics, relationships, and life.* New York: Oxford University Press.

Srivastva, S., & Cooperrider, D.L. (1990). *Appreciative management and leadership: The power of positive thought and action in organizations.* San Francisco: Jossey-Bass.

Tenkasi, R.V. (2000). The dynamics of cultural knowledge and learning in creating viable theories of global change and action. *Organization Development Journal,* 18:74–90.

Trivers, R.L. (1971). The evolution of reciprocal altruism. *The Quarterly Review of Biology,* 46:35–57.

Vaillant, G.E. (1993). *The wisdom of the ego.* Cambridge: Harvard University Press.

de Waal, F.B.M. (2000). Attitudinal reciprocity in food sharing among brown capuchin monkeys. *Animal Behaviour,* 60:253–261.

Westermarck, E. (1932). *Ethical relativity.* New York: Harcourt, Brace.

White, P. (1996). Gratitude, citizenship, and education. *Studies in Philosophy and Education,* 18:43–52.

Whitney, D., & Cooperrider, D.L. (1998). The appreciative inquiry summit: Overview and applications. *Employment Relations Today,* 25:17–28.

Wright, T.A., & Staw, B.M. (1999). Affect and favorable work outcomes: Two longitudinal tests of the happy-productive worker thesis. *Journal of Organizational Behavior,* 2:1–23.

Chapter 7

Bandura, A. (1998). *Self-efficacy: The exercise of control.* 2nd ed. New York: W.H.Freeman.

Barnett, C.S., & Pratt, M.G. (2000). From threat-rigidity to flexibility: Toward a learning model of autogenic crisis in organizations. *Journal of Organizational Change Management,* 13:74–88.

Bigley, G.A., & Roberts, K.H. (2001). The incident command system: Highreliability organizing for complex and volatile task environments. *Academy of Management Journal,* 44:1281–1299.

Bourrier, M. (1996). Organizing maintenance work at two nuclear power plants. *Journal of Contingencies and Crisis Management,* 4:104–112.

Bower, G.H., & Hilgard, E.R. (1981). *Theories of learning.* Englewood Cliffs, NJ: Prentice-Hall.

Bunderson, J.S., & Sutcliffe, K.M. (2002a). Comparing alternative conceptualizations of functional diversity in management teams: Process and performance effects. *Academy of Management Journal,* 45:975–893.

_____(2002b). Why some teams emphasize learning more than others: Evidence from business unit management teams. In Neal, M., Mannix, E., & Sondak, H. (Eds.), *Research on managing groups and teams,* vol.4 (pp.49–84). New York: Elsevier Science.

_____(in press). Management team learning orientation and business unit performance. *Journal of Applied Psychology.*

Caproni, P.J. (2001). *The practical coach: Management skills for everyday life.* Upper Saddle River, NJ: Prentice-Hall.

Cicchetti, D., & Garmezy, N. (1993). Prospects and promises in the study of resilience. *Development and Psychopathlogy,* 5:497–502.

Cohen, W.M., & Levinthal, D.A. (1990). Absorptive capacity: A new perspective on learning and innovation. *Administrative Science Quarterly,* 35:128–152.

Daft, R.L., & Lengel, R.H. (1984). Information richness: A new approach to managerial

274

behavior and organization design. In Staw, B., & Cummings, L.L. (Eds.), *Research in organizational behavior,* vol.6 (pp.191–233). Greenwich, CT: JAI.

Dweck, C.S. (1986). Motivational processes affecting learning. *American Psychologist,* 41:1040–1048.

Dweck, C.S., & Leggett, E.L. (1988). A social-cognitive approach to motivation and personality. *Psychological Review,* 95:256–273.

Edmondson, A.C. (1999). Psychological safety and learning behavior in work teams. *Administrative Science Quarterly,* 44:350–383.

Egeland, B., Carlson, E., & Sroufe, L.A. (1993). Resilience as process. *Development and Psychopathology,* 5:517–528.

Eisenhardt, K.M., & Martin, J.A. (2000). Dynamic capabilities: What are they? *Strategic Management Journal,* 21:1105–1121.

Garmezy, N. (1991). Resilience in children's adaptation to negative life events and stressed environments. *Pediatric Annals,* 20:459–466.

275

Gittell, J.H., & Cameron, K. (2002).
Compassionate leader behavior, relationships,
and resilience: Airline responses to the crisis
of September 11th. Paper presented at the
annual meeting of the Academy of
Management, Denver.

Heyman, G.D., & Dweck, C.S. (1992).
Achievement goals and intrinsic motivation:
Their relation and their role in adaptive
motivation. *Motivation and Emotion,*
16:231–247.

Jackson, S.E., & Dutton, J.E. (1988).
Discerning threats and opportunities.
Administrative Science Quarterly, 33:370–387.

Kobasa, S.C. (1979). Stressful life events,
personality, and health: An inquiry into
hardiness. *Personality and Social Psychology,*
37:1–11.

Leana, C.R., & Van Buren, H.J. (1999).
Organizational social capital and employment
practices. *Academy of Management Review,*
24:538–555.

Leonard-Barton, D. (1992). Core capabilities
and core rigidities: A paradox in managing

276

new product development. *Strategic Management Journal,* 13:111–125.

Levinthal, D.A., & March, J.G. (1981). A model of adaptive organizational search. *Journal of Economic Behavior and Organization,* 2:307–333.

_____(1993). The myopia of learning. *Strategic Management Journal,* 14:95–112.

Luthar, S.S., Cicchetti, D., & Becker, B. (2000). The construct of resilience: A critical evaluation and guidelines for future work. *Child Development,* 71:543–562.

MacLean, N. (1992). *Young men and fire.* Chicago: University of Chicago Press.

March, J.G. (1991). Exploration and exploitation in organizational learning. *Organization Science,* 2:71–87.

Masten, A.S. (1994). Resilience in individual development: Successful adaptation despite risk and adversity. In Wang, M.C., & Gordon, E.W. (Eds.), *Educational resilience in inner city America: Challenges and prospects* (pp.3–25). Hillsdale, NJ: Erlbaum.

_____(2001). Ordinary magic: Resilience processes in development. *American Psychologist,* 56:227–238.

Masten, A.S., & Coatsworth, J.D. (1995). Competence, resilience, and psychopathology. In Cicchetti, D., & Cohen, D. (Eds.), *Developmental psychopathology,* vol.2, *Risk, disorder, and adaptation* (pp.715–752). New York: Wiley.

Masten, A.S., & Reed, M.J. (2002). Resilience in development. In Snyder, C.R., & Lopez, S.J. (Eds.), *Handbook of positive psychology* (pp.74–88). New York: Oxford University Press.

McGrath, R.G., MacMillan, I.C., & Venkatraman, S. (1995). Defining and developing competence: A strategic process paradigm. *Strategic Management Journal,* 13:137–161.

Meyer, A.D. (1982). Adapting to environmental jolts. *Administrative Science Quarterly,* 27:515–537.

Miller, D.M. (1993). The architecture of simplicity. *Academy of Management Review,* 18:116–138.

Porac, J.F. (2002). Organizing for resilience: Discussant comments. Paper presented at the annual meeting of the Academy of Management, Denver.

Rochlin, G.I. (1989). Informal organizational networking as a crisis avoidance strategy: U.S. naval flight operations as a case study. *Industrial Crisis Quarterly,* 3:159–176.

Rudolph, J.W., & Repenning, N.P. (2002). Disaster dynamics: Understanding the role of quantity in organizational collapse. *Administrative Science Quarterly,* 47:1–30.

Sandage, S.J., & Hill, P.C. (2001). The virtues of positive psychology: The rapprochment and challenges of an affirmative postmodern perspective. *Journal for the Theory of Social Behavior,* 31:241–259.

Schulman, P. (1993). The negotiated order of organizational reliability. *Administration and Society,* 25:353–372.

Seligman, M.E.P., & Csikszentmihalyi, M. (2000). Positive psychology: An introduction. *American Psychologist,* 55:5–14.

Sitkin, S.B. (1992). Learning through failure: The strategy of small losses. In Staw, B.M., & Cummings, L.L. (Eds.), *Research in organizational behavior,* vol.14 (pp.231–266). Greenwich, CT: JAI Press.

Staudinger, U.M., Marsiske, M., & Baltes, P.B. (1993). Resilience and levels of reserve capacity in later adulthood: Perspectives from life-span theory. *Development and Psychopathology,* 5:541–566.

Staw, B.M., Sandelands, L.E., & Dutton, J.E. (1981). Threat-rigidity effects in organizational behavior: A multi-level analysis. *Administrative Science Quarterly,* 26:501–524.

Sternberg, R.J., & Kolligian, J. (1990). *Competence considered.* New Haven, CT: Yale University Press.

Teece, D.J., Pisano, G., & Shuen, A. (1997). Dynamic capabilities and strategic management. *Strategic Management Journal,* 18:509–533.

Thomas, J.B., & McDaniel, R.R. (1990). Interpreting strategic issues: Effects of strategy and top management team information processing structure. *Academy of Management Journal,* 33:286–306.

Thompson, J.D., & Hawkes, R.W. (1962). Disaster, community organization, and administrative process. In Baker, G.W., & Chapman, D.W. (Eds.), *Man and society in disaster* (pp.268–300). New York: Basic Books.

Virany, B., Tushman, M.L., & Romanelli, E. (1992). Executive succession and organization outcomes in turbulent environments: An organizational learning approach. *Organization Science,* 3:72–91.

Wanberg, C.R., & Banas, J.T. (2000). Predictors and outcomes of openness to changes in a reorganizing workplace. *Journal of Applied Psychology,* 85:132–142.

Weick, K.E. (1979). *The social psychology of organizing.* New York: McGraw-Hill.

_____(1993). The collapse of sensemaking in organizations: The Mann Gulch disaster. *Administrative Science Quarterly,* 38:628–652.

_____(2003). Positive organizing and organizational tragedy. In Cameron, K., Dutton, J.E., & Quinn, R.E. (Eds.), *Positive*

organizational scholarship. San Francisco: Berrett-Koehler.

Weick, K.E., & Roberts, K.H. (1993). Collective mind in organizations: heedful interrelating on flight decks. *Administrative Science Quarterly,* 38:357–381.

Weick, K.E., & Sutcliffe, K.M. (2001). *Managing the unexpected: Assuring high performance in an age of complexity.* San Francisco: Jossey-Bass.

Weick, K.E., Sutcliffe, K.M., & Obstfeld, D. (1999). Organizing for high reliability: Processes of collective mindfulness. In Sutton, R., & Staw, B. (Eds.), *Research in organizational behavior,* vol.21 (pp.81–124). Greenwich, CT: JAI.

Westrum, R. (1991). *Technologies and society: The shaping of people and things.* Belmont, CA: Wadsworth.

Wildavsky, A. (1988). *Searching for safety.* New Brunswick, NJ: Transaction Books.

Wood, R., & Bandura, A. (1989). Social cognitive theory of organizational management. *Academy of Management Review,* 14:361–384.

Worline, M.C., Dutton, J.E., Frost, P.J., Kanov, J., Lilius, J, & Maitlis, S. (2002). Creating fertile soil: The organizing dynamics of resilience. Paper presented at the annual meeting of the Academy of Management, Denver.

Wruck, K., & Jensen, M. (1994). Science, specific knowledge, and total quality management. *Journal of Accounting and Economics,* 18:247–287.

Chapter 8

Aldwin, C.M., Sutton, K.J., & Lachman, M. (1996). The development of coping resources in adulthood. *Journal of Personality,* 64:837–871.

Arvey, R.D., Bouchard, T.J., Jr., Segal, N.L., & Abraham, L.M. (1989). Job satisfaction: Environmental and genetic components. *Journal of Applied Psychology,* 74:187–192.

Black, B. (2001). The road to recovery. *Gallup Management Journal,* 1:10–12.

Bouchard, T.J., Lykken, D.T., McGue, M., Segal, N.L., & Tellegen, A. (1990). Sources of human psychological differences: The

Minnesota study of twins reared apart. *Science,* 250:223–228.

Bouchard, T.J., Jr. (1997). Genetic influence on mental abilities, personality, vocational interests and work attitudes. *International Review of Industrial and Organizational Psychology,* 12:373–395.

Buckingham, M., & Clifton, D.O. (2001). *Now, discover your strengths.* New York: Free Press.

Cassandro, V.J., & Simonton, D.K. (2002). Creativity and genius. In Keyes & Haidt (Eds.), *Flourishing: Positive psychology and the life well lived* (pp.163–184).

Clausen, J.A. (1998). Life reviews and the life stories. In Giele, J.Z., & Elder, G.H. (Eds.), *Methods of life course research: Qualitative and quantitative approaches* (pp.189–212).

Connelly, S. (2002). All together now. *Gallup Management Journal,* 2:12–18.

Csikszentmihalyi, M. (1990). *Flow: The psychology of optimal experience.* New York: HarperCollins.

Diener, E. (2000). Subjective well-being: The science of happiness and a proposal for a natural index. *American Psychologist,* 55(1):34–43.

Fredrickson, B.L. (2000). Why positive emotions matter in organizations: Lessons from the broaden-and-build model. *Psychologist Manager Journal,* 4(2):131–142.

Gallup Organization. (2001). Summary of selection research item bank. Internal Company Database.

_____(2002). Workplace poll. Internal Research Document, July.

Glock, J.W. (1955). The relative value of three methods of improving reading: Tachistoscope, films, and determined effort. Ph.D. thesis, University of Nebraska–Lincoln.

Harter, J.K. (1998). Gage Park High School research study. Gallup Technical Report.

Harter, J.K., & Schmidt, F.L. (2002). Employee engagement, satisfaction, and business-unit-level outcomes: Meta-analysis. Gallup Technical Report.

Harter, J.K., Schmidt, F.L., & Hayes, T.L. (2002). Business-unit-level relationship between employee satisfaction, employee engagement, and business outcomes: A meta-analysis. *Journal of Applied Psychology,* 87:2.

Hodges, T. (2002). An experimental study of strengths investment and changes in state hope. Technical Report.

Peterson, C. (2002). The future of optimism. *American Psychologist,* 55(1):44–55.

Rath, T.C. (2002). Measuring the impact of Gallup's strength-based development program for students. Technical Report.

Salovey, P., Rothman, A.J., Detweiler, J.B., & Steward, W.T. (2000). Emotional states and physical health. *American Psychologist,* 55(1):99–109.

Schmidt, F.L., Hunter, J.E., McKenzie, R.C., & Muldrow, T.W. (1979). Impact of valid selection procedures on work-force productivity. *Journal of Applied Psychology,* 64(6):609–626.

Schmidt, F.L., & Rader. (1999). Exploring the boundary conditions for interview validity: Meta-analytic validity findings for a new interview type. *Personnel Psychology,* 52:445–464.

Schmidt, F.L., & Rauschenberger, J. (1986). Utility analysis for practitioners. Paper presented at the first annual conference of the Society for Industrial and Organizational Psychology, Chicago, April.

Seligman, M.E.P. (1994). *What you can change and what you can't.* New York: Knopf.

_____(1998). Positive social sciences. *APA Monitor,* 29(4):2–5.

_____(1999). Positive psychology. Presidential address delivered at the 107th annual convention of the American Psychological Association, Boston.

Seligman, M.E.P., & Csikszentmihalyi, M. (2000). Positive psychology: An introduction. *American Psychologist,* 55(1):5–14.

Shippmann, J.S., Ash, R.A., Carr, L., Hesketh, B., Pearlman, K., Battista, M., Eyde, L.D., Kehoe, J., Prien, E.P., & Sanchez, J. (2000). The practice of competency modeling. *Personnel Psychology,* 53:703–740.

Snyder, C.R., Sympson, S.C., Ybasco, F.C., Borders, T.F., Babyak, M.A., & Higgins, R.L. (1996). Development and validation of the state hope scale. *Journal of Personality and Social Psychology,* 70(2):321–335.

Williamson, J. (2002). Assessing student strengths: Academic performance and persistence of first-time college students at a private, church affiliated college. Diss., Mount Vernon Nazarene University.

Chapter 9

Amabile, T.M. (1988). A model of creativity and innovation in organizations. In Staw, B.M., & Cummings, L.L., III (Eds.), *Research in organizational behavior,* vol.10 (pp.123–167). San Francisco: JAI Press.

Andersson, L., & Bateman, T. (2000). Individual environmental initiatives: Championing natural environmental issues in U.S. business

288

organizations. *Academy of Management Journal,* 43:548–570.

Aspinwall, L.G., Richter, L., & Hoffman, R.R. (in press). Understanding how optimism "works": An examination of optimists' adaptive moderation of belief and behavior. In Chang, E.C. (Ed.), *Optimism and pessimism: Theory, research, and practice.* Washington, DC: American Psychological Association.

Aspinwall, L.G., & Taylor, S.E. (1997). A stitch in time: Self-regulation and proactive coping. *Psychological Bulletin,* 121:417–436.

Avolio, B.J., & Locke, E.E. (2002). Contrasting different philosophies of leader motivation: Altruism versus egoism. *Leadership Quarterly,* 13:169–191.

Baltes, P.B., & Staudinger, U.M. (2000). Wisdom: A metaheuristic (pragmatic) to orchestrate mind and virtue toward excellence. *American Psychologist,* 55:122–135.

Bandura, A. (1982). Self-efficacy mechanism in human agency. *American Psychologist,* 37:122.

_____(1986). *The social foundations of thought and action.* Englewood Cliffs, NJ: Prentice-Hall.

_____(1997). *Self-efficacy: The exercise of control.* New York: W.H.Freeman.

_____(2000). Cultivate self-efficacy for personal and organizational effectiveness. In Locke, E.A. (Ed.), *The Blackwell handbook of principles of organizational behavior.* Oxford, UK: Blackwell.

_____(2001). Social cognitive theory: An agentic perspective. *Annual Review of Psychology,* 52:1–26.

Barrick, M .R., & Mount, M.K. (1991). The big five personality dimensions of job performance: A meta-analysis. *Personnel Psychology,* 44:1–26.

Bateman, T., & Crant, M. (1993). The proactive component of organizational behavior. *Journal of Organizational Behavior,* 14:103–118.

_____(2003). Revisiting intrinsic and extrinsic motivation. Working paper.

Bateman, T., O'Neill, H., & Kenworthy-U'Ren, A. (2002). The goals of the top executive: A comprehensive taxonomy. *Journal of Applied Psychology,* 87, 1134–1148.

Blau, P.M. (1964). *Exchange and power in social life.* New York: John Wiley.

Bolino, M., Turnley, W., & Bloodgood, J. (2002). Citizenship behavior and the creation of social capital in organizations. *Academy of Management Review,* 27:505–522.

Bradley, C.L., & Marcia, J.E. (1998). Generativity-stagnation: A five-category model. *Journal of Personality,* 66:39–64.

Calkins, G. (2000). Dean Jernigan. *Fast Company,* November, pp.170–184.

Cantor, N., & Sanderson, C.A. (1999). Life task participation and well-being: The importance of taking part in daily life.

Carver, C.S., & Scheier, M.F. (1985). Aspects of self, and the control of behavior. In Schlenker, B.R., (Ed.), *The self and the social life* (pp.146–174). New York: McGraw-Hill.

Cawley, M.J., III, Martin, J., & Johnson, J. (2000). A virtues approach to personality. *Personality and Individual Differences,* 28:997–1013.

Colarelli, S.M., Dean, R.A., & Konstans, C. (1987). Comparative effects of personal and situational influences on job outcomes of new professionals. *Journal of Applied Psychology,* 72:558–566.

Crant, J.M. (2000). Proactive behavior in organizations. *Journal of Management,* 26:435–462.

Cropanzano, R., James, K., & Citera, M. (1993). A goal hierarchy model of personality, motivation, and leadership. In Staw, B., & Cummings, L. (Eds.), *Research in organizational behavior,* vol.15 (pp.267–322). Greenwich, CT: JAI Press.

Csikszentmihalyi, M. (1990). *Flow: The psychology of optimal experience.* New York: Harper & Row.

_____(1997). *Finding flow: The psychology of engagement with everyday life.* New York: Basic Books.

Deci, E.L., & Ryan, R.M. (2000). The "what" and the "why" of goal pursuits: Human needs and the self-determination of behavior. *Psychological Inquiry,* 11:227–268.

Diener, D. (2000). Subjective well-being: The science of happiness and a proposal for a national index. *American Psychologist,* 55:34–43.

Dienstbier, R.A., & Zillig, L.M. (2002). Toughness. In Snyder, C.R., & Lopez, S.J. (Eds.), *Handbook of positive psychology* (pp.515–540). New York: Oxford University Press.

Dutton, J.E., & Ashford, S.J. (1993). Selling issues to top management. *Academy of Management Review,* 18:397–428.

Eisenberger, R., Pierce, W.D., & Cameron, J. (1999). Effects of reward on intrinsic motivation: Negative, neutral, and positive—Comment on Deci, Koestner, and Tyan, 1999. *Psychological Bulletin,* 125:677–691.

Erickson, E.H. (1950). *Childhood and society.* New York: Norton.

Frese, M., Kring, W., Soose, A., & Zempel, J. (1996). Personal initiative at work: Differences between East and West Germany. *Academy of Management Journal,* 39:37–63.

Frost, P., Dutton, J., Worline, M., & Wilson, A. (2000). Narratives of compassion in organizations. In Fineman, S. (Ed.), *Emotions in organizations* (pp.25–45). Beverly Hills, CA: Sage.

Gardner, H. (1995). *Leading minds: An anatomy of leadership.* New York: Basic Books.

Greenblatt, E. (in press). Work/life balance: Wisdom or whining? *Organizational Dynamics.*

Hackman, J.R., & Oldham, G.R. (1976). Motivation through the design of work: Test of a theory. *Organizational Behavior and Human Performance,* 16:250–279.

Haidt, J., & Keltner, J. (2002). Awe/reponsiveness to beauty and excellence. Working paper.

Haidt, J., & Rodin, J. (1999). Control and efficacy as interdisciplinary bridges. *Review of General Psychology,* 3:317–337.

Hamel, G. (2000). *Leading the revolution.* Boston: Harvard Business School Press.

Higgins, E.T., Grant, H., & Shah, J. (1999). Self-regulation and the quality of life: Emotional and non-emotional life experiences. In Kahneman, D., Diener, E., and Schwarz, N. (Eds.), *Well-being: The foundations of hedonic psychology* (pp.244–266). New York: Russell Sage.

House, R., & Shamir, B. (1993). Toward the integration of transformational, charismatic, and visionary theories. In Chemers, M.M., & Ayman, R. (Eds.), *Leadership theory and research: Perspectives and directions* (pp.81–107). San Diego: Academic Press.

Howell, J., & Higgins, C. (1990). Champions of technological innovation. *Administrative Science Quarterly,* 35:317–341.

Karoly, P. (1993). Mechanisms of self regulation: A systems view. In Rosenzweig, M., & Porter, L. (Eds.), *Annual Review of Psychology,* 44:23–52.

Kohlberg, L. (1969). Stage and sequence: The cognitive-developmental approach to socialization. In Goslin, D.A. (Ed.), *Handbook of socialization theory and research* (pp.347–380). Chicago: Rand McNally.

Kouzes, J., & Posner, B. (1995). *The leadership challenge.* San Francisco: Jossey-Bass.

Kristof-Brown, A., & Stevens, C.K. (2001). Goal congruence in project teams: Does the fit between members' personal mastery and performance goals matter? *Journal of Applied Psychology,* 86:1083–1095.

Kruger, P. (2000). Helena Luczywo and Wanda Rapaczynski. *Fast Company,* November, pp.152–166.

Langer, E.J. (1989). *Mindfulness.* Reading, MA: Addison-Wesley.

Lewin, K. (1951). *Field theory in social science.* New York: Harper.

Luthans, F. (2002). Positive organizational behavior: Devloping and managing psychological strengths. *Academy of Management Executive,* 16:57–72.

McClelland, D.C., & Boyatzis, R.E. (1982). Leadership motive pattern and longterm success in management. *Journal of Applied Psychology,* 67:737–743. McGregor, I., & Little, B. (1998). Personal projects, happiness, and meaning: On doing well and being yourself. *Journal of Personality and Social Psychology,* 74:494–512.

Miller, D.T. (1999). The norm of self-interest. *American Psychologist,* 54:1053–100.

Morrison, E.W., & Phelps, C.C. (1999). Taking charge at work: Extra-role efforts to initiate workplace change. *Academy of Management Journal,* 42: 403–419.

Muraven, M., & Baumeister, R.F. (2000). Self-regulation and depletion of limited resources: Does self-control resemble a muscle? *Psychological Bulletin,* 126:247–259.

Nadler, D.A. (1998). *Champions of change: How CEOs and their companies are mastering the skills of radical change.* San Francisco: Jossey-Bass.

Nahapiet, J., & Ghoshal, S. (1998). Social capital, intellectual capital, and the organizational advantage. *Academy of Management Review,* 23:242–266.

Peikoff, L. (1991). *Objectivism: The philosophy of Ayn Rand.* New York: Dutton.

Perttula, K. (2003). The POW factor: Understanding passion for one's work. Unpublished diss.

Phillips, J., Hollenbeck, J., & Ilgen, D. (1996). Prevalence and prediction of positive discrepancy creation: Examining a discrepancy between two self-regulation theories. *Journal of Applied Psychology,* 81:498–511.

Pinder, C. (1998). *Work motivation in organizational behavior.* Upper Saddle River, NJ: Prentice Hall.

Pottruck, D., & Pearce, T. (2000). *Clicks and mortar: Passion driven growth in an Internet driven world.* San Francisco: Jossey-Bass.

Ryan, R.M., & Deci, E.L. (2000). Self-determination theory and the facilitation of intrinsic motivation, social development, and well-being. *American Psychologist,* 55:68–78.

Scheier, M.F., & Carver, C.S. (1985). Optimism, coping, and health: Assessment and implications of generalized outcome expectancies. *Health Psychology,* 4:219–247.

Schmuck, P., & Sheldon, K.M. (2001). Life goals and well-being. Seattle: Hogrefe & Huber.

Schulman, P. (1999). Applying learned optimism to increase sales productivity. *Journal of Personal Selling & Sales Management,* 19:31–37.

Seligman, M.E.P., & Csikszentmihalyi, M. (2000). Positive psychology: An introduction. *American Psychologist,* 55:5–14.

Sheldon, K.M. (2001). The self-concordance model of healthy goal striving: When personal goals correctly represent the person. In Schmuck, P., & Sheldon, K. (Eds.), *Life goals and well-being* (pp.18–36). Seattle: Hogrefe & Huber.

Sheldon, K.M., & Bettencourt, B.A. (2002). Psychological needs and subjective well-being in social groups. *British Journal of Social Psychology,* 41(1): 25–38.

Simonton, D.K. (2000). Creativity: Cognitive, personal, developmental and social aspects. *American Psychologist,* 55:151–158.

Spreitzer, G.M., & Sonenshein, S. (2003). Positive deviance and extraordinary organizing. In Cameron, K., Dutton, J., & Quinn, R. (Eds.), *Positive organizational scholarship.* San Francisco: Berrett-Koehler.

Staw, B.M., & Boettger, R.D. (1990). Task revision: A neglected form of work performance. *Academy of Management Journal,* 33:534–559.

Stewart, R. (1982). *Choices for the manager.* Englewood Cliffs, NJ: Prentice-Hall.

Sutcliffe, K., & Vogus, T. (2003). Organizing for resilience. In Cameron, K., Dutton, J., & Quinn, R. (Eds.), *Positive organizational scholarship.* San Francisco: Berrett-Koehler.

Thoms, P., & Greenberger, D.B. (1995). Training business leaders to create positive organizational visions of the future: Is it successful? *Academy of Management Best Paper Proceedings,* 212–216.

Van Maanen, J., & Schein, E.H. (1979). Toward a theory of organizational socialization. In Staw, B.M. (Ed.), *Research in organizational behavior,* vol.1 (pp.209–264). Greenwich, CT: JAI Press.

Winner, E. (2000). The origins and ends of giftedness. *American Psychologist,* 55:159–169.

Worline, M., Wrzesniewski, A., & Rafaeli, A. (2002). Courage and work: Breaking routines to improve performance. In Loard, R., Klimoski, R., & Kanfer, R. (Eds.), *Emotions in the workplace: Understanding the structure and role of emotions in organizational behavior* (pp.295–330). San Francisco: Jossey-Bass.

Wrzesniewski, A., & Dutton, J. (2001). Crafting a job: Revisioning employees as active crafters of their work. *Academy of Management Review,* 26:179–201.

Zimbardo, P.G., & Boyd, J.N. (1999). Putting time in perspective: A valid, reliable individual-differences metric. *Journal of Personality and Social Psychology,* 77:1271–1288.

Chapter 10

American heritage dictionary of the English language (2000). 4th ed. Boston: Houghton Mifflin.

Ashford, S.J., Rothbard, N.P., Piderit, S.K., & Dutton, J.E. (1998). Out on a limb: The role of context and impression management in selling gender-equity issues. *Administrative Science Quarterly,* 23(3):23–57.

Baker, W.E., Faulkner, R.R., & Fisher, G.A. (1998). Hazards of the market: The continuity and dissolution of interorganizational market relationships. *American Sociological Review,* 63:147–177.

Barker, J.R. (1993). Tightening the Iron Cage: Concertive control in selfmanaging teams. *Administrative Science Quarterly,* 38(3):408–437.

Bateman, T., & Porath, C. (2003). Transcendent behavior. In Cameron, K.S., Dutton, J.E., & Quinn, R.E. (Eds.), *Positive organizational scholarship.* San Francisco: Barrett-Koehler.

Barnard, C. (1968). *The functions of the executive.* Cambridge: Harvard University Press.

Becker, E. (1973). *The denial of death.* New York: Free Press.

Bell, D. (2002). *Ethical ambition: Living a life of meaning and worth.* New York: Bloomsbury USA.

Berger, P.L., & Luckmann, T. (1990). *The social construction of reality.* New York: Anchor Books.

Cameron, K.S., Dutton, J.E., & Quinn, R.E. (2003). Foundations of positive organizational scholarship. In Cameron, K.S., Dutton, J.E., & Quinn, R.E. (Eds.), *Positive organizational scholarship.* San Francisco: Berrett-Koehler.

Clemens, E.S. (1993). Organizational repertoires and institutional change: Women's groups and the transformation of U.S. politics, 1890–1920. *American Journal of Sociology,* 98(4):755–798.

Cohen, M.D., March, J.G., & Olsen, J.P. (1972). A garbage can model of organizational choice. *Administrative Science Quarterly,* 17(1):1–25.

Creed, W.E.D., & Scully, M.A. (2001). Songs of ourselves: Employees' deployment of social identity in everyday workplace encounters. *Journal of Management Inquiry,* 9:391–412.

Durkheim, E. (1954). *The elementary forms of religious life.* New York: Free Press.

Dutton, J.E., & Heaphy, E.D. (2003). The power of high quality connections. In Cameron, K.S., Dutton, J.E., & Quinn, R.E. (Eds.), *Positive*

organizational scholarship. San Francisco: Berrett-Koehler.

Eisenberg, E.M. (1984). Ambiguity as strategy in organizational communication. *Communication Monographs,* 51:227–242.

Fama, E.F., & Jensen, M.C. (1983). Separation of ownership and control. *Journal of Law and Economics,* 26(June):327–349.

Feldman, M.S., & Khademian, A.M. (2003). Empowerment and cascading vitality. In Cameron, K.S., Dutton, J.E., & Quinn, R.E. (Eds.), *Positive organizational scholarship.* San Francisco: Berrett-Koehler.

Fitzgibbons, A. (1996). *Adam Smith's system of liberty, wealth, and virtue: The moral and political foundations of the wealth of nations.* Christchurch, New Zealand: Clarendon Press.

Fredrickson, B. (2003). Positive emotions and upward spirals in organizations. In Cameron, K.S., Dutton, J.E., & Quinn, R.E. (Eds.), *Positive organizational scholarship.* San Francisco: Berrett-Koehler.

Giddens, A. (1979). *Central problems in social theory.* Berkeley: University of California Press.

Glazer, M.P., & Glazer, P.M. (1989). *The whistleblowers: Exposing corruption in government and industry.* New York: Basic Books.

Goffman, E. (1974). *Frame analysis: An essay on the organization of experience.* Cambridge: Harvard University Press.

Graham, J.W. (1986). Principled organizational dissent: A theoretical essay. In Staw, B.M., & Cummings, L.L. (Eds.), *Research in organizational behavior,* vol.8 (pp.1–52). Greenwich, CT: JAI Press.

Granovetter, M. (1985). Economic action and social structure: The problem of embeddedness. *American Journal of Sociology,* 91(3):481–510.

Hackman, J.R. (1992). Group influences on individuals in organizations. In Dunnette, M.D., & Hough, L.M. (Eds.), *Handbook of industrial and organizational psychology,* 2nd ed. (pp.199–267). Palo Alto, CA: Consulting Psychologists Press.

Haidt, J. (2000). The positive emotion of elevation. *Prevention and Treatment,* 3(3).

Heilbroner, R.L. (1986). *The worldly philosophers: The lives, times, and ideas of the great economic thinkers,* 6th ed. New York: Simon & Schuster.

Heimer, C.A., & Staffen, L.R. (1998). *For the sake of the children: The social organization of responsibility in the hospital and the home.* Chicago: University of Chicago Press.

Kramer, R.M., & Tyler, T.R. (1996). *Trust in organizations: Frontiers of theory and research.* Thousand Oaks, CA: Sage.

Larson, A. (1992). Network dyads in entrepreneurial settings: A study of the governance of exchange relationships. *Administrative Science Quarterly,* 37(1):76–104.

March, J.G., & Simon, H.A. (1958). *Organizations.* New York: John Wiley & Sons.

McAdam, D., McCarthy, J.D., & Zald, M.N. (1996). *Comparative perspectives on social movements: Political opportunities, mobilizing structures, and cultural framings.* New York: Cambridge University Press.

Meyerson, D.E. (2001). Radical change the quiet way. *Harvard Business Review,* 79(9):92–97.

Meyerson, D.E., & Scully, M.A. (1995). Tempered radicalism and the politics of ambivalence and change. *Organization Science,* 6(5):585–600.

Miller, D. (1992). *The Icarus paradox: How exceptional companies bring about their own downfall.* New York: HarperCollins.

Miller, W.I. (2000). *The mystery of courage.* Cambridge: Harvard University Press .

Olsen, J.P. (1976). Choice in an organized anarchy. In March, J.G., & Olsen, J.P. (Eds.), *Ambiguity and choice in organizations* (pp.82–139). Bergen, Norway: Universitetsforlaget.

Orlikowski, W.J. (2000). Using technology and constituting structures: A practice lens for studying technology in organizations. *Organization Science,* 11(4):404–428.

Ouchi, W.G. (1980). Markets, bureaucracies, and clans. *Administrative Science Quarterly,* 25(1):129–141.

Powell, W.W., & Dimaggio, P.J. (1991). *The new institutionalism in organizational analysis.* Chicago: University of Chicago Press.

Quinn, R.E. (1988). *Beyond rational management: Mastering the paradoxes and competing demands of high performance.* San Francisco: Jossey-Bass.

Rachman, S.J. (1990). *Fear and courage.* 2nd ed. New York: W.H. Freeman.

Roth, N.L., Sitkin, S.B., & House, A. (1994). Stigma as a determinant of legalization. In Sitkin, S.B., & Bies, R.J. (Eds.), *The legalistic organization* (pp.137–168). Thousand Oaks, CA: Sage.

Rothschild, J., & Miethe, T.D. (1999). Whistle-blower disclosures and management retaliation: The battle to control information about organization corruption. *Work and Occupations,* 26(1):107–128.

Scott, W.R. (1997). *Organizations: Rational, natural, and open systems.* 4th ed. Englewood Cliffs, NJ: Prentice Hall.

Shelp, E.E. (1984). Courage: A neglected virtue in the patient-physician relationship. *Social Science and Medicine,* 18(4):351–360.

Smith, A. (1991). *An enquiry into the nature and causes of the wealth of nations.* Amherst, NY: Prometheus Books. Original work published in 1776.

Spreitzer, G.M., & Sonenschein, S. (2003). Positive deviance and extraordinary organizing. In Cameron, K.S., Dutton, J.E., & Quinn, R.E. (Eds.), *Positive organizational scholarship.* San Francisco: Berrett-Koehler.

Szagun, G., & Schauble, M. (1997). Children's and adults' understanding of the feeling experience of courage. *Cognition and Emotion,* 11(3):291–306.

Thompson, J.D. (1967). *Organizations in action.* New York: McGraw-Hill.

Thoreau, H.D. (1993). Civil disobedience. In Thoreau, H.D., *Civil disobedience and other essays* (pp.1–18). New York: Dover.

Tillich, P. (1952). *The courage to be.* New Haven, CT: Yale University Press.

Uzzi, B. (1997). Social structure and competition in interfirm networks: The paradox of embeddedness. *Administrative Science Quarterly,* 42:35–67.

Vaughan, D. (1996). *The Challenger launch decision.* Chicago: University of Chicago Press.

Walton, D.N. (1986). *Courage: A philosophical investigation.* Berkeley: University of California Press.

Weber, M. (1947). *The theory of social and economic organization.* New York: Oxford University Press.

Weick, K.E. (1995). *Sensemaking in organizations.* Foundations for Organizational Science. Thousand Oaks, CA: Sage.

Williamson, O. (1975). *Markets and hierarchies: A study of the economics of internal organizations.* New York: Free Press.

Worline, M., Wrzesniewski, A., & Rafaeli, A. (2002). Courage and work: Breaking routines to improve performance. In Lord, R., Klimoski, R., & Kanfer, R. (Eds.), *Emotions in the workplace: Understanding the structure and role of emotions in organizational behavior* (pp.295–330). San Francisco: Jossey-Bass.

Chapter 11

Aron, A., Norman, C.C., Aron, E.N., McKenna, C., & Heyman, R.E. (2000). Couple's shared participation in novel and arousing activities and experienced relationship quality. *Journal of Personality and Social Psychology,* 78:273–284.

Ashby, F.G., Isen, A.M., & Turken, A.U. (1999). A neuropsychological theory of positive affect and its influence on cognition. *Psychological Review,* 106:529–550.

Aspinwall, L.G. (1998). Rethinking the role of positive affect in self-regulation. *Motivation and Emotion,* 22:1–32.

_____(2001). Dealing with adversity: Self-regulation, coping, adaptation, and health. In Tesser, A., & Schwarz, N. (Eds.), *The Blackwell handbook of social psychology,* vol.1, *Intraindividual processes* (pp.591–614). Malden, MA: Blackwell.

Baron, R.A. (1993). Affect and organizational behavior: When and why feeling good (or bad) matters. In Murnighan, K. (Ed.), *Social psychology in organizations: Advances in theory* (pp.63–88). New York: Prentice Hall.

Bonanno, G.A., & Keltner, D. (1997). Facial expressions of emotion and the course of conjugal bereavement. *Journal of Abnormal Psychology,* 106:126–137.

Boulton, M.J., & Smith, P.K. (1992). The social nature of play fighting and play chasing: Mechanisms and strategies underlying cooperation and compromise. In Barkow, J.H., Cosmides, L., & Tooby, J. (Eds.), *The adapted mind: Evolutionary psychology and the generation of culture* (pp.429–444). New York: Oxford University Press.

Caro, T.M. (1988). Adaptive significance of play: Are we getting closer? *Tree,* 3:50–54.

Csikszentmihalyi, M. (1990). *Flow: The psychology of optimal experience.* New York: HarperCollins.

Diener, E., Sandvik, E., & Pavot, W. (1991). Happiness is the frequency, not the intensity, of positive versus negative affect. In Strack, F. (Ed.), *Subjective well-being: An*

312

interdisciplinary perspective (pp.119–139). Oxford, UK: Pergamon Press.

Dolhinow, P.J. (1987). At play in the fields. In Topoff, H. (Ed.), *The natural history reader in animal behavior* (pp.229–237). New York: Columbia University Press.

Estrada, C.A., Isen, A.M., & Young, M.J. (1997). Positive affect facilitates integration of information and decreases anchoring in reasoning among physicians. *Organizational Behavior and Human Decision Processes,* 72:117–135.

Folkman, S. (1997). Positive psychological states and coping with severe stress. *Social Science Medicine,* 45:1207–1221.

Folkman, S., & Moskowitz, J.T. (2000). Positive affect and the other side of coping. *American Psychologist,* 55:647–654.

Fredrickson, B.L. (1998). What good are positive emotions? *Review of General Psychology,* 2:300–319.

_____(2000). Cultivating positive emotions to optimize health and well-being.

Prevention and Treatment, 3. Available at http://journals.apa.org/ prevention.

_____(2001). The role of positive emotions in positive psychology: The broadenand-build theory of positive emotions. *American Psychologist,* 56:218–226.

_____(2002). Positive emotions. In Snyder, C.R., & Lopez, S.J. (Eds.), *Handbook of positive psychology* (pp.120–134). New York: Oxford University Press.

_____(in press). Gratitude and other positive emotions broaden and build. In Emmons, R.A. (Ed.), *Kindling the science of gratitude.* New York: Oxford University Press.

Fredrickson, B.L., & Branigan, C. (2001). Positive emotions. In Mayne, T.J., & Bonnano, G.A. (Eds.), *Emotion: Current issues and future directions* (pp.123–151). New York: Guilford.

_____(2002). Positive emotions broaden the scopes of attention and thoughtaction repertoires. Manuscript under review.

Fredrickson, B.L., Johnson, K.J., & Waugh, C.E. (2002). *Smiling predicts broadened attention.* Manuscript in preparation.

Fredrickson, B.L., & Joiner, T. (2002). Positive emotions trigger upward spirals toward emotional well-being. *Psychological Science,* 13:172–175.

Fredrickson, B.L., & Levenson, R.W. (1998). Positive emotions speed recovery from the cardiovascular sequelae of negative emotions. *Cognition and Emotion,* 12:191–220.

Fredrickson, B.L., Mancuso, R.A., Branigan, C., & Tugade, M. (2000). The undoing effect of positive emotions. *Motivation and Emotion,* 24:237–258.

Fredrickson, B.L., Maynard, K.E., Helms, M.J., Haney, T.L., Seigler, I.C., & Barefoot, J.C. (2000). Hostility predicts magnitude and duration of blood pressure response to anger. *Journal of Behavioral Medicine,* 23:229–243.

Fredrickson, B.L., Tugade, M.M., Waugh, C.E., & Larkin, G. (2003). What good are positive emotions in crises? A prospective study of resilience and emotions following the terrorist attacks on the United States on September

11th, 2001. *Journal of Personality and Social Psychology* 84, 365–376.

Frijda, N.H. (1986). *The emotions.* Cambridge: Cambridge University Press.

Frijda, N.H., Kuipers, P., & Schure, E. (1989). Relations among emotion, appraisal, and emotional action readiness. *Journal of Personality and Social Psychology,* 57:212–228.

Gasper, K. & Clore, G.L. (2002). Attending to the big picture: Mood and global verses local processing of visual information. *Psychological Science,* 13:34-40.

George, J.M. (1991). State or trait: Effects of positive mood on prosocial behavior at work. *Journal of Applied Psychology,* 76:299–307.

_____(1995). Leader positive mood and group performance: The case of customer service. *Journal of Applied Social Psychology,* 25:778–794.

_____(1998). Salesperson mood at work: Implications for helping customers. *Journal of Personal Selling and Sales Management,* 18:23–30.

Gross, J.J., Fredrickson, B.L., & Levenson, R.W. (1994). The psychophysiology of crying. *Psychophysiology,* 31:460–468.

Haidt, J. (2000). The positive emotion of elevation. *Prevention and Treatment.* Available at http://journals.apa.org/prevention.

_____(2003). Elevation and the positive psychology of morality. In Keyes, C.L., & Haidt, J. (Eds.), *Flourishing: The positive person and the good life* (pp.275–289). Washington, DC: American Psychological Association.

Hatfield, E., Cacioppo, J.T., & Rapson, R.L. (1993). Emotional contagion. *Current Directions in Psychological Science,* 2:96–99.

Isen, A.M. (1987). Positive affect, cognitive processes, and social behavior. *Advances in Experimental Social Psychology,* 20:203–253.

_____(2002). A role for neuropsychology in understanding the facilitating influence of positive affect on social behavior and cognitive processes. In Snyder, C.R., & Lopez, S.J. (Eds.), *Handbook of positive psychology* (pp.528–540). New York: Oxford University Press.

Isen, A.M., & Daubman, K.A. (1984). The influence of affect on categorization. *Journal of Personality and Social Psychology,* 47:1206–1217.

Isen, A.M., Daubman, K.A., & Nowicki, G.P. (1987). Positive affect facilitates creative problem solving. *Journal of Personality and Social Psychology,* 52:1122–1131.

Isen, A.M., Johnson, M.M.S., Mertz, E., & Robinson, G.F. (1985). The influence of positive affect on the unusualness of word associations. *Journal of Personality and Social Psychology,* 48:1413–1426.

Isen, A.M., & Means, B. (1983). The influence of positive affect on decisionmaking strategy. *Social Cognition,* 2:18–31.

Isen, A.M., Rosenzweig, A.S., & Young, M.J. (1991). The influence of positive affect on clinical problem solving. *Medical Decision Making,* 11:221–227.

Kahn, B.E., & Isen, A.M. (1993). The influence of positive affect on varietyseeking among safe, enjoyable products. *Journal of Consumer Research,* 20:257–270.

Keltner, D., & Bonanno, G.A. (1997). A study of laughter and dissociation: Distinct correlates of laughter and smiling during bereavement. *Journal of Personality and Social Psychology,* 73:687–702.

Larsen, R.J., & Fredrickson, B.L. (1999). Measurement issues in emotion research. In Kahneman, D., Diener, E., & Schwarz, N. (Eds.), *Well-being: Foundations of hedonic psychology* (pp.40–60). New York: Russell Sage.

Lazarus, R.S. (1991). *Emotion and adaptation.* New York: Oxford University Press.

Lee, P.C. (1983). Play as a means for developing relationships. In Hinde, R.A. (Ed.), *Primate social relationships* (pp.82–89). Oxford, UK: Blackwell.

Leslie, A.M. (1987). Pretense and representation: The origins of "theory of mind." *Psychological Review,* 94:412–426.

Levenson, R.W. (1994). Human emotions: A functional view. In Ekman, P., & Davidson, R. (Eds.), *The nature of emotion:*

Fundamental questions (pp.123–126). New York: Oxford University Press.

Levenson, R.W., Ekman, P., & Friesen, W.V. (1990). Voluntary facial action generates emotion-specific autonomic nervous system activity. *Psychophysiology,* 27:363–384.

Lundqvist, L.O., & Dimberg, U. (1995). Facial expressions are contagious. *Journal of Psychophysiology,* 9:203–211.

McCullough, M.E., Kilpatrick, S.D., Emmons, R.A., & Larson, D.B. (2001). Is gratitude a moral affect? *Psychological Bulletin,* 127:249–266.

Moskowitz, J.T. (2001). Emotion and coping. In Mayne, T.J., & Bonnano, G.A. (Eds.), *Emotion: Current issues and future directions* (pp.311–336). New York: Guilford.

Oatley, K., & Jenkins, J.M. (1996). *Understanding emotions.* Cambridge, MA: Blackwell.

Ohman, A. (2000). Fear and anxiety: Evolutionary, cognitive, and clinical perspectives. In Lewis, M., & Haviland-Jones,

J.M. (Eds.), *Handbook of emotions,* 2nd ed. (pp.573–593). New York: Guilford.

Panksepp, J. (1998). Attention deficit hyperactivity disorders, psychostimulants, and intolerance of childhood playfulness: A tragedy in the making? *Current Directions in Psychological Science,* 7:91–98.

Peterson, C., & Seligman, M.E.P. (1984). Causal explanations as a risk factor for depression: Theory and evidence. *Psychological Review,* 91:347–374.

Quinn, R.E. (2000). *Change the world: How ordinary people can achieve extraordinary results.* San Francisco: Jossey-Bass.

Reed, M.B., & Aspinwall, L.G. (1998). Self-affirmation reduces biased processing of health-risk information. *Motivation and Emotion,* 22:99–132.

Rosenberg, E.L. (1998). Levels of analysis and the organization of affect. *Review of General Psychology,* 2:247–270.

Ryff, C.D., & Singer, B. (1998). Contours of positive human health. *Psychological Inquiry,* 9:1–28.

Sherrod, L.R., & Singer, J. L (1989). The development of make-believe play. In Goldstein, J. (Ed.), *Sports, games, and play* (pp.1–38). Hillsdale, NJ: Lawrence Erlbaum.

Simons, C.J.R., McCluskey-Fawcett, K.A., & Papini, D.R. (1986). Theoretical and functional perspective on the development of humor during infancy, childhood, and adolescence. In Nahemow, L., McCluskey-Fawcett, K.A., & McGhee, P.E. (Eds.), *Humor and aging* (pp.53–77). San Diego: Academic Press.

Staw, B.M., Sutton, R.I., & Pellod, L.H. (1994). Employee positive emotion and favorable outcomes at the workplace. *Organizational Science,* 5:51–71.

Staw, B.M., & Barsade, S.G. (1993). Affect and managerial performance: A test of the sadder-but-wiser vs. happier-and-smarter hypotheses. *Administrative Science Quarterly,* 38:304–331.

Stein, N.L., Folkman, S., Trabasso, T., & Richards, T.A. (1997). Appraisal and goal processes as predictors of psychological well-being in bereaved caregivers. *Journal of Personality and Social Psychology,* 72:872–884.

Tooby, J., & Cosmides, L. (1990). The past explains the present: Emotional adaptations and the structure of ancestral environments. *Ethology and Sociobiology,* 11:375–424.

Trope, Y., & Pomerantz, E.M. (1998). Resolving conflicts among self-evaluative motives: Positive experiences as a resource for overcoming defensiveness. *Motivation and Emotion,* 22:53–72.

Watson, D., Clark, L.A., McIntyre, C.W., & Hamaker, S. (1992). Affect, personality, and social activity. *Journal of Personality and Social Psychology,* 63:1011–1025.

Waugh, C.E., & Fredrickson, B.L. (2003). Feeling good and feeling close: The effect of positive emotion on self-other overlap. Manuscript under review.

Wright, T.A., & Staw, B.M. (1999). Affect and favorable work outcomes: Two longitudinal tests of the happy-productive worker thesis. *Journal of Organizational Behavior,* 20:1–23.

Chapter 12

Aristotle (1985). *Nicomachean ethics* Trans T. Irwin. Indianapolis: Hackett.

Ashkanasy, N.M., & Daus, C.S. (2002). Emotion in the workplace: The new challenge for managers. *Academy of Management Executive,* 16:76–86.

Bagozzi, R.P. (1999). Happiness. In Levinson, D., Ponzetti, J.J., Jr., & Jorgensen, P.F. (Eds.), *Encyclopedia of human emotions,* vol.1 (pp.317–324). New York: Macmillan.

_____(2000). On the concept of intentional social action in consumer behavior. *Journal of Consumer Research,* 27:388–396.

Bagozzi, R.P., Baumgartner, H., & Pieters, R. (1998). Goal-directed emotions. *Cognition and Emotion,* 12:1–26.

Bagozzi, R.P., & Dholakia, U.M. (2002). Intentional social action in virtual communities. *Journal of Interactive Marketing,* 16:2–21.

_____(2003). Brand communities and intentional social action. Unpublished working paper, Rice University.

Bagozzi, R.P., Dholakia, U.M., & Basuroy, S. (2003). How effortful decisions get enacted: The motivating role of decision processes, desires, and anticipated emotions. Unpublished working paper, Rice University.

Bagozzi, R.P., & Lee, K-H. (2002). Multiple routes for social influence: The role of compliance, internalization, and social identity. *Social Psychology Quarterly,* 65:226–247.

Bagozzi, R.P., & Verbeke, W. (2002). Determinants and effects of guilt and shame by salespeople and the moderating roles of empathy and distraction cognitive style. Unpublished working paper. Rice University.

Bagozzi, R.P., & Verbeke, W., & Gavino, J.C., Jr. (2003). Culture moderates the self-regulation of shame and its effects on performance: The case of salespersons in the Netherlands and the Philippines. *Journal of Applied Psychology,* 88.

Bagozzi, R.P., Wong, N., & Yi, Y. (1999). The role of culture and gender in the relationship between positive and negative affect. *Cognition and Emotion,* 13:641–672.

Barret, K.C. (1995). A functionalist approach to shame and guilt. In Tangney, J.P., and Fischer, K.W. (Eds.), *Self-conscious emotions* (pp.25–63). New York: Guilford.

Barrett, L.F., & Gross, J.J. (2001). Emotional intelligence: A process model of emotion representation and regulation. In Mayne, T.J., & Bonanno, G.A. (Eds.), *Emotions: Current issues and future directions* (pp.286–310). New York: Guilford.

Barrett, L.F., & Russell, J.A. (1998). Independence and bipolarity in the structure of current affect. *Journal of Personality and Social Psychology,* 74:967–984.

Bergami, M., & Bagozzi, R.P. (2000). Self-categorization, affective commitment, and group self-esteem as distinct aspects of social identity in the organization. *British Journal of Social Psychology,* 39:555–577.

Brown, S.P., Cron, W.L., & Slocum, J.W., Jr. (1997). Effects of goal-directed emotions on salespeople volitions, behavior, and performance: A longitudinal study. *Journal of Marketing,* 61:39–50.

Carver, C.S., & Scheier, M.F. (1998). *On the self-regulation of behavior* Cambridge: Cambridge University Press.

Fischer, K.W., & Tangney, J.T. (1995). Self-conscious emotions and the affect revolution: Framework and overview. In Tangney, J.P., & Fischer, K.W. (Eds.), *Self-conscious emotions* (pp.3–24). New York: Guilford.

Fredrickson, B.L., & Branigan, C. (2001). Positive emotions. In Mayne, T.J., & Bonanno, G.A. (Eds.), *Emotions: Current issues and future directions* (pp.123–151). New York: Guilford.

Frijda, N.H. (1993). Moods, emotion episodes, and emotions. In Lewis, M., & Haviland, J.M. (Eds.), *Handbook of emotions* (pp.381–403). New York: Guilford.

Frijda, N.H., Kuipers, P., & ter Schure, E. (1989). Relations among emotion, appraisal, and emotional action readiness. *Journal of Personality and Social Psychology,* 57:212–228.

Frijda, N.H., Manstead, A.S.R., & Bem, S. (2000). The influence of emotions on beliefs. In Frijda, N.H., Manstead, A.S.R., & Bem, S. (Eds.), *Emotions and beliefs: How feelings influence thoughts* (pp.1–9). Cambridge: Cambridge University Press.

George, J.M. (2000). Emotions and leadership: The role of emotional intelligence. *Human Relations,* 53:1027–1055.

Goleman, D. (1998). What makes a leader? *Harvard Business Review,* November–December, pp.92–102.

_____(2000). Leadership that gets results. *Harvard Business Review,* March–April, pp.79–90.

Green, D.P., Goldman, S.L., & Salovey, P. (1993). Measurement error masks bipolarity in affect ratings. *Journal of Personality and Social Psychology,* 64:1029–1041.

Huy, Q.N. (1999). Emotional capability, emotional intelligence, and radical change. *Academy of Management Review,* 14:325–345.

Kristjansson, K. (2002). *Justifying emotions: Pride and jealousy.* London: Routledge.

Lazarus, R.S. (1991). *Emotion and adaptation.* New York: Oxford University Press.

Locke, E.A., & Latham, G.P. (1990). *A theory of goal-setting and task performance.* Englewood Cliffs, NJ: Prentice-Hall.

Luthans, F. (2002). Positive organizational behavior: Developing and managing psychological strengths. *Academy of Management Executive,* 16:57–72.

Miller, R.S. (1996). *Embarrassment.* New York: Guilford.

Oatley, K. (1992). *Best laid schemes: The psychology of emotions.* Cambridge: Cambridge University Press.

Oatley, K., & Johnson-Laird, P.N. (1987). Towards a cognitive theory of emotions. *Cognition and Emotion,* 1:29–50.

_____(1996). The communicative theory of emotions: Empirical tests, mental models, and implications for social interaction. In Martin, L.L., & Tesser, A. (Eds.), *Striving and feeling: Interactions among goals, affect, and selfregulation* (pp.363–393). Mahwah, NJ: Erlbaum.

Perugini, M., & Bagozzi, R.P. (2001). The role of desires and anticipated emotions in goal-directed behavior: Broadening and deepening the theory of planned behavior. *British Journal of Social Psychology,* 40:79–98.

Pugh, S.D. (2001). Service with a smile: Emotional contagion in service encounters. *Academy of Management Journal,* 44:1018–1027.

Rousseau, D.M. (1997). Organizational behavior in the new organizational era. *Annual Review of Psychology,* 48:515–546.

Russell, J.A. (1980). A circumplex model of affect. *Journal of Personality and Social Psychology,* 39:1161–1178.

Russell, J.A., & Carroll, J.M. (1999). On the bipolarity of positive and negative affect. *Psychological Bulletin,* 125:3–30.

Salovey, P., & Mayer, J.D. (1990). Emotional intelligence. *Imagination, Cognition, and Personality,* 9:185–211.

Schneider, S.L. (2001). In search of realistic optimism: Meaning, knowledge, and warm fuzziness. *American Psychologist,* 56:250–263.

330

Seligman, M.E.P. (2002). *Authentic happiness.* New York: Free Press.

Seligman, M.E.P., & Csikszentmihalyi, M. (2000). Positive psychology: An introduction. *American Psychologist,* 55:5–14.

Tajfel, H. (1978). Social categorization, social identity, and social comparison. In Tajfel, H. (Ed.), *Differentiation between social groups: Studies in the social psychology of intergroup relations* (pp.61–76). London: Academic Press.

Tangney, J.P., & Salovey, P. (1999). Problematic social emotions: Shame, guilt, jealousy, and envy. In Kowalski, R.M., & Leary, M.R. (Eds.), *The social psychology of emotional and behavioral problems* (pp.167–195). Washington, DC: American Psychological Association.

Thoits, P.A. (1990). Emotion deviance: Research agenda. In Kemper, T.D. (Ed.), *Research agendas in the sociology of emotions* (pp.180–206). Albany: State University of New York Press.

Verbeke, W., & Bagozzi, R.P. (2000). Sales call anxiety: Exploring what it means when fear rules a sales encounter. *Journal of Marketing,* 64:88–101.

_____(2002). A situational analysis on how salespeople experience and cope with shame and embarrassment. *Psychology & Marketing,* 19:713–741.

_____(2003a). Adaptive and maladaptive consequences of envy and pride in personal selling. Unpublished working paper, Rice University.

_____(2003b). Exploring the role of self- and customer-provoked embarrassment in personal selling. *International Journal of Research in Marketing.*

Verbeke, W., Belschak, F., & Bagozzi, R.P. (2003). Exploring emotional competence: Its effects on coping, social capital, and performance of salespeople. Unpublished working paper, Rice University.

Watson, D., & Tellegen, A. (1985). Toward a consensual structure of mood. *Psychological Bulletin,* 98:219–235.

Chapter 13

Allen, T.J. (1977). *Managing the flow of technology.* Cambridge: MIT Press.

Amabile, T.M., Conti, R., Coon, H., Lazenby, J., & Herron, M. (1996). Assessing the work environment for creativity. *Academy of Management Journal,* 39(5):1154–1184.

Argote, L., & Ingram, P. (2000). Knowledge transfer: A basis for competitive advantage in firms. *Organizational Behavior & Human Decision Processes,* special issue, *The psychological foundations of knowledge transfer in organizations,* 82(1):150–169.

Argyris, C. (1985). *Strategy, change, and defensive routines.* Boston: Pitman.

Ashford, S., & Northcraft, G. (1992). Conveying more (or less) than we realize: The role of impression-management in feedback-seeking. *Organizational Behavior & Human Decision Processes,* 53(3):310–334.

Ashford, S.J., & Tsui, A.S. (1991). Self regulation for managerial effectiveness: The role of active feedback seeking. *Academy of Management Journal,* 34(2):251–280.

Blau, P.M. (1955). *The dynamics of bureaucracy: A study of interpersonal relationships in two government agencies.* Chicago: University of Chicago Press.

Brown, S.L., & Eisenhardt, K.M. (1997). The art of continuous change: Linking complexity theory and time-paced evolution in relentlessly shifting organizations. *Administrative Science Quarterly,* 42:1–34.

Cameron, K., & Caza, A. (2002). Organizational and leadership virtues and the role of forgiveness. *Journal of Leadership and Organizational Studies,* 9:33–48.

Capers, B., & Lipton. C. (1993). Hubble space telescope disaster. *Academy of Management Executive,* 7(3):23–37.

Ciborra, C. (1996). The platform organization: Recombining strategies, structures, and surprises. *Organization Science,* 7(2):103–118.

Clark, K.B., & Fujimoto, T. (1989). Lead time in automobile development: Explaining the Japanese advantage. *Journal of Technology and Engineering Management,* 6:25–58.

Collins, J.C., & Porras, J.I. (1994). *Built to last: Successful habits of visionary companies.* New York: HarperCollins.

Daft, R.L. (1982). Bureaucratic versus nonbureaucratic structure and the process of innovation and change. *Research in the Sociology of Organizations,* 1:129–166.

de Gues, A. (1991). *The living company.* Boston: Harvard Business School Press.

Duncan, R.B. (1976.) The ambidextrous organization: Designing dual structures for innovation. In Kilman, R.H., Pondy, L.R., & Slevin, D.P. (Eds.), *The management of organizational design: Strategies and implementation* (pp.167–188). New York: North-Holland.

Depret, E., & Fiske, S. (1999). Perceiving the powerful: Intriguing individuals versus threatening groups. *Journal of Experimental Social Psychology,* 35(5):461–480.

Diener, E. (2000). Subjective well-being: The science of happiness and a proposal for a national index. *American Psychologist,* 55(1):34–43.

Druian, P.R., & DePaulo, B.M. (1977). Asking a child for help. *Social behavior and Personality,* 5(1):33–39.

Dutton, J.E., Frost, P.J., & Worline, M.C. (2002). Leading in times of trauma: Creating a compassionate organization. *Harvard Business Review,* 80(1): 54–61.

Dweck, C.S. (1986). Motivational processes affecting learning. *American Psychologist,* special issue, *Psychological science and education,* 41(10):1040–1048.

Dweck, C.S., & Leggett, E.L. (1988). A social-cognitive approach to motivation and personality. *Psychological Review,* 95(2):256–273.

Eagly, A., Makhijani, M., & Klonsky, B. (1992). Gender and the evaluation of leaders: A meta-analysis. *Psychological Bulletin,* 111(1):3–22.

Edmondson, A.C. (1996). Learning from errors is easier said than done: Group and organizational influences on the detection and correction of human error. *Journal of Applied Behavioral Science,* 32(1): 5–32.

_____(1999). Psychological safety and learning behavior in work teams. *Administrative Science Quarterly, 44:* 350–383.

Elliot, E.S., & Dweck, C.S. (1988). Goals: An approach to motivation and achievement. *Journal of Personality and Social Psychology,* 54(1):5–12.

Emerson, R.M. (1962). Power-dependence relations. *American Sociological Review,* 27:31–40.

Feldman, D. (1984). The development and enforcement of group norms. *Academy of Management Review,* 9:47–53.

Frankl, V.E. (1970). *Man's search for meaning: An introduction to logogtherapy.* New York: Washington Square Press.

Fredrickson, B.L. (1998). What good are positive emotions? *Review of General Psychology,* 2:300–319.

_____(2001). The role of positive emotions in positive psychology: The broadenand-build theory of positive emotions. *American Psychologist,* 56:218–226.

Fredrickson, B.L., & Joiner, T. (2002). Positive emotions trigger upward spirals toward emotional well-being. *Psychological Science,* 13(2):172–175.

French, J.R.P., & Raven, B.H. (1959). The bases of social power. In Cartwright, D. (Ed.), *Studies of social power* (pp.118–149). Ann Arbor, MI: Institute of Social Research.

Gilligan, C. (1982). *In a different voice.* Cambridge: Harvard University Press.

Hackman, J.R. (1992). Group influences on individuals in organizations. In Dunnette, M.D., & Hough, L.M. (Eds.), *Handbook of industrial and organizational psychology,* vol.3 (pp.199–255). Palo Alto: Consulting Psychologists Press.

Hong, Y, Y., Chiu, C.Y., Dweck, C.S., Lin, D.M., & Wan, W. (1999). Implicit theories, attributions, and coping: A meaning system approach. *Journal of Personality and Social Psychology,* 77(3):588–599.

Karabenick, S., & Knapp, J. (1988). Help seeking and the need for academic assistance. *Journal of Educational Psychology,* 80(3):406–408.

Kaplan, R.E. (1979). The conspicuous absence of evidence that process consultation enhances task performance. *Journal of Applied Behavioral Science,* 15:346–360.

Lee, F. (1997). When the going gets tough, do the tough ask for help? Help seeking and power motivation in organizations. *Organizational Behavior and Human Decision Processes,* 72(3):336–363.

_____(2001). The fear factor. *Harvard Business Review,* 79(1):29–30.

_____(2002). The social costs of seeking help. *Journal of Applied Behavioral Science,* 38(1):17–35.

Lee, F., Edmondson, A., Thomke, S., & Worline, M. (2000). Promoting experimentation in organizations: The hidden dilemma of supportive conditions. Paper presented at the Academy of Management Conference, August 2000, Toronto, Canada.

Lee, F., & Tiedens, L. (2001). Is it lonely at the top? Independence and interdependence of power-holders. In Staw, B., & Sutton, R. (Eds.), *Research in organizational behavior,* vol.23 (pp.43–91). Greenwich, CT: JAI Press.

Lee, F., Worline, M., & Tyre, M. (2002). When does help seeking help? The effects of status and accessibility on help seeking and learning outcomes. Unpublished manuscript, University of Michigan.

Leonard-Barton, D. (1989). Implementing new production technologies: Exercises in corporate learning. In Von Glinow, M., & Mohrmans, S. (Eds.), *Managing complexity in high technology industries: Systems and people.* New York: Oxford Press.

Markus, H., & Kitayama, S. (1991). Culture and the self: Implications for cognition, emotion, and motivation. *Psychological Review,* 98(2):224–253.

May, R. (1975). *The courage to create.* New York: Bantam Books.

Morrison, E.W. (1993). Newcomer information seeking: Exploring types, modes, sources, and outcomes. *Academy of Management Journal,* 36(3):557–589.

Newman, R., & Goldin, L. (1990). Children's reluctance to seek help with schoolwork. *Journal of Educational Psychology,* 82(1):92–100.

340

Nonaka, I., & Takeuchi, H. (1995). *The knowl-edge-creating company.* New York: Oxford University Press.

Peterson, C. (2000). The future of optimism. *American Psychologist,* 55(1):44–55.

Pfeffer, J., & Sutton, R. (2000). *The knowing-doing gap: How smart companies turn knowledge into action.* Boston: Harvard Business School Press.

Rogers, C.R. (1970). *On encounter groups.* New York: Harrow Books. _____(1980). *A way of being.* Boston: Houghton Mifflin.

Rosenthal, R., & Rosnow, R.L. (1992). *Essentials of behavioral research: Methods and data analysis.* 2nd ed. New York: McGraw-Hill.

Salancik, G., & Pfeffer, J. (1977). Who gets power—and how they hold on to it: A strategic-contingency model of power. *Organizational Dynamics,* 5(3):2–21.

Seligman, M.E.P., & Csikszentmihalyi, M. (2000). Positive psychology: An introduction. *American Psychologist,* 55(1):5–14.

Sitkin, S.B. (1992). Learning through failure: The strategy of small losses. *Research in Organizational Behavior,* 14:231–266.

Thomke, S. (1998). Managing experimentation in the design of new products. *Management Science,* 44(6):743–762.

Thomke, S., von Hippel, E., & Franke, R. (1998). Modes of experimentation: An innovation process—and competitive—variable. *Research Policy,* 27:315–332.

Thompson, J.D. (1967). *Organizations in action.* New York: McGraw Hill.

Triandis, H.C. (1994). *Culture and social behavior.* San Francisco: McGraw-Hill.

Tushman, M.L., & Anderson, P. (1986). Technological discontinuities and organizational environments. *Administrative Science Quarterly,* 31:439–465.

Tushman, M.L., & O'Reilly, C.A. (1996). Ambidextrous organizations: Managing evolutionary and revolutionary change. *California Management Review,* 38(4):8–30.

_____(1997). *Winning through innovation: A practical guide to leading organizational change and renewa* l. Boston: Harvard Business School Press.

Tyre, M., & Ellis, S. (1993). Determinants of helping and help-seeking among developers and users of new technologies. Paper presented at the fifty-third Academy of Management Conference, Atlanta, GA, August.

Vincente, W. (1990). *What engineers know and how they know it.* Baltimore: Johns Hopkins University Press.

Wheelwright, S.C., & Clark, K.B. (1992.) *Revolutionizing product development.* New York: Free Press.

Willis, T. (1983). Social comparison in coping and help seeking. In DePaulo, B., Nadler, A., & Fisher, J. (Eds.), *New directions in helping,* vol.2 (pp.190–192). New York: Academic Press.

Wilson, J.Q. (1966). Innovation in organizations: Notes toward a theory. In Thompson, J.D. (Ed.), *Approaches to organizationaldesign* (pp.193–218).Pittsburgh: University of Pittsburgh Press.

Worline, M.C., Wrzesniewski, A., & Rafaeli, A. (2002). Courage at work: Breaking routines to improve performance. In Lord, R.G., Klimoski, R.J., & Kanfer, R. (Eds.), *Emotions in the workplace: Understanding the structure and role of emotions in organizational behavior* (pp.295–330). San Francisco: Jossey-Bass.

Chapter 14

Bandura, A. (1977). Self-efficacy: Toward a unifying theory of behavioral change. *Psychological Review,* 84:191–215.

_____(1989). Human agency in social cognitive theory. *American Psychologist,* 44(9):1175–1184.

Bass, B.M. 1996. *A new paradigm of leadership.* Alexandria, VA: U.S. Army Research Institute.

Bateman, T.S., & Crandt, J.M. (1993). The proactive component of organizational behavior: A measure and correlates. *Journal of Organizational Behavior,* 14:103–118.

Bateman, T.S., & Porath, C. (2003). Transcendent behavior. In Cameron, K., Dutton, J., & Quinn, R. (Eds.), *Positive*

organizational scholarship. San Francisco: Berrett-Koehler.

Becker, H.S. (1963). *Outsiders: Studies in the sociology of deviance.* London: Free Press of Glencoe.

Ben-Yehuda, N. (1990). Positive and negative deviance: More fuel for a controversy. *Deviant Behavior,* 11(3):221–243.

Bennett, R.J., & Robinson, S.L. (2000). Development of a measure of workplace deviance. *Journal of Applied Psychology,* 85(3):349–360.

Brief, A.P., & Motowidlo, S.J. (1986.) Prosocial organizational behaviors. *Academy of Management Review,* 11:710–725.

Business Enterprise Trust (1991). Merck & Co., Inc. In Donaldson, T., & Werhane, P., (Eds.), *Ethical issues in business: A philosophical approach* (pp.215–220). Upper Saddle River, NJ: Prentice-Hall.

Cameron, K. (2003). Organizational virtuousness and performance. In Cameron, K., Dutton, J., & Quinn, R. (Eds.), *Positive*

organizational scholarship. San Francisco: Berrett-Koehler.

Cameron, K., Dutton, J., & Quinn, R. (Eds.) (2003). *Positive organizational scholarship.* San Francisco: Berrett-Koehler.

Chappell, T. (1996). *The soul of a business: Managing for profit and the common good.* New York: Bantam Books.

Clinard, M.B., & Meier, R.F. (2001). *Sociology of deviant behavior.* 11th ed. Fort Worth, TX: Harcourt.

Deci, E.L., & Ryan, R.M. (1985). *Intrinsic motivation and self-determination in human behavior.* New York: Plenum Press.

Diener, D. (2000). Subjective well-being: The science of happiness and a proposal for a national index. *American Psychologist,* 55:34–43.

Dodge, D. (1985). The over-negativized conceputalization of deviance: A programmatic exploration. *Deviant Behavior,* 6(1):17–37.

Donaldson, T., & Dunfee, D. (1999). *The ties that bind.* Boston: Harvard University Press.

Douglas, J.D. (1977). Shame and deceit in creative deviance. In Sagarin, E. (Ed.), *Deviance and social change* (pp.59-86). Thousand Oaks, CA: Sage.

Dutton, J.E., Frost, P., Worline, M., Kanov, J., & Lilius, J. (2002). Leading in times of trauma. *Harvard Business Review,* January, pp.55–61.

Dutton, J.E., & Heaphy, E.D. (2003). The power of high quality connections. In Cameron, K., Dutton, J., & Quinn, R. (Eds.), *Positive organizational scholarship.* San Francisco: Berrett-Koehler.

Dutton, J.E., Quinn, R., & Pasick, R. (2001). The heart of Reuters. Paper presented at the Conference on Positive Organizational Scholarship, University of Michigan, December 12-14, 2001.

Elangovan, A.R., & Shapiro, D. (1998). Betrayal of trust in organizations. *Academy of Management Review,* 23:547–566.

Freeman, R.E. (1984). *Strategic management: A stakeholder approach.* Boston: Pitman.

Frese, M., Garst, H., & Fay, D. 2000. Control and complexity in work and the development of personal initiative: A four wave longitudinal study of occupational socialization. Working paper, University of Giessen, Germany.

Friedman, M. (1970). The social responsibility of business is to increase its profits. *New York Times Magazine,* September 13, 1970.

Gibbs, J.P. (1965). Norms: The problem of definition and classification. *American Journal of Sociology,* 70(5):586–594.

Gist, M.E., & Mitchell, T.R. (1992). Self-efficacy: A theoretical analysis of its determinants and malleability. *Academy of Management Review,* 17:183–211.

Goode, E. (1991). Positive deviance: A viable concept. *Deviant Behavior,* 12(3): 289–309.

Greenleaf, R. K, & Spears, L. (2002). *Servant leadership: A journey into the nature of legitimate power and greatness.* Mahwah, NJ: Paulist Press.

Heckert, D.M. (1998). Positive deviance: A classificatory model. *Free Inquiry in Creative Sociology,* 26(1):23–30.

Howell, J.M., & Higgins, C.A. (1990). Champions of technology innovation. *Administrative Science Quarterly,* 35:317–341.

Hughes, R., & Coakley, J. (1991). Positive deviance among athletes: The implications of overconformity to the sport ethic. *Sociology of Sport Journal,* 8:307–325.

Jones, A.L. (1998). Random acts of kindness: A teaching tool for positive deviance. *Teaching Sociology,* 26:179–188.

Katz, J. (1972). Deviance, charisma, and rule-defined behavior. *Social Problems,* 20:186–201.

Katzenbach, J.R. (1996). *Real change leaders.* New York: Random House.

Lutnick, H., & Barbash, T. (2002). *Top of the world: Cantor-Fitzgerald and 9/11.* New York: HarperCollins.

Mathews, R., & Wacker, W. (2002). *The deviant's advantage.* New York: Crown Business.

Mead, G.H. (1934). *Mind, self, and society.* Chicago: University of Chicago Press.

Merton, R.K. (1968). *Social theory and social structure.* New York: Free Press.

Mischel, W. (1980). *Essentials of psychology* (2nd ed.). New York: Random House.

Morrison, E.W. (2002). Sometimes you've got to break the rules: Prosocial rule breaking at work. Working paper, New York University.

Park, N., & Peterson, C.M. (2003). Virtues and organizations. In Cameron, K., Dutton, J., & Quinn, R. (Eds.), *Positive organizational scholarship.* San Francisco: Berrett-Koehler.

Parker, S.K., & Axtell, C.M. (2001). Seeing another viewpoint: Antecedents and outcomes of employee perspective taking. *Academy of Management Journal,* 44:1085–1100.

Pascale, R.T., Milleman, M., & Gioja, L. (2000). *Surfing the edge of chaos: The laws of nature and the new laws of business.* New York: Crown.

Perlow, R., & Latham, L. (1993). Relationship of client abuse with locus of control and gender: A longitudinal study in mental retardation facilities. *Journal of Applied Psychology,* 78:831–834.

Peterson, C., & Seligman, M.E.P. (2003). *The VIA classification of strengths and virtues.* Washington, DC: American Psychological Association.

Posner, J. (1976). The stigma of excellence: On being just right. *Sociological Inquiry,* 46(2):141–144.

Quinn, R.E. (1996). *Deep change: Discovering the leader within.* San Francisco: Jossey-Bass.

Quinn, R.E., & Quinn, G.T. (2002). *Letters to Garrett: Stories of change, power, and possibility.* San Francisco: Jossey-Bass.

Robinson, S.L., & Bennett, R.J. (1995). A typology of workplace behaviors: A multidimensional scaling study. *Academy of Management Journal,* 38:555–572.

Rushdie, S. (1990). Interview in *The Guardian* (London), November 8. As cited on the webpage http://www.bartleby.com/66/49/475 49.html

Ryan, R.M., & Deci, E.L. (2000). Self-determination theory and the facilitation of intrinsic motivation, social development, and well-being. *American Psychologist,* 55:68–78.

Sagarin, E. (1985). Positive deviance: An oxymoron. *Deviant Behavior,* 6:169–181.

Sandage, S.J., & Hill, P.C. (2001). The virtues of positive psychology: The rapprochement and challenges of an affirmative postmodern perspective. *Journal for the Theory of Social Behaviour,* 31:241–260.

Spreitzer, G.M. (1995). Psychological empowerment in the workplace: Dimensions, measurement, and validation. *Academy of Management Journal,* 38:1442–1465.

Spreitzer, G.M., & Sonenshein, S. (2003). Positive deviance: Construct development.

352

Working paper, University of Michigan Business School.

Staw, B.M., & Boetteger, R. (1990). Task revision: A neglected form of work performance. *Academy of Management Journal,* 33:534–559.

Storms, P.L., & Spector, P.E. (1987). Relationships of organizational frustration with reported behavioral reactions: The moderating effects of locus of control. *Journal of Occupational Psychology,* 60:227–234.

Thomas, K.W., & Velthouse, B.A. (1990). Cognitive elements of empowerment: An interpretive model of intrinsic task motivation. *Academy of Management Review,* 15:666–681.

Vandewalle, D., Van Dyne, L., & Kostova, T. (1995). Psychological ownership: An empirical examination of its consequences. *Group and Organization Management,* 29:210–226.

Warren, D. (in press). Constructive and destructive deviance in organizations. *Academy of Management Review.*

Webster's New World Dictionary (2nd Concise Edition). 1982. New York: Webster's New World.

Wilkins, L.T. (1964). *Social deviance: Social policy, action, and research.* London: Tavistock.

Withey, M.J., & Cooper, W.H. (1989). Predicting exit, voice, loyalty, and neglect. *Administrative Science Quarterly,* 34:521–540.

Worline, M. (In press). Valor. In Peterson, C., & Seligman, M. (Eds.), *Values in Action classification of strengths.* Cincinnati, OH: Values in Action Coalition.

Worline, M., Wrzesniewski, A., & Rafaeli, A. (2002). Courage and work: Breaking routines to improve performance. In Lord, R., Klimoski, R., & Kanfer, R. (Eds.), *Emotions in the workplace: Understanding the structure and role of emotions in organizational behavior* (pp.295–330). San Francisco: Jossey-Bass.

Wrzesniewski, A. (2003). Finding positive meaning in work. In Cameron, K., Dutton, J., & Quinn, R. (Eds.), *Positive organizational scholarship.* San Francisco: Berrett-Koelher.

Wrzesniewski, A., McCauley, C.R., Rosin, P., & Schwartz, B. (1997). Jobs, careers, and callings: People's relations to their work. *Journal of Research in Personality,* 31:21–33.

Chapter 15

Bennis, W.G. (1963). A new role for the behavioral sciences: Effecting organizational change. *Administrative Science Quarterly,* 8(2):125–165.

Cameron, K. (2002). Organizational virtues: Implications for performance. Symposium presented at the Academy of Management, Denver, CO, August 2002.

Cavanagh, G.F., & Moberg, D.J. (1999). The virtue of courage within the organization. In Pava, M.L., & Primeaux, P.P. (Eds.), *Research in ethical issues in organizations,* vol.1 (pp.1–25). Stamford, CT: JAI Press.

Chin, R., & Benne, K.D. (2000). General strategies for effecting changes in human systems. In French, W.L. , Bell, C.H., Jr., &

Zawacki, R.A. (Eds.), *Organization development and transformation: Managing effective change,* 5th ed. (pp.43–63). New York: Irwin McGraw-Hill.

Cooperrider, D.L. (1986). *Appreciative Inquiry: Toward a methodology for understanding and enhancing organization innovation.* Unpublished Ph.D. diss., Case Western Reserve University, Cleveland, OH.

_____(1999). Positive image, positive action: The affirmative basis of organizing. In Srivastva, S., & Cooperrider, D.L. (Eds.), *Appreciative management and leadership: The power of positive thought and action in organization,* rev. ed. (pp.91–125). Cleveland, OH: Lakeshore Communications.

_____(2000). The inter-religious friendship group: A visible force for peace. *Weatherhead :* The Magazine of the Weatherhead School of Management. Cleveland, OH: Case Western Reserve University.

_____(2001). *AI: The beginnings (Toward a methodology for understanding and enhancing organizational innovation).* Cleveland, OH: Lakeshore Communications.

Cousins, N. (1998). Therapeutic value of laughter. *Integrative Psychiatry,* 3(2):112.

Cooperrider, D.L., & Whitney, D. (1999). A positive revolution in change: Appreciative inquiry. In Cooperrider, D.L., Sorensen, P.F., Jr., Whitney, D., & Yaeger, T.F. (Eds.), *Appreciative inquiry: Rethinking human organization toward a positive theory of change* (p.18). Champaign, IL: Stipes Publishing.

Folkman, S., & Moskowitz, J.T. (2000). Positive affect and the other side of coping. *American Psychologist,* 55:647–654.

Fredrickson, B.L. (1998). What good are positive emotions? *Review of General Psychology,* 2(3):300–319.

_____(2000). Cultivating positive emotions to optimize health and well-being. *Prevention & Treatment,* 3:n.p.

_____(2001). The role of positive emotions in positive psychology: The broadenand-build theory of positive emotions. *American Psychologist,* 56(3): 218–226.

Fredrickson, B.L., Mancuso, R.A., Branigan, C., & Tugade, M.M. (2000). *Motivation & Emotion,*

24(4):237–258. Available at http://olc3.ohioli nk.edu/bin/
gate.exe?f=doc&state=o2ttam.62.4.

Fry, R., Barrett, F., Seiling, J., & Whitney, D. (2001). *Appreciative inquiry and organizational transformation: Reports from the field.* Westport, CT: Quorum Books.

Gergen, K.J. (1997). Social psychology as social construction: The emerging vision. In McGarty, C., & Haslam, S.A. (Eds.), *The message of social psychology: Perspectives on mind in society* (pp.113–128). Malden, MA: Blackwell.

Grudin, R. (1990). *The grace of GREAT things: Creativity and innovation.* New York: Ticknor & Fields.

Haidt, J. (2000). The positive emotion of elevation. *Prevention & Treatment,* 3:n.p.

Hatfield, E., Cacioppo, J.T., & Rapson, R.L. (1994) *Emotional contagion: Studies in emotion and social interaction.* New York: Cambridge University Press.

Hubbard, B.M. (1998). *Conscious evolution: Awakening the power of our social potential.* Novato, CA: New World Library.

Hock, D. (1999). *Birth of the chaordic age.* San Francisco: Berrett-Koehler.

Isen, A.M., Daubman, K.A., & Nowicki, G.P. (1987). Positive affect facilitates creative problem solving. *Journal of Personality and Social Psychology,* 52:1122–1131.

Jackson, S.E., & Dutton, J.E. (1988). Discerning threats and opportunities. *AdministrativeSciencequarterly,*33:370–387.

Kast, V. (1994). *Joy, inspiration, and hope.* New York: Fromm International.

Khandwalla, P.N. (1998). Thorny Glory: Toward organizational greatness. In Srivastva, S., & Cooperrider, D.L., *Organizational wisdom and executive courage* (pp.157–204). San Francisco: New Lexington Press.

Kotter, J. (1998). Leading change: Why transformation efforts fail. *Harvard Business Review of Change,* pp.1–20.

Kung, H. (1996). *Great Christian thinkers.* New York: Continuum. Originally titled *Grosse christliche Denker.*

Ludema, J.D., Wilmot, T.B., & Srivastva, S. (1997). Organizational hope: Reaffirming the constructive task of social and organizational inquiry. *Human relations,* 50:1015–1052.

May, R. (1975). *The courage to create.* New York: Norton.

Quinn, R.E. (2000). *Change the world: How ordinary people can achieve extraordinary results.* San Francisco: Jossey-Bass.

Schneider, K.J., & May, R. (1995). *The psychology of existence: An integrative clinical perspective.* New York: McGraw-Hill.

Srivastva, S., & Cooperrider, D.L. (Eds.) (1998). *Organizational wisdom and executive courage.* San Francisco: New Lexington Press.

Tugade, M.M., & Fredrickson, B.L. (in press). Positive emotions and health. To appear in Anderson, N. (Ed.), *Encyclopedia of health and behavior.* Thousand Oaks, CA: Sage.

Whitney, D., & Cooperrider, D.L. (2000). The appreciative inquiry summit: An emerging methodology for whole system positive change. *OD Practitioner: Journal of the*

Organization Development Network,
32(1):13–26.

Weick, K.E. (1984). Small wins: Redefining the scale of social problems. *American Psychology,* 39(1):40–49.

Wright, R. (2001). *Nonzero: The logic of human destiny.* New York: Vintage Books.

Chapter 16

Allen, B.P., & Potkay, C.R. (1981). On the arbitrary distinction between states and traits. *Journal of Personality and Social Psychology,* 41:916–928.

Atwater, L.E., Waldman, D., Atwater, D., & Cartier, J. (2000). An upward feedback field experiment: Supervisors' cynicism, follow-up, and commitment to subordinates. *Personnel Psychology,* 53:275–297.

Avolio, B.J. (1999). *Full leadership development: Building the vital forces in organizations.* Newbury Park, CA: Sage.

_____(in press). Examining the full range model of leadership: Looking back to transform forward. In Day, D., & Zaccarro, S. (Eds.),

Leadership development for transforming organizations. Mahwah, NJ: Erlbaum.

_____(in press). *Made/born: Leadership development in balance.* Mahwah, NJ: Erlbaum.

Avolio, B.J., & Gibbons, T.C. (1988). Developing transformational leaders: A life span approach. In Conger, J.A., Kanungo, R.N., et al. (Eds.), *Charismatic leadership: The elusive factor in organizational effectiveness* (pp.276–308). San Francisco: Jossey-Bass.

Avolio, B.J., Kahai, S., & Dodge, G. (2000). E-leadership and its implications for theory, research, and practice. *Leadership Quarterly,* 11:615–670.

Bandura, A. (1986). *Social foundations of thought and action.* Englewood Cliffs, NJ: Prentice-Hall.

_____(1997). *Self-efficacy: The exercise of control.* New York: Freeman.

_____(1999). Social cognitive theory of personality. In Pervin, L., & John, O. (Eds.), *Handbook of personality,* 2nd ed. (pp.154–196). New York: Guilford.

_____(2000). Cultivate self-efficacy for personal and organizational effectiveness. In Locke, E.A. (Ed.), *The Blackwell handbook of principles of organizational behavior* (pp.120–136). Oxford, UK: Blackwell.

_____(2002). Psychology is not destiny: Social scientist swims against the tide of negativity. *Campus Report: Stanford University.*

Barrick, M.R., & Mount, M.K. (1991). The big five personality dimensions and job performance: A meta-analysis. *Personnel Psychology,* 44:1–26.

Bass, B.M. (1985). *Leadership and performance beyond expectations.* New York: Free Press.

Bass, B.M., & Avolio, B.J. (1994). *Improving organizational effectiveness through transformational leadership.* Thousand Oaks, CA: Sage.

Bass, B.M., & Steidlmeier, P. (1999). Ethics, character, and authentic transformational leadership behavior. *Leadership Quarterly,* 10:181–217.

Bennis, W., & Nanus, B. (1985). *Leaders: The strategies for taking charge.* New York: Harper & Row.

Buckingham, M., & Clifton, D. (2001). *Now, discover your strengths.* New York: Free Press.

Buckingham, M., & Coffman, C. (1999). *First, break all the rules.* New York: Simon & Schuster.

Burns, J.M. (1978). *Leadership.* New York: Free Press.

Chemers, M.M., Watson, C.B., & May, S.T. (2000). Dispositional affect and leadership effectiveness: A comparison of self-esteem, optimism, and efficacy. *Personality and Social Psychology Bulletin,* 26:267–277.

Coffman, C., & Gonzales-Molina, G. (2002). *Follow this path.* New York: Time Warner.

Conger, J.A. (1990). The dark side of leadership. *Organizational Dynamics,* 19:44–55.

Coutu, D.L. (2002). How resilience works. *Harvard Business Review,* May, pp.46–55.

Day, D.B. (2000). Leadership development: A review in content. *Leadership Quarterly,* 11:581–614.

Doe, P.J. (1994). Creating a resilient organization. *Canadian Business Review,* 21:22–26.

Egeland, B., Carlson, E., & Stroufe, L.A. (1993). Resilience as a process. *Development and Psychopathology,* 5:517–528.

Erickson, R.C., Post, R.D., & Paige, A.B. (1975). Hope as a psychiatric variable. *Journal of Clinical Psychology,* 31:324–330.

Gardner, D., & Avolio, B.J. (1998). The charismatic relationship: A dramaturgical perspective. *Academy of Management Review,* 23(1):32–58.

Gillham, J. (2000). *The science of optimism and hope: Research essays in honor of Martin E.P.Seligman.* Philadelphia: Templeton Foundation Press.

Harter, J.K., Schmidt, F.L., & Hayes, T.L. (2002). Business-unit-level relationship between employee satisfaction, employee engagement, and business outcomes: A meta-analysis. *Journal of Applied Psychology,* 87:268–279.

Harter, S. (2002). Authenticity. In Snyder, C.R., & Lopez, S.J. (Eds.), *Handbook of positive psychology* (pp.382–394). Oxford, UK: Oxford University Press.

Horne, J.F., & Orr, J.E. (1998). Assessing behaviors that create resilient organizations. *Employment Relations Today,* Winter:29–39.

House, R.V., & Aditya, R.N. (1997). The social scientific study of leadership: Quo vadis? *Journal of Management,* 23:409–473.

House, R.V., & Shamir, B. (1993). Towards the integration of transformational, charismatic, and visionary theories. In Chemers, M.M., & Ayman, R. (Eds.), *Leadership theory and research: Perspectives and directions* (pp.81–108). San Diego, CA: Academic Press.

Howell, J.P. (1992). Two faces of charisma: Socialized and personalized leadership in organizations. In Conger, J.A., & Kanungo, R.N. (Eds.), *Charismatic leadership: The elusive factor in organizational effectiveness* (pp.213–236). San Francisco: Jossey-Bass.

Howell, J.M., & Avolio, B.J. (1992). The ethics of charismatic leadership: Submission or Liberation? *Academy of Management Executive,* 6:43–53.

Huey, S.J., Jr., & Weisz, J.R. (1997). Ego control, ego resiliency, and the fivefactor model as predictors of behavioral and emotional problems in clinicreferred children and adolescents. *Journal of Abnormal Psychology,* 106:404–415.

Hunter, A.J., & Chandler, G.E. (1999). Adolescent resilience. *Image: Journal of Nursing Scholarship,* 31:243–247.

Judge, T.A., & Bono, J.E. (2001). Relationship of core self-evaluations traits—selfefficacy, locus of control, and emotional stability—with job satisfaction and job performance: A meta-analysis. *Journal of Applied Psychology,* 86:80–92.

Judge, T.A., Erez, A., & Bono, J.E. (1998). The power of being positive: The relation between positive self-concept and job performance. *Human Performance,* 11:167–187.

Kark, R., & Shamir, B. (2002). The dual effect of transformational leadership: Priming relational and collective selves and further effects on followers. In Avolio, B.J., & Yammarino, F.J. (Eds.), *Transformational and charismatic leadership: The road ahead* (pp.67–91). Oxford, UK: Elsevier.

Kegan, J. (1982). *The evolving self: Problem and process in human development.* Cambridge: Harvard University Press.

Kuhnert, K.W., & Lewis, P. (1987). Transactional and transformational leadership: A constructive/developmental analysis. *Academy of Management Review,* 12:648–657.

Lazarus, R.S. (1999). *Stress and emotion: A new synthesis.* New York: Springer.

London, M. (2002). *Leadership development: Paths to self-insight and professional growth.* Mahwah, NJ: Erlbaum.

Lopez, S., Prosser, E.C., Edwards, L.M., Magyar-Moe, J.L., Neufeld, J.E., & Rasmussen, H.N. (2002). Putting positive psychology in a multicultural context. In Snyder, C.R., & Lopez, S.J. (Eds.), *Handbook of positive psychology* (pp.700–714). Oxford, UK: Oxford University Press.

Luthans, F. (2002a). The need for and meaning of positive organizational behavior. *Journal of Organizational Behavior,* 23:695–706.

_____(2002b). Positive organizational behavior: Developing and managing psychological strengths. *Academy of Management Executive,* 16:57–72.

_____(2002c). Positive psychology approach to OB. In Luthans, F., *Organizational behavior,* 9th ed. (pp.286–322). New York: McGraw-Hill/Irwin.

_____(2003). Positive organizational behavior (POB): Implications for leadership and HR development and motivation. In Steers, R.M., Porter, L.W., & Begley, G.A. (Eds.), *Motivation and leadership at work* (in press). New York: McGraw-Hill/Irwin.

Luthans, F., & Jensen, S.M. (2002). Hope: A new positive strength for human resource development. *Human Resource Development Review,* 1:304–322.

Luthans, F., Luthans, K.W., Hodgetts, R.M., & Luthans, B.C. (2002). Positive approach to leadership (PAL): Implications for today's organizations. *Journal of Leadership Studies,* 8:3–20.

Luthans, F., Peterson, S.J., & Ibrayeva, E. (1998). The potential for the "dark side" of leadership in post-communist countries. *Journal of World Business,* 33:185–201.

Luthar, S.S., Cicchetti, D., & Becker, B. (2000). The construct of resilience: A critical evaluation and guidelines for future work. *Child Development,* 71:543–562.

Maddux, J.E. (2002). Self-efficacy. In Snyder, C.R., & Lopez, S.J. (Eds.), *Handbook of positive psychology* (pp.277–287). Oxford, UK: Oxford University Press.

Magaletta, P.R., & Oliver, J.M. (1999). The hope construct, will and ways: Their relations with self-efficacy, optimism, and well-being. *Journal of Clinical Psychology,* 55:539–551.

Mallak, L. (1998). Putting organizational resilience processes to work. *Industrial Management,* 40:8–14.

Masten, A.S. (2001). Ordinary magic: Resilience process in development. *American Psychologist,* 56:227–239.

Masten, A.S., & Reed, M.J. (2002). Resilience in development. In Snyder, C.R., & Lopez, S.J. (Eds.), *Handbook of positive psychology* (pp.74–88). Oxford, UK: Oxford University Press.

McCormick, M.J. (2001). Self-efficacy and leadership effectiveness: Applying social cognitive theory to leadership. *Journal of Leadership Studies,* 8:22–33.

Meyers, D.G. (2000). Hope and happiness. In Gillman, J. (Ed.), *The science of optimism and hope* (pp.323–336). Philadelphia: Templeton Foundation Press.

Miller, D.T. (1999). The norm of self-interest. *American Psychologist,* 54:1053– 1060.

Mischel, W. (1973). Toward a cognitive social learning reconceptualization of personality. *Psychological Review,* 80:252–283.

Nicholsen, N. (1998). How hardwired is human behavior? *Harvard Business Review,* July–August, pp.135–147.

Peterson, C. (2000). The future of optimism. *American Psychologist,* 55:44–55.

Peterson, S.J., & Luthans, F. (2003). Does the manager's level of hope matter? *Leadership and Organizational Development Journal,* 24.

Pierce, B.D., & White, R. (1999). The evolution of social structure: Why biology matters. *Academy of Management Review,* 24:843–853.

Quinn, R.E., Spreitzer, G.M., & Brown, M.V. (2000). Changing others through changing ourselves: The transformation of human systems. *Journal of Management Inquiry,* 9:147–164.

Rutter, M. (1987). Psychosocial resilience and protective mechanisms. *American Journal of Orthopsychiatry,* 57:316–331.

Sandage, S.J., & Hill, P.C. (2001). The virtues of positive psychology: The rapprochement and challenges of an affirmative postmodern perspective. *Journal of the Theory of Social Behaviour,* 31:241–259.

Scheier, M.F., & Carver, C.S. (1992). Effects of optimism on psychological and physical well-being. *Cognitive Therapy and Research,* 16:201–228.

372

Schneider, S.L. (2001). In search of realistic optimism: Meaning, knowledge, and warm fuzziness. *American Psychologist,* 56:250–263.

Schulman, M. (2002). How we become moral. In Snyder, C.R., & Lopez, S.J. (Eds.), *Handbook of positive psychology* (pp.499–512). Oxford, UK: Oxford University Press.

Schulman, P. (1999). Applying learned optimism to increase sales productivity. *Journal of Personal Selling and Sales Management,* 19:31–37.

Seligman, M.E.P. (1998a). Building human strengths: Psychology's forgotten mission. *APA Monitor,* January, p.2.

_____(1998b). *Learned optimism.* New York: Pocket Books.

_____(1999). The president's address. *American Psychologist,* 54:559–562.

_____(2002). *Authentic happiness.* New York: Free Press.

Seligman, M.E.P., & Csikszentmihalyi, M. (2000). Positive psychology. *American Psychologist,* 55:5–14.

Sheldon, K.M., & King, L. (2001). Why positive psychology is necessary. *American Psychologist,* 56:216–217.

Snyder, C.R. (2000). *Handbook of hope.* San Diego, CA: Academic Press.

Snyder, C.R., Harris, C., Anderson, J.R., Holleran, S.A., Irving, L.M., Sigmon, S.T., Yoshinobu, L., Gibb, J., Langelle, C., & Harney, P. (1991). The will and the ways. *Journal of Personality and Social Psychology,* 60:570–585.

Snyder, C.R., Irving, L., & Anderson, J.R. (1991). Hope and health. In Snyder, C.R., & Forsyth, D.R. (Eds.), *Handbook of social and clinical psychology* (pp.285–305). Elmsforth, NY: Pergamon.

Snyder, C.R., & Lopez, S.J. (2002). *Handbook of positive psychology.* Oxford, UK: Oxford University Press.

Snyder, C.R., Rand, K.L., & Sigmon, D.R. (2002). Hope theory. In Snyder, C.R., & Lopez, S.J. (Eds.), *Handbook of positive psychology* (pp.257–276). Oxford, UK: Oxford University Press.

374

Snyder, C.R., Sympson, S.C., Ybasco, F.C., Borders, T.F., Babyak, M.A., & Higgins, R.L. (1996). Development and validation of the state hope scale. *Journal of Personality and Social Psychology,* 70:321–335.

Snyder, C.R., Tran, T., Schroeder, L., Pulvers, K., Adams III, V., & Laub, L. (2000). Teaching children the hope recipe: Setting goals, finding routes to those goals, and getting motivated. *Today's Youth,* 4, 46–50.

Stajkovic, A.D., & Luthans, F. (1998a). Self-efficacy and work-related performance: A meta-analysis. *Psychological Bulletin,* 124:240–261.

_____(1998b). Social cognitive theory and self-efficacy: Going beyond traditional motivational and behavioral approaches. *Organizational Dynamics,* 26:62–74.

Stewart, M., Reid, G., & Mangham, C. (1997). Fostering children's resilience. *Journal of Pediatric Nursing,* 12:21–31.

Turner, N., Barling, J., Epitropaki, O., Butcher, V., & Miller, C. (2002). Transformational leadership and moral reasoning. *Journal of Applied Psychology,* 87:304–311.

Turner, N., Barling, J., & Zacharatos, A. (2002). Positive psychology at work. In Snyder, C.R., & Lopez, S.J. (Eds.), *Handbook of positive psychology* (pp.715–730). Oxford, UK: Oxford University Press.

Wanburg, C.R. (1997). Antecedents and outcomes of coping behavior among unemployed and reemployed individuals. *Journal of Applied Psychology,* 82:731–744.

Wood, R.E., & Bandura, A. (1989). Social cognitive theory of organizational management. *Academy of Management Review,* 14:361–384.

Wunderley, L.J., Reddy, W.B., & Dember, W.N. (1998). Optimism and pessimism in business leaders. *Journal of Applied Social Psychology,* 28:751–760.

Chapter 17

Adler, H.M. (2002). The sociophysiology of caring in the doctor-patient relationship. *Journal of General Internal Medicine,* 17:883–890.

Altemus, M., Redwin, L., Leong, Y.M., Yoshikawa, T., Yehuda, R., Deterea-Wadleigh, S., & Murphy, D.L. (1997). Reduced sensitivity to glucorticoid feedback and reduced glucorticoid receptor mRNA expression in the luteal phase of the menstrual cycle. *Neuropsychopharmacology,* 17:100–109.

Ashforth, B.E., & Johnson, S.A. (2001). Which hat to wear? The relative salience of multiple identities in organizational contexts. In Hogg, M.A., & Terry, D.J. (Eds.), *Social identity processes in organizational contexts* (pp.31–48). Philadelphia: Psychology Press.

Baker, W. (2000). *Achieving success through social capital.* San Francisco: Jossey-Bass.

Baker, W., Cross, R., & Wooten, M. (2003). Positive organizational network analysis and energizing relationships. In Cameron, K.E., Dutton, J.E., & Quinn, R.E. (Eds.), *Positive organizational scholarship.* San Francisco: Berrett-Koehler.

Baron, J.N., & Pfeffer, J. (1994). The social psychology of organizations and inequality. *Social Psychology Quarterly,* 57(3):190–209.

Bartel, C., & Dutton, J. (2001). Ambiguous organizational memberships: Constructing organizational identities in interactions with others. In Hogg, M., & Terry, D. (Eds.),

Social identity processes in organizational contexts (pp.115–130). Philadelphia: Psychology Press.

Bauer, T.N., & Green, S.G. (1996). Development of leader-member exchange: A longitudinal test. *Academy of Management Journal,* 39(6):1538–1567.

Baumeister, R.F., & Leary, M.R. (1995). The need to belong: Desire for interpersonal attachments as a fundamental human motivation. *Psychological Bulletin,* 117(3):497–529.

Berscheid, E. (1999). The greening of relationship science. *American Psychologist,* 54(4):260–266.

Berscheid, E., & Lopes, J. (1997). A temporal model of relationship satisfaction and stability. In Sternberg, R.J., & Hojjat, M. (Eds.), *Satisfaction in close relationships* (pp.129–159). New York: Guilford Press.

Blake, S. (1999). At the crossroads of race and gender: Lessons from the mentoring experiences of professional black women. In Murrell, A.J., Crosby, F.J., & Ely, R.J. (Eds.), *Mentoring dilemmas: Developmental*

378

relationships within multicultural organizations (pp.83–104). Mahwah, NJ: Erlbaum.

Blau, P. (1964). *Exchange and power in social life.* New York: Wiley.

Blumer, H. (1966). Sociological implications of the thought of George Herbert Mead. *American Journal of Sociology,* 71:535–548.

Bowlby, J. (1969). *Attachment and loss.* Vol.1. *Attachment.* New York: Basic Books.

_____(1973). *Attachment and loss.* Vol.2. *Separation anxiety and anger.* New York: Basic Books.

Bradbury, H., & Lichtenstein, B.M. (2000). Relationality in organizational research: Exploring the space between. *Organization Science,* 11(5):551–564.

Brass, D.J. (1984). Being in the right place: A structural analysis of individual influence in an organization. *Administrative Science Quarterly,* 29(4): 518–539.

Brown, J.S., & Duguid, P. (1991). Organizationallearningandcommunities-ofprac-tice: Toward a unified view of working, learning, and innovation. *Organization Science,* 2:40–57.

Cameron, K., Caza, A., & Bright, D. (2002). *Positive deviance, organizational virtuousness, and performance.* Working paper, University of Michigan.

Cohen, S. (2001). Social relationships and the susceptibility to the common cold. In Ryff, C., & Singer, B. (Eds.), *Emotion, social relationships, and health* (pp.221–232). Oxford, UK: Oxford University Press.

Cooley, C. (1902). *Human nature and the social order.* New York: Charles Scribner's Sons.

Creed, W.E., & Scully, M.A. (2000). Songs of ourselves: Employees' deployment of social identity in workplace encounters. *Journal of Management Inquiry,* 9(4):391–412.

Csikszentmihalyi, M. (1990). *Flow: The psychology of optimal experience.* New York: Harper & Row.

Duck, S. (1990). Relationships as unfinished business: Out of the frying pan and into the fire. *Journal of Social and Personal Relationships,* 7:5–28.

Dutton, J.E. (2003). *Energizing your workplace: Building and sustaining high quality relationships at work.* San Francisco: Jossey-Bass.

Dutton, J.E., Worline, M.C., Frost, P.J., & Lilius, J.M. (2002). *The organizing of compassion.* Working paper, University of Michigan.

Eisenhardt, K.M., & Martin, J.A. (2000). Dynamic capabilities: What are they? *Strategic Management Journal,* 21:1105–1122.

Emerson, R.M. (1976). Social exchange theory. *Annual Review of Sociology,* 2:335–362.

Emirbayer, M. (1997). Manifesto for a relational psychology. *American Journal of Sociology,* 103(2):281–317.

Fletcher, J. (1999). *Disappearing acts.* Cambridge: MIT Press.

Fredrickson, B.L. (1998). What good are positive emotions? *Review of General Psychology,* 2(3):300–319.

_____(2002). Positive emotions. In Snyder, C.R., & Lopez, S.J. (Eds.), *Handbook of positive psychology* (pp.120–134). New York: Oxford University Press.

Frost, P.J. (2003). *Toxic emotions at work: How compassionate managers handle pain and conflict.* Cambridge: Harvard Business School Press.

Gabarro, J. (1987). The development of working relationships. In Lorsch, J.W. (Ed.), *Handbook of organizational behavior* (pp.172–189). Englewood Cliffs, NJ: Prentice-Hall.

Gergen, K. (1994). *Realities and relationships: Soundings in social construction.* Cambridge: Harvard University Press.

Gersick, C.J.G., Bartunek, J., & Dutton, J.E. (2000). Learning from academia: The importance of relationships in professional life. *Academy of Management Journal,* 43(6):1026–1044.

Gittell, J.H. (2001). Supervisory span, relational coordination, and flight departure performance: Reassessing post-bureaucracy theory. *Organization Science,* 12(4):467–482.

Gottman, J. (2001). Meta-emotion, children's emotional intelligence, and buffering children from marital conflict. In Ryff, C., & Singer, B. (Eds.), *Emotion, social relationships, and health* (pp.23–39). Oxford, UK: Oxford University Press.

Graen, G.B., & Scandura, T.A. (1987). Toward a psychology of dyadic organizing. In Cummings, L.L., & Staw, B.M. (Eds.), *Research in organizational behavior,* vol.9 (pp.175–208). Greenwich, CT: JAI Press.

Granovetter, M. (1973). The strength of weak ties. *American Journal of Sociology*78(May):1360–1380.

Gutek, B.A. (1995). *The dynamics of service.* San Francisco: Jossey-Bass.

Hallowell, E.M. (1999). *Connect.* New York: Pantheon Books.

Higgins, M., & Kram, K. (2001). Reconceptualizing mentoring at work: A developmental network perspective. *Academy of Management Review,* 26(2):264–288.

Hochschild, A. (1997). *The time bind: When work becomes home and home becomes work.* New York: Metropolitan Books.

Homans, G. (1974). *Social behavior.* Rev. ed. New York: Harcourt Brace.

House, J.S., Landis, K.R., & Umberson, D. (1988). Social relationships and health. *Science,* 241:540–545.

Ibarra, H. (1999). Provisional selves: Experimenting with image and identity in professional adaptation. *Administrative Science Quarterly,* 44:764–791.

_____(2003). *Working identity: Unconventional strategies for reinventing your career.* Cambridge: Harvard Business School Press.

Jacques, R. (1993). Untheorized dimensions of caring work: Caring as structural practice and caring as a way of seeing. *Nursing Administration Quarterly,* 17:1–10.

Josselson, R. (1996). *The space between us: Exploring human dimensions of human relationships.* Thousand Oaks, CA: Sage.

384

Kahn, W.A. (1990). Psychological conditions of personal engagement and disengagement at work. *Academy of Management Journal,* 33(4):692–724.

_____(1993). Caring for the caregivers: Patterns of organizational caregiving. *Administrative Science Quarterly,* 38(4):539–563.

_____(1998). Relational systems at work. In Staw, B.M., & Cummings, L.L. (Eds.), *Research in organizational behavior,* vol.20 (pp.39–76). Greenwich, CT: JAI Press.

Kaplan, A.G., Miller, J.B., Jordan, J.V., Surrey, J.L., & Stiver, I.P. (1991). *Women's growth in connection: Writings from the Stone Center.* New York: Guilford Press.

Kram, K. (1985). *Mentoring at work: Developmental relationships in organizational life.* Glenville, IL: Scott Foresman.

Kram, K.E., & Isabella, L.A. (1985). Mentoring alternatives: The role of peer relationships in career development. *Academy of Management Journal,* 28(1):110–132.

Lampert, M. (2001). *Teaching problems and the problems of teaching.* New Haven, CT: Yale University Press.

Lave, J., & Wenger, E. (1991). *Situated learning: Legitimate peripheral participation.* New York: Cambridge University Press.

Lawler, E.J., & Yoon, J. (1998). Network structure and emotion in exchange relations. *American Sociological Review,* 63(6):871–894.

Lepore, S.J., Mata-Allen, K.A., & Evans, G.W. (1993). Social support lowers cardiovascular reactivity to an acute stressor. *Psychosomatic Medicine,* 55:518–524.

Levinson, D.J., Darrow, C.N., Klein, E.B., Levinson, M.H., & McKee, B. (1978). *The seasons of a man's life.* New York: Alfred A. Knopf.

Lewis, T., Amini, F., & Lannan, R. (2000). *A general theory of love.* New York: Random House.

Losada, M. (1999). The complex dynamics of high performance teams. *Mathematical and Computer Modeling,* 30:179–192.

Markus, H. (1977). Self-schemata and processing information about the self. *Journal of Personality and Social Psychology,* 35(2):63–78.

McEwen, B.S. (1998). Protective and damaging effects of stress mediators. *New England Journal of Medicine,* 338:171–179.

Mead, G.H. (1934). *Mind, self, and society: From the standpoint of a social behaviorist.* Chicago: University of Chicago Press.

Mendoza S. (1991). Sociophysiology of well-being in non-human primates *Lab Animal Science,* 41:344–349.

Miller, J.B. (1988). Connections, disconnections, and violations. Stone Center Working Paper Series, Work in Progress no.33, Wellesley, MA.

Miller, J.B., & Stiver, I.P. (1997). *The healing connection: How women form relationships in therapy and in life.* Boston: Beacon Press.

Mills, J., & Clark, M.S. (1982). Communal and exchange relationships. *Review of Personality and Social Psychology,* 3:121–144.

Nix, G., Ryan, R.M., Maly, J.B., & Deci, E.L. (1999). Revitalization through selfregulation: The effects of autonomous versus controlled motivation on happiness and vitality. *Journal of Experimental Social Psychology,* 35:266–284.

Ornish, D. (1998). *Love and survival: The scientific basis for the healing power of intimacy.* New York: HarperCollins.

Orr, J. (1996). *Talking about machines: An ethnography of a modern job.* Ithaca, NY: IRL Press.

Pearson, C.M., Andersson, L.A., & Porath, C.L. (2000). Assessing and attacking workplace incivility. *Organizational Dynamics,* 29(2):123–137.

Potter, J., & Wetherell, M. (1998). Social representations, discourse analysis, and racism. In Flick, U. (Ed.), *The psychology of the social* (pp.138–155). New York: Cambridge University Press.

Powell, W.W., Koput, K.W., & Smith-Doerr, L. (1996). Interorganizational collaboration and the locus of innovation: Networks of learning in biotechnology. *Administrative Science Quarterly,* 41:116–145.

Pratt, M.P. (2000). The good, the bad, and the ambivalent: Managing identification among Amway distributors. *Administrative Science Quarterly,* 45(3):456–493.

Prus, R. (1996). *Symbolic interaction and ethnographic research.* Albany: State University of New York Press. Quinn, R., & Dutton, J.E. (2002). Coordination as energy-in-conversation: A process theory of organizing. *Academy of Management Review.*

Quinn, R.E., & Quinn, G.T. (2002). *Letters to Garrett: Stories of change, power, and possibility.* San Francisco: Jossey-Bass.

Ragins, B.R., Cotton, J.L., & Miller, J.S. (2000). Marginal mentoring: The effects of type of mentor, quality of relationship, and program design on work and career attitudes. *Academy of Management Journal,* 43(5):1177–1194.

Reicher, S. (1995). Three dimensions of the social self. In Oosterwegel, A. (Ed.), *The self in European and North American culture: Development and processes* (pp.277–290). Dordrecht, Netherlands: Kluwer.

Reis, H. (2001). Relationship experiences and emotional well-being. In Ryff, C., & Singer, B. (Eds.), *Emotion, social relationships, and health* (57–86). Oxford, UK: Oxford University Press.

Reis, H., & Gable, S. (2003). Toward a positive psychology of relationships. In Keyes, C.L.M., and Haidt, J. (Eds.), *Flourishing: Positive psychology and the life well-lived* (pp.129–159). Washington, DC: American Psychological Association.

Rogers, C.R. (1951). *Client-centered therapy.* New York: Houghton Mifflin.

Ryan, R.M., & Frederick, C. (1997). On energy, personality, and health: Subjective vitality as a dynamic reflection of well-being. *Journal of Personality,* 65(3):529–566.

Ryff, C.D., & Singer, B. (1998). The contours of positive human health. *Psychological Inquiry,* 9:1–28.

_____(2000). Interpersonal flourishing: A positive health agenda for the new millennium. *Personality Social Psychological Review,* 4:30–44.

Sampson, E.E. (1993). *Celebrating the other: A dialogical account of human nature.* Boulder, CO: Westview Press.

Sandelands, L.E. (2002). *Thinking about social life.* Unpublished manuscript, University of Michigan.

Schlenker, B.R. (1985). Identity and self-identification. In Schlenker, B.R. (Ed.), *The self in social life* (pp.65–99). New York: McGraw-Hill.

Schrieshiem, C.A., Castro, S.L., & Cogliser, C.C. (1999). Leader-member exchange (LMX) research: A comprehensive review of theory, measurement, and data-analytic practices. *Leadership Quarterly,* 10(1):63–113.

Seeman, T.E. (1996). Social ties and health: The benefits of social integration. *Annals of Epidemiology,* 6:442–451.

Seeman, T.E., Singer, B.H., Rowe, J.W., Horwitz, R.I., & McEwan, B.S. (1997). The price of adaptation: Allostatic load and its health consequences. MacArthur Studies of

Successful Aging. *Archives of Internal Medicine,* 157:2259–2268.

Shellenbarger, S., (2000). From our readers: The bosses that drove me to quit my job. *Wall Street Journal,* February 9, p. B1.

Srivastva, S., & Cooperrider, D.L. (1998). *Organizational wisdom and executive courage.* Lanham, MD: Lexington Books.

Sutcliffe, K.M., & Vogus, T. (2003). Organizing for resilience. In Cameron, K., Dutton, J., & Quinn, R. (Eds.), *Positive organizational scholarship.* San Francisco: Berrett-Koehler.

Swann, W.B. (1987). Identity negotiation: Where two roads meet. *Journal of Personality and Social Psychology,* 53:1038–1051.

Taylor, S.E., Dickerson, S.S., & Klein, L.C. (2002). Toward a biology of social support. In Snyder, C.R., & Lopez, S.L. (Eds.), *Handbook of positive psychology* (pp.556–572). Oxford, UK: Oxford University Press.

Thibaut, J., & Kelley, H.H. (1959). *The social psychology of groups.* New York: Wiley.

Uchino, B., Cacioppo, J., & Kiecolt-Glaser, J. (1996). The relationship between social support and physiological processes: A review with emphasis on underlying mechanisms and implications for health. *Psychological Bulletin,* 199(3):488–531.

Uvnas-Moberg, K. (1997). Physiological and endocrine effects of social contact. *Annals of the New York Academy of Sciences* 807:140–163.

Uzzi, B. (1997). Social structure and competition in interfirm networks: The paradox of embeddedness. *Administrative Science Quarterly,* 42:35–67.

von Krogh, G., Ichijo, K., & Nonaka, I. (2000). *Enabling knowledge creation.* New York: Oxford University Press.

Weick, K.E., & Roberts, K.H. (1993). Collective mind in organizations: Heedful interrelating on flight decks. *Administrative Science Quarterly,* 38(3):357– 381.

Weick, K.E., Sutcliffe, K.M., & Obstfeld, D. (1999). Organizing for high reliability: Processes of collective mindfulness. *Research in organizational behavior,* vol.21 (pp.81–123). Stamford, CT: JAI Press.

Wenger, E. (2000). Communities of practice and social learning systems. *Organization,* 7(2):225–246.

Williams, M., & Dutton, J. (1999). Corrosive political climates: The heavy toll of negative political behavior in organizations. In Quinn, R.E., O'Neill, R.M., & St. Clair, L. (Eds.), *The pressing problems of modern organizations: Transforming the agenda for research and practice* (pp.3–30). New York: American Management Association.

Winnicott, D.W. (1960). The theory of the patient-infant relationship. *International Journal of Psychoanalysis,* 41:585–595.

_____(1965). *The maturational processes and the facilitating environment.* New York: International University Press.

Worline, M., Dutton, J., Frost, P., Lilius, J., Kanov, J., & Maitlis, S. (2002). Fertile soil: The organizing dynamics of resilience. Paper presented at the National Academy of Management, Denver, CO, August.

394

Young-Bruehl, E., & Bethelard, F. (2000). *Cherishment: A psychology of the heart.* New York: Free Press.

Zahra, S.A., & George, G. (2002). Absorptive capacity: A review, reconceptualization, and extension. *Academy of Management Review,* 27(2):185–203.

Chapter 18

Adams, J.S. (1976). The structure and dynamics of behavior in organizational boundary roles. In Dunnette, M.D. (Ed.), *Handbook of industrial and organizational psychology* (pp.1175–1199). Chicago: Rand McNally.

Adler, P., & Borys, B. (1996). Two types of bureaucracy: Enabling and coercive. *Administrative Science Quarterly,* 41:62–89.

Aldrich, H., & Herker, D. (1977). Boundary spanning roles and organization structure. *Academy of Management Review,* 2(2):217–230.

Ancona, D.G., & Caldwell, D.F. (1992). Bridging the boundary: External activity and performance in organizational teams.

Administrative Science Quarterly, 37:634–665.

Appelbaum, E., & Batt, R. (1994). *The new American workplace.* Ithaca, NY: ILR Press.

Appelbaum, E., & Berg, P. (1997). Hierarchical organization and horizontal coordination: Evidence from a worker survey. Economic Policy Institute working paper.

Applegate, L.M. (1999). In search of a new organizational model: Lessons from the field. In DeSanctis, G., & Fulk, J. (Eds.), *Shaping organization form: Communication, connection, and community* (pp.33–70). Newbury Park, CA: Sage.

Argote, L. (1982). Input uncertainty and organization coordination in hospital emergency units. *Administrative Science Quarterly,* 27:420–434.

Bahde, K. (2003). *Charting the course: A social constructionist approach to the mergers and acquisitions integration process and the role of the integration manager.* Ph.D. diss., Benedictine University.

Bahde, K., & Gittell, J.H. (2002). Boundary spanners: A relational, social constructionist perspective. Unpublished manuscript.

Batt, R. (1996). From bureaucracy to enterprise? The changing jobs and careers of managers in telecommunications service. In Osterman, P. (Ed.), *Broken ladders: Managerial careers in the new economy.* New York: Oxford University Press.

Beekun, R.I. (1989). Assessing the effectiveness of sociotechnical interventions: Antidote or fad? *Human Relations,* 47:877–897.

Blau, P. (1968). The hierarchy of authority in organizations. *American Journal of Sociology,* 73:453–467.

_____(1972). Interdependence and hierarchy in organizations. *Social Science Research,* 1:1–24.

Caldwell, D.H., & O'Reilly, C.A., III (1982). Boundary spanning and individual performance: The impact of self-monitoring. *Journal of Applied Psychology,* 67(1):124–127.

Currall, S.C., & Judge, T.A. (1995). Measuring trust between organizational boundary role persons. *Organizational Behavior and Human Decision Processes,* 64(2):151–170.

Deming, W.E. (1986). *Beyond the crisis.* Cambridge: MIT Press.

Donnellon, A. (1994). Team work: Linguistic models of negotiations. In Sheppard, B., Lewicki, R., & Bies, R. (Eds.), *Research in negotiations in organizations.* Greenwich, CT: JAI Press.

Dougherty, D. (1992). Interpretive barriers to successful product innovation in large firms. *Organization Science,* 3(2):179–202.

Dutton, J.E., & Heaphy, E.D. (2003). The power of high-quality connections. In Cameron K.S., Dutton, J.E. & Quinn, R.E. (Eds.), *Positive organizational scholarship.* San Francisco, CA: Berrett-Koehler.

Eisenberg, E. (1990). Jamming: Transcendence through organizing. *Communication Research,* 17:139–164.

Feldman, M.S., & Rafaeli, A. (2002). Organizational routines as sources of connections and understandings. *Journal of Management Studies,* 39(3):309–331.

Ford, J.D. (1981). Department context and formal structure as constraints on leader behavior. *Academy of Management Journal,* 24:274–288.

Friedman, R.A., & Podolny, J. (1992). Differentiation of boundary spanning roles: Labor negotitions and implications for role conflict. *Administrative Science Quarterly,* 37(1):28–47.

Galbraith, J. (1973). *Designing complex organizations.* Reading, MA: Addison-Wesley.

_____(1977). *Organization design.* Reading, MA: Addison-Wesley.

_____(1995). *Competing with flexible lateral organizations.* Reading, MA: Addison-Wesley.

Gittell, J.H. (2000). Paradox of coordination and control. *California Management Review,* 423:1–17.

_____(2001). Supervisory span, relational coordination, and flight departure performance: A reassessment of post-bureaucracy theory. *Organization Science,* 12(4):467–484.

_____(2002). Coordinating mechanisms in care provider groups: Relational coordination as a mediator and input uncertainty as a moderator of performance effects. *Management Science,* 48(11):1408–1426.

_____(2003). *The Southwest Airlines way: Using the power of relationships to achieve high performance* (pp.25–43). New York: McGraw-Hill.

Goodstadt, B.E., & D. Kipnis. (1970). Situational influences on the use of power. *Journal of Applied Psychology,* 54:201–207.

Granovetter, M.S. (1973). The strength of weak ties. *American Journal of Sociology,* 78:1360–1380.

Hackman, R., & Oldham, G. (1980). *Work redesign.* New York: Addison-Wesley.

Heckscher, C., & Donnellon, A. (Eds.) (1994). *The post-bureaucratic organization.* Thousand Oaks, CA: Sage.

Heller, F., & G. Yukl. (1969). Participation, managerial decision-making, and situational variables. *Organizational Behavior and Human Performance,* 4:227–241.

Hickson, D.J. (1966). A convergence in organization theory. *Administrative Science Quarterly,* pp.224–237.

Hunt, R.G. (1970). Technology and organization. *Academy of Management Journal,* pp.235–252.

Jermier, J., & Berkes, L. (1979). Leader behavior in a police command bureaucracy: A closer look at the quasi-military model. *Administrative Science Quarterly,* 24:1–23.

Katz, D., & Kahn, R.L. (1966). *The social psychology of organizations.* New York: Wiley.

Katz, R., & Tushman, M.L. (1983). A longitudinal study of the effects of boundary spanning supervision on turnover and promotion in research and development. *Academy of Management Journal,* 26(3):437–456.

Kipnis, D., & Cosentino, J. (1969). Use of leadership powers in industry. *Journal of Applied Psychology,* 53:460–466.

Kipnis, D., & Lane, W.P. (1962). Self confidence and leadership. *Journal of Applied Psychology,* 46:291–295.

Krackhardt, D. (1994). Constraints on the interactive organization as an ideal type. In Heckscher, C., & Donnellon, A. (Eds.), *The post-bureaucratic organization: New perspectives on organizational change* (pp.211–222). Beverly Hills, CA: Sage.

Lawrence, P.R., & Lorsch, J.W. (1968). *Organization and environment: Managing differentiation and integration.* Boston: Graduate School of Business Administration, Harvard University.

Levitt, B., & March, J. (1986). Organizational learning. *Annual Review of Sociology,* 14:319–340. Palo Alto, CA: Annual Reviews.

Likert, R. (1961). *New patterns of management.* New York: McGraw-Hill.

402

Lord, R.G., & Rouzee, M. (1979). Task interdependence, temporal phase, and cognitive heterogeneity as determinant of leadership behavior and behavior-performance relations. *Organizational Behavior and Human Performance,* 23:182–200.

MacDuffie, J.P. (1996). Automotive white collar: The changing status and roles of salaried employees in the North American auto industry. In Osterman, P. (Ed.), *Broken ladders: Managerial careers in the new economy.* New York: Oxford University Press.

March, J., & Simon, H. (1958). *Organizations.* New York: Wiley.

McGregor, D. (1960). *The human side of enterprise.* New York: McGraw-Hill.

Mohrman, S.A. (1993). Integrating roles and structure in the lateral organization. In Galbraith, J.R., Lawler, E.E., III, & Associates (Eds.), *Organizing for the future: The new logic of managing complex organizations* (pp.109–141). San Francisco: Jossey-Bass.

Mowday, R., Porter, L., & Steers, R. (1982). *Employee organization linkages.* New York: Academic Press.

Nadler, D., & Tushman, M. (1988). Strategic linking: Designing formal coordination mechanisms. In Nadler, D., & Tushman, M. (Eds.), *Strategic organization design* (pp.89–116). New York: Scott Foreman.

Nelson, R., & Winter, S. (1981). *An evolutionary theory of economic change.* Cambridge: Belknap/Harvard University Press.

Nohria, N., & Berkeley, J.D. (1994). The virtual organization: Bureaucracy, technology, and the implosion of control. In Heckscher, C., & Donnellon, A. (Eds.), *The post-bureaucratic organization: New perspectives on organizational change* (pp.223–252). Beverly Hills, CA: Sage.

O'Reilly, C., & Roberts, K. (1977). Task group structure, communication, and effectiveness in three organizations. *Journal of Applied Psychology,* 62: 674–681.

Orlikowski, W., & Yates, J. (1991). Genre repertoire: The structuring of communicative practices in organizations. *Administrative* Science Quarterly, 394: 541–574.

Piore, M., & Sabel, C. (1984). *The second industrial divide.* New York: Basic Books.

Podolny, J., & Baron, J. (1996). Resources and relationships: Social networks and mobility in the workplace. *American Sociological Review,* 62:673–693.

Pondy, L. (1967). Organizational conflict: Concepts and models. *Administrative Science Quarterly,* pp.297–320.

Porter, L., & Lawler, E. (1964). The effects of "tall" versus "flat" organization structures on managerial job satisfaction. *Personnel Psychology,* pp.135–148.

Powell, W.W., Koput, K.W., & Smith-Doerr, L. (1996). Interorganizational collaboration and the locus of innovation: Networks of learning in biotechnology. *Administrative Science Quarterly,* 41:116–145.

Rubenstein, A., Barth, R.T., & Douds, C.F. (1971). Ways to improve communications between R&D groups. *Research Management,* 14:49.

Rubinstein, S.A. (2000). The impact of co-management on quality performance: The case of the Saturn Corporation. *Industrial and Labor Relations Review,* 531:197–220.

Saavedra, R., Earley, P.D., & Van Dyne, L. (1993). Complex interdependence in task-performing groups. *Journal of Applied Psychology,* 781:61–72.

Tannenbaum, A. (1968). *Control in organizations.* New York: McGraw-Hill.

Taylor, F.W. (1998). *The principles of scientific management.* Toronto: Dover. Original work published in 1911.

Thompson, J. (1967). *Organizations in action.* New York: McGraw-Hill.

Tushman, M.L., & Nadler, D.A. (1978). Information processing as an integrating concept in organizational design. *Academy of Management Review,* 3(3): 613–624.

Tushman, M.L., & Scanlan, T.J. (1981a). Boundary spanning individuals: Their role in information transfer and their antecedents. *Academy of Management Journal,* 24(2):289–305.

_____(1981b). Characteristics and external orientations of boundary spanning individuals. *Academy of Management Journal,* 24(1):83–98.

Udy, S.H. (1959). *Organization of work.* New Haven, CT: HRAF Press.

Uzzi, B. (1997). Social structure and competition in interfirm networks: The paradox of embeddedness. *Administrative Science Quarterly,* 42:35–67.

Van de Ven, A. (1975). A framework for organization assessment. *Academy of Management Review,* 1(1):64–78.

Van de Ven, A., Delbecq, A., & Koenig, R., Jr. (1976). Determinants of coordination modes within an organization. *American Sociological Review,* 41:322–338.

Van de Ven, A., & Ferry, D. (1980). *Measuring and assessing organizations.* New York: Wiley.

Van Maanen, J., & Barley, S.R. (1984). Occupational communities: Culture and control in organizations. In Staw, B.M., & Cummings, L.L. (Eds.), *Research in Organizational Behavior,* vol.6 (pp.287–365). Greenwich, CT: JAI Press.

von Bertalanffy, L. (1950). The theory of open systems in physics and biology. *Science,* 111:23–29.

Wageman, R. (1995). Interdependence and group effectiveness. *Administrative Science Quarterly,* 40:145–180.

Wall, T.D., Kemp, N.J., Jackson, P.R., & Clegg, C.W. (1986). Outcomes of autonomous workgroups: A long-term field experiment. *Academy of Management Journal,* 29(2):280–305.

Waller, M. (1999). The timing of adaptive group responses to non-routine events. *Academy of Management Journal,* 422:127–137.

Walton, R. (1985). From control to commitment in the workplace. *Harvard Business Review,* March–April, pp.76–84.

Walton, R., & Hackman, R. (1986). Groups under contrasting management strategies. In Goodman, P., et al. (Eds.), *Designing effective work groups.* San Francisco: Jossey-Bass.

Walton, R., & Schlesinger, L. (1979). Do supervisors thrive in participative work systems?*OrganizationalDynamics,*7(3):25–38.

Weick, K. (1993). The collapse of sense-making in organizations: The Mann Gulch disaster. *Administrative Science Quarterly,* 38:628–652.

Weick, K.E., & Roberts, K.H. (1993). Collective mind in organizations: Heedful interrelating on flight decks. *Administrative Science Quarterly,* 38(3):357–381.

Woodward, J. (1965). *Industrial organization: Theory and practice.* New York: Oxford University Press.

Zuboff, S. (1988). *In the age of the smart machine: The future of work and power.* New York: Basic Books.

Chapter 19

Alderfer, C. (1972). *Human needs in organizational settings.* New York: Free Press.

Amabile, T.M., Hill, K.G., Hennessey, B.A., & Tighe, E.M. (1994). The work preference inventory: Assessing intrinsic and extrinsic motivational orientations. *Journal of Personality and Social Psychology,* 66:950–967.

Arvey, R.D., Bouchard, T.J., Segal, N.L., & Abraham, L.M. (1989). Job satisfaction: Environmental and genetic components. *Journal of Applied Psychology,* 74(2):187–192.

Bagozzi, R.P., & Bergami, M. (2000). Self-categorization and commitment as distinct aspects of social identity in the organization: Conceptualization, measurement, and relation to antecedants and consequences. *British Journal of Social Psychology,* 39: 555–577.

Baumeister, R.F. (1991). *Meanings of life.* New York: Guilford Press.

Baumeister, R.F., & Vohs, K.D. (2002). The pursuit of meaningfulness in life. In Snyder, C.R., & Lopez, S.J. (Eds.), *The handbook of positive psychology* (pp.608–618). New York: Oxford University Press.

Bellah, R.N., Madsen, R., Sullivan, W.M., Swidler, A., & Tipton, S.M. (1985). *Habits of the heart: Individualism and commitment in American life.* New York: Harper & Row.

Bowe, J., Bowe, M., & Streeter, S. (2000). *Gig: Americans talk about their jobs at the turn of the millennium.* New York: Crown.

Casey, C. (1995). *Work, self, and society: After industrialism.* New York: Routledge.

Colby, A., Sippola, L., & Phelps, E. (2002). Social responsibility and paid work in contemporary American life. In Rossi, A. (Ed.), *Caring and doing for others: Social responsibility in the domains of family, work, and community* (pp.463–501). Chicago: University of Chicago Press.

Cook, J., & Wall, T.D. (1980). New work attitude measures of trust, organizational commitment, and personal need non-fulfillment. *Journal of Occupational Psychology,* 53:39–52.

Davidson, J.C., & Caddell, D.P. (1994). Religion and the meaning of work. *Journal for the Scientific Study of Religion,* 33:135–147.

Dubin, R. (1956). Industrial workers' worlds: A study of the "central life interests" of industrial workers. *Social Problems,* 3:131–142.

Gillham, J.E., Shatte, A.J., Reivich, K.J., & Seligman, M.E.P. (2001). Optimism, pessimism, and explanatory style. In Chang, E.C. (Ed.), *Optimism and pessimism: Implications for theory, research, and practice* (pp.53–75). Washington, DC: American Psychological Association.

Griffin, R.W. (1987). Toward an integrated theory of task design. *Research in Organizational Behavior,* 9:79–120.

Hackman, J.R. (1990). *Groups that work (and those that don't): Creating conditions for effective teamwork.* San Francisco: Jossey-Bass.

Hackman J.R., & Oldham, G.R. (1976). Motivation through the design of work: Test of a theory. *Organization Behavior and Human Decision Processes,* 16:250–279.

_____(1980). *Work redesign.* Reading, MA: Addison-Wesley.

Herzberg, F., Mausner, B., & Snyderman, B.B. (1959). *The motivation to work.* New York: Wiley.

Judge, T.A., Thoresen, C.J., Bono, J.E., & Patton, G.K. (2001). The job satisfaction-job performance relationship: A qualitative and quantitative review. *Psychological Bulletin,* 127(3):376–407.

Kanungo, R.N. (1981). Work alienation and involvement: Problems and prospects.

International Review of Applied Psychology, 30:1–15.

_____(1982). Measurement of job and work involvement. *Journal of Applied Psychology,* 67:341–349.

Kanungo, R.N., & Hartwick, J. (1987). An alternative to the intrinsic-extrinsic dichotomy of work rewards. *Journal of Management,* 13:751–766.

Kohn, M.L., Schooler, C., Miller, J., Miller, K.A., & Schoenberg, R. (1983). *Work and personality: An inquiry into the impact of social stratification.* Norwood, NJ: Ablex.

Lodahl, T.M., & Kejner, M. (1965). The definition and measurement of job involvement. *Journal of Applied Psychology,* 49:24–33.

Loscocco, K.A. (1989). The interplay of personal and job characteristics in determining work commitment. *Social Science Research,* 18:370–394.

McCrae, R.R., & Costa, P.T. (1999). A Five-Factor theory of personality. In Pervin, L.A. (Ed.), *Handbook of personality: Theory and research,* 2nd ed. (pp.139–153). New York: Guilford Press.

Morse, N.C., & Weiss, R.S. (1955). The function and meaning of work and the job. *American Sociological Review,* 20:191–198.

MOW International Research Team (1987). *The meaning of working.* New York: Academic Press.

Mowday, R.T., Steers, R.M., & Porter, L.W. (1979). The measurement of organizational commitment. *Journal of Vocational Behavior,* 14:224–247.

Nord, W.R., Brief, A.P., Atieh, J.M., & Doherty, E.M. (1990). Studying meanings of work: The case of work values. In Brief, A., & Nord, W. (Eds.), *Meanings of occupational work: A collection of essays* (pp.21–64). Lexington: Lexington Books.

Oldham, G.R., & Hackman, J.R. (1981). Relationships between organizational structure and employee reactions: Comparing alternative frameworks. *Administrative Science Quarterly,* 26:66–83.

Pratt, M.G., & Ashforth, B.E. (2003). Fostering meaningfulness in working and at work. In Cameron, K., Dutton, J.E., & Quinn, R.E. (Eds.), *Positive organizational scholarship.* San Francisco: Berrett-Koehler.

Rawsthorne, L.J., & Elliott, A.J. (1999). Achievement goals and intrinsic motivation: A meta-analytic review. *Personality & Social Psychology Review,* 3:326–344.

Roberson, L. (1990). Functions of work meanings in organizations: Work meanings and work motivation. In Brief, A., & Nord, W. (Eds.), *Meanings of occupational work: A collection of essays* (pp.107–134). Lexington, MA: Lexington Books.

Schwartz, B. (1986). *The battle for human nature: Science, morality, and modern life.* New York: W.W. Norton.

_____(1994). *The costs of living: How market freedom erodes the best things in life.* New York: W.W.Norton.

Seligman, M.E.P. (2002). *Authentic happiness: Using the new positive psychology to realize your potential for lasting fulfillment.* New York: Free Press.

Staw, B.M., Bell, N.E., & Clausen, J.A. (1986). The dispositional approach to job attitudes. *Administrative Science Quarterly,* 31:56–77.

Taylor, J.C., & Bowers, D.G. (1972). *Survey of organizations: A machine scored standardized questionnaire instrument.* Ann Arbor: Institute for Social Research, University of Michigan.

Tropp, L.R., & Wright, S.C. (1999). Ingroup identification as the inclusion of ingroup in the self. *Personality and Social Psychology,* 5: 585–600.

Vecchio, R.P. (1980). The function and meaning of work and the job: Morse and

Weiss (1955) revisited. *Academy of Management Journal,* 23:361–367.

Weber, M. (1958). *The Protestant ethic and the spirit of capitalism.* New York: Scribner.

_____(1963). *The sociology of religion.* Boston: Beacon.

Wrzesniewski, A. (1999). Jobs, careers, and callings: Work orientation and job transitions. Unpublished Ph.D. diss., University of Michigan.

Wrzesniewski, A., & Dutton, J.E. (2001). Crafting a job: Revisioning employees as active crafters of their work. *Academy of Management Review,* 26:179–201.

Wrzesniewski, A., & Landman, J. (2000). Occupational choice and regret: Decision antecedents and their outcomes. Unpublished manuscript.

Wrzesniewski, A., McCauley, C.R., Rozin, P., & Schwartz, B. (1997). Jobs, careers, and callings: People's relations to their work. *Journal of Research in Personality,* 31:21–33.

Zhou, J., & George, J.M. (2001). When job dissatisfaction leads to creativity: Encouraging the expression of voice. *Academy of Management Journal,* 44: 682–696.

Chapter 20

Albert, S., & Whetten, D.A. (1985). Organizational identity. In Cummings, L.L., & Staw, B.M. (Eds.), *Research in organizational behavior,* vol.7 (pp.263–295). Greenwich, CT: JAI Press.

Ashforth, B.E. (2001). *Role transitions in organizational life: An identity-based perspective.* Mahwah, NJ: Erlbaum.

Ashforth, B.E., & Kreiner, G.E. (1999). "How can you do it?": Dirty work and the challenge of constructing a positive identity. *Academy of Management Review,* 24:413–434.

Ashforth, B.E., & Pratt, M.G. (2002). Institutionalized spirituality: An oxymoron? In Giacalone, R.A., & Jurkiewicz, C.L. (Eds.), *The handbook of workplace spirituality and organizational performance* (pp.93–107). Armonk, NY: M.E. Sharpe.

Ashforth, B.E., & Vaidyanath, D. (2002). Work organizations as secular religions. *Journal of Management Inquiry,* 11:359–370.

Barber, A.E. (1998). *Recruiting employees: Individual and organizational perspectives.* Thousand Oaks, CA: Sage.

Bauer, T.N., Morrison, E.W., & Callister, R.R. (1998). Organizational socialization: A review and directions for future research. In Ferris, G.R. (Ed.), *Research in personnel*

418

and human resources management, vol.16 (pp.149–214). Greenwich, CT: JAI Press.

Baumeister, R.F. (1991). *Meanings of life.* New York: Guilford Press.

Baumeister, R.F., & Leary, M.R. (1995). The need to belong: Desire for interpersonal attachments as a fundamental human motivation. *Psychological Bulletin,* 117:497–529.

Bowen, D., Ledford, G., Jr., & Nathan, B. (1991). Hiring for the organization, not the job. *Academy of Management Executive,* 5(4):35–51.

Braverman, H. (1974). *Labor and monopoly capital: The degradation of work in the twentieth century.* New York: Monthly Review Press.

Brief, A., & Nord, W. (Eds.) (1990). *Meanings of occupational work.* Lexington, MA: Lexington Books.

Brooker, K. (2002). Starting over. *Fortune,* January 21, pp.50–62ff.

Cheney, G. (1983). The rhetoric of identification and the study of organizational communication. *Quarterly Journal of Speech,* 69:143–158.

Conger, J.A., & Kanungo, R.N. (1987). Toward a behavioral theory of charismatic leadership in organizational settings. *Academy of Management Review,* 12:637–647.

Cooley, C.H. (1922). *Human nature and the social order.* Rev. ed. New York: Scribner.

Davidson, J.C., & Caddell, D.P. (1994). Religion and the meaning of work. *Journal for the Scientific Study of Religion,* 33:135–147.

Dunn, D.S. (1996). Well-being following amputation: Salutary effects of positive meaning, optimism, and control. *Rehabilitation Psychology,* 41(4):285–302.

Edmondson, A. (1999). Psychological safety and learning behavior in work teams. *Administrative Science Quarterly,* 44:350–383.

Ehrenreich, B. (2001). *Nickel and dimed: On (not) getting by in America.* New York: Metropolitan Books.

Emmons, R.A. (1999). *The psychology of ultimate concerns: Motivation and spirituality in personality.* New York: Guilford Press.

England, G.W., & Harpaz, I. (1990). How working is defined: National contexts and demographic and organizational role influences. *Journal of Organizational Behavior,* 11:253–266.

Feldt, T., Kinnunen, U., & Mauno, S. (2000). A mediational model of sense of coherence in the work context: A one-year follow-up study. *Journal of Organizational Behavior,* 21:461–476.

Fox, S., & Spector, P.E. (1999). A model of work frustration-aggression. *Journal of Organizational Behavior,* 20:915–931.

Frankl, V.E. (1962). *Man's search for meaning: An introduction to logotherapy.* Trans. I. Lasch. Boston: Beacon.

Frost, P.J., Dutton, J.E., Worline, M.C., & Wilson, A. (2000). Narratives of compassion in organizations. In Fineman, S. (Ed.), *Emotion in organizations,* 2nd ed. (pp.25–45). London: Sage.

Furey, R.J. (1997). *The road to you.* New York: Alba House.

Gardner, H., Csikszentmihalyi, M., & Damon, W. (2001). *Good work: When excellence and ethics meet.* New York: Basic Books.

Gill, F. (1999). The meaning of work: Lessons from sociology, psychology, and political theory. *Journal of Socio-Economics,* 28:725–743.

Gini, A. (2000). *My job, my self: Work and the creation of the modern individual.* New York: Routledge.

Gittell, J.H., & O'Reilly, C. (2001). *JetBlue Airways: Starting from scratch.* Case no.9-801-354. Boston: Harvard Business School, October 29.

Gouldner, A.W. (1957). Cosmopolitans and locals: Toward an analysis of latent social roles—I. *Administrative Science Quarterly,* 2:281–306.

Guevara, K., & Ord, J. (1996). The search for meaning in a changing work context. *Futures,* 28:709–722.

422

Gunther, M. (2001) God and business. *Fortune,* July 9, pp.58–61ff.

Hackman, J.R., & Oldham, G.R. (1980). *Work redesign.* Reading, MA: Addison-Wesley.

Hackman, J.R., & Wageman, R. (1995). Total quality management: Empirical, conceptual, and practical issues. *Administrative Science Quarterly,* 40: 309–342.

Harpaz, I., & Fu, X. (2002). The structure of the meaning of work: A relative stability amidst change. *Human Relations,* 55:639–667.

Hartley, J.F. (1983). Ideology and organizational behavior. *International Studies of Management and Organizations,* 13(3):7–34.

Heise, D.R. (1977). Social action as the control of affect. *Behavioral Science,* 22:163–177.

Hodson, R. (2001). *Dignity at work.* Cambridge: Cambridge University Press.

House, R.J. (1997). Path-goal theory of leadership: Lessons, legacy, and a reformulated theory. *Leadership Quarterly,* 7:323–352.

Jones, G.R. (1986). Socialization tactics, self-efficacy, and newcomers' adjustments to organizations. *Academy of Management Journal,* 29:262–279.

Kahn, W.A. (1990). Psychological conditions of personal engagement and disengagement at work. *Academy of Management Journal,* 33:692–724.

Kirkpatrick, S.A., & Locke, E. (1996). Direct and indirect effects of three core charismatic leadership components on performance and attitudes. *Journal of Applied Psychology,* 81:36–51.

Kramer, R.M. (1996). Divergent realities and convergent disappointments in the hierarchic relation: Trust and the intuitive auditor at work. In Kramer, R.M., & Tyler, T.R. (Eds.), *Trust in organizations: Frontiers of theory and research* (pp.216–245). Thousand Oaks, CA: Sage.

Kristof, A.L. (1996). Person-organization fit: An integrative review of its conceptualizations, measurement, and implications. *Personnel Psychology,* 49:1–49.

Lawler, E.E., III. (1994). Total quality management and employee involvement: Are they compatible? *Academy of Management Executive,* 8(1):68–76.

Lawler, E.E., III, Mohrman, S.A., & Benson, G. (2001). *Organizing for high performance: Employee involvement, TQM, reengineering, and knowledge management in the Fortune 1000.* San Francisco: Jossey-Bass.

Markus, H. (1977). Self-schemata and processing information about the self. *Journal of Personality and Social Psychology,* 35:63–78.

MOW International Research Team. (1987). *The meaning of work.* New York: Academic Press.

Nord, W., Brief, A., Atieh, J., & Doherty, E. (1990). Studying meanings of work: The case of work values. In Brief, A., & Nord, W. (Eds.), *Meanings of occupational work* (pp.21–64). Lexington, MA: Lexington Books.

O'Brien, G.E. (1992). Changing meanings of work. In Hartley, J.F., & Stephenson, G.M. (Eds.), *Employment relations: The psychology of influence and control at work* (pp.44–66). Oxford, UK: Blackwell.

O'Reilly, C.A., III. (1989). Corporations, culture, and commitment: Motivation and social control in organizations. *California Management Review,* 31(4):9–25.

O'Reilly, C.A., III, & Pfeffer, J. (1995). *Southwest Airlines: Using human resources for competitive advantage.* Case no. HR1A. Stanford, CA: Graduate School of Business, Stanford University, March 6.

_____(2000). *Hidden value: How great companies achieve extraordinary results with ordinary people.* Boston: Harvard Business School Press.

Pratt, M.G. (2000a). Building an ideological fortress: The role of spirituality, encapsulation, and sensemaking. *Studies in Cultures, Organizations, and Societies,* 6:35–69.

_____(2000b). The good, the bad, and the ambivalent: Managing identification among Amway distributors. *Administrative Science Quarterly,* 45:456–493.

_____(2001). Social identity dynamics in modern organizations: An organizational psy-chology/organizational behavior perspective. In Hogg, M.A., & Terry, D.J. (Eds.), *Social*

426

identity processes in organizational contexts (pp.13–30). Philadelphia: Psychology Press.

Pratt, M.G., & Barnett, C.K. (1997). Emotions and unlearning in Amway recruiting techniques: Promoting change through "safe" ambivalence. *Management Learning,* 28:65–88.

Pratt, M.G., Rock, K.W., & Kaufmann, J. (2001). Making sense of socialization: How multiple social identities shape members' experiences of work. *Academy of Management Proceedings* (MOC): A1–A6.

Pratt, M.G., & Rosa, J.A. (in press). Transforming work-family conflict into commitment in network marketing organizations. *Academy of Management Journal.*

Roberson, L. (1990). Functions of work meanings. In Brief, A., & Nord, W. (Eds.), *Meanings of occupational work* (pp.107–134). Lexington, MA: Lexington Books.

Ricks, T.E. (1997). *Making the corps.* New York: Scribner.

Ryff, C.D., & Singer, B. (1998a). The contours of positive human health. *Psychological Inquiry,* 9:1–28.

_____(1998b). The role of purpose in life and personal growth in positive human health. In Wong, P.T.P., & Fry, P.S. (Eds.), *The human quest for meaning: A handbook of psychological research and clinical applications* (pp.213–235). Mahwah, NJ: Erlbaum.

Saks, A.M., & Ashforth, B.E. (1997). Organizational socialization: Making sense of the past and present as a prologue for the future. *Journal of Vocational Behavior,* 51:234–279.

Schein, E.H. (1970). *Organizational psychology.* 2nd ed. Englewood Cliffs, NJ: Prentice-Hall.

Shamir, B. (1991). Meaning, self, and motivation in organizations. *Organization Studies,* 12:405–424.

Shamir, B., House, R.J., & Arthur, M.B. (1993). The motivational effects of charismatic leadership: A self-concept based theory. *Organization Science,* 4:577–594.

428

Simons, T. (2002). Behavioral integrity: The perceived alignment between managers' words and deeds as a research focus. *Organizational Science,* 13(1):18–35.

Spreitzer, G.M. (1995). Psychological empowerment in the workplace: Dimensions, measurement, and validation. *Academy of Management Journal,* 38:1442–1465.

Starbuck, W.H., & Milliken, F.J. (1988). Executives' perceptual filters: What they notice and how they make sense. In Hambrick, D.C. (Ed.), *The executive effect: Concepts and methods for studying top managers* (pp.35–65). Greenwich, CT: JAI Press.

Stead, E. (2001). *A way of working: Essays on the practice of medicine.* Ed. B. Haynes. Durham, NC: Carolina Academic Press.

Stryker, S., & Serpe, R.T. (1982). Commitment, identity salience, and role behavior: Theory and research example. In Ickes, W., & Knowles, E.S. (Eds.), *Personality, roles, and social behavior* (pp.199–218). New York: Springer-Verlag.

ˇSverko, B., & Vizek-Vidoviæ, V. (1995). Studies of the meaning of work: Approaches, models, and some of the findings. In Super, D.E., & ˇ Sverko, B. (Eds.), *Life roles, values, and careers* (pp.3–21). San Francisco: Jossey-Bass.

Tajfel, H., & Turner, J.C. (1979). An integrative theory of intergroup conflict. In Austin, W.G., & Worchel, S. (Eds.), *The social psychology of group relations* (pp.33–47). Monterey, CA: Brooks-Cole.

Tausky, C. (1995). The meanings of work. In Simpson, R.L., & Simpson, I.H. (Eds.), *Research in the sociology of work,* vol.5 (pp.15–27). Greenwich, CT: JAI Press.

Treadgold, R. (1999). Transcendent vocations: Their relationship to stress, depression, and clarity of self-concept. *Journal of Humanistic Psychology,* 39(1): 81–105.

Trice, H.M., & Beyer, J.M. (1993). *The cultures of work organizations.* Englewood Cliffs, NJ: Prentice Hall.

USA Today (2002). http://careers.usatoday.co m/service/usa/national/content/news/ onthe-job/2002-08-22-job-satisfaction.

Weick, K.E. (1993). The collapse of sensemaking in organizations: The Mann Gulch disaster. *Administrative Science Quarterly,* 38:628–652.

_____(1995). *Sensemaking in organizations.* Thousand Oaks, CA: Sage.

Wong, P.T.P. (1998). Implicit theories of meaningful life and the development of the personal meaning profile. In Wong, P.T.P., & Fry, P.S. (Eds.), *The human quest for meaning: A handbook of psychological research and clinical applications* (pp.111–140). Mahwah, NJ: Erlbaum.

Wrzesniewski, A. (2002). "It's not just a job": Shifting meaning of work in the wake of 9/11. *Journal of Management Inquiry,* 11:230–234.

Wrzesniewski, A., & Dutton, J. (2001). Crafting a job: Revisioning employees as active crafters of their work. *Academy of Management Review,* 26(2):179–201.

Wrzesniewski, A., McCauley, C., Rozin, P., & Schwartz, B. (1997). Jobs, careers, and callings: People's relations to their work. *Journal of Research in Personality,* 31:21–33.

Zohar, D. (1999). When things go wrong: The effect of daily work hassles on effort, exertion and negative mood. *Journal of Occupational and Organizational Psychology,* 72:265–283.

Chapter 21

Adler, P.S., & Kwon, S. (2002). Social capital: Prospects for a new concept. *Academy of Management Review,* 27:17–40.

Allen, T. (1977). *Managing the flow of technology.* Cambridge: MIT Press.

Baker, W. (2000). *Achieving success through social capital.* San Francisco: Jossey-Bass.

Baum, J.A.C. (Ed.) (2002). *Companion to organizations.* Malden, MA: Blackwell.

Berger, P., & Luckman, T. (1966). *The social construction of reality.* New York: Anchor Books.

Brass, D.J., & Burkhardt, M.E. (1992). Centrality and power in organizations. In Nohria, N., & Eccles, R.G. (Eds.), *Networks and organizations* (pp.191–215). Boston: Harvard Business School Press.

Burt, R. (1992). *Structural holes.* Cambridge: Harvard University Press._____(2000). The network structure of social capital. *Research in Organizational Behavior.* Greenwich, CT: JAI Press.

Cameron, K., Dutton, J., & Quinn, R. (n.d.). *A new orientation to organizational scholarship.* Available at www.bus.umich.edu/positiveorga nizationalscholarship/neworientation.html.

Campbell, D.T. (1969). Ethnocentrism and the fish-scale model of omniscience. In Sherif, M., & Sherif, C.W. (Eds.), *Interdisciplinary relationships in the social sciences* (pp.328–348). Chicago: Aldine.

Castells, M. (2000). *The rise of the network society.* 2nd ed. Vol.1. Malden, MA: Blackwell.

Collins, R. (1993). Emotional energy as the common denominator of rational action. *Rationality and Society,* 5:203–230.

Cross, R., & Baker, W. (2003). Energy in organizational networks. Working paper.

Cross, R., Baker, W., & Parker, A. (2002). Charged up: The creation and depletion of energy in social networks. Working paper, Institute for Knowledge-Based Organizations.

Dougherty, D. (1992). Interpretive barriers to successful product innovation in large firms. *Organization Science,* 3:179–202.

Dutton, J., & Heaphy, E. (2003). The power of high quality connections. In Cameron, K., Dutton, J., & Quinn, R. (Eds.), *Positive organizational scholarship.* San Francisco: Berret-Koehler.

Freeman, L., Romney, K., & Freeman, S. (1987). Cognitive structure and informant accuracy. *American Anthropologist,* 89:310–325.

Granovetter, M. (1973). The strength of weak ties. *American Journal of Sociology,* 78:1360–1380.

Hansen, M.T. (1999). The search-transfer problem: The role of weak ties in sharing knowledge across organization subunits. *Administrative Science Quarterly,* 44:82–111.

Higgins, M., & Kram, K. (2001). Reconceptualizing mentoring at work: A developmental network perspective. *Academy of Management Review,* 26:264–288.

Ibarra, H. (1992). Homophilly and differential returns: Sex differences in network structure and access in an advertising firm. *Administrative Science Quarterly,* 37:422–447.

Kilduff, M. (1992). The friendship network as a decision-making resource: Dispositional moderators of social influences on organizational choice. *Journal of Personality and Social Psychology,* 62:168–180.

Krackhardt, D. (1992). The strength of strong ties: The importance of philos in organizations. In Nohria, N., & Eccles, R. (Eds.), *Networks and organizations: Structures, form, and action* (pp.216–239). Boston: Harvard Business School Press.

Labianca, G., Brass, D.J., & Gray, B. (1998). Social networks and perceptions of intergroup conflict: The role of negative relationships and third parties. *Academy of Management Journal,* 41:55–67.

Lave, J., & Wenger, E. (1991). *Situated learning: Legitimate peripheral participation.* Cambridge: Cambridge University Press.

Lincoln, J.R., & Miller, J. (1979). Work and friendship ties in organizations: A comparative analysis of relational networks. *Administrative Science Quarterly,* 24:181–199.

Marks, S.R. (1977). Multiple roles and role strain: Some notes on human energy, time, and commitment. *American Sociological Review,* 42:921–936.

Marsden, P. (1990). Network data and measurement. *Annual Review of Sociology,* 16:435–463.

McPherson, M., Smith-Lovin, L., & Cook, J.M. (2001). Birds of a feather: Homophily in social networks. *Annual Review of Sociology,* 27:415–444.

Miller, J.B., & Stiver, I.P. (1997). *The healing connection: How women form relationships in therapy and in life.* Boston: Beacon Press.

Monge, P., & Contractor, N. (2001). Emergence of communication networks. In Jablin, F., & Putnam, L. (Eds.), *Handbook of organizational communication,* 2nd ed. (pp.440–502). Thousand Oaks, CA: Sage.

New York Times (1993). Emotions mapped by new geography. April 3, p. L17.

Orr, J.E. (1996). *Talking about machines: An ethnography of a modern job.* Ithaca, NY: Cornell University Press.

Quinn, R., & Dutton, J. (2002). Coordination as energy-in-conversation: A process theory of organizing. Working paper, University of Michigan.

Raudenbush, S., & Bryk, A. (2002). *Hierarchical linear models: Applications and data analysis methods.* 2nd ed. Thousand Oaks, CA: Sage.

Ryan, R.M., & Frederick, C. (1997). On energy, personality, and health: Subjective vitality as a dynamic reflection of well-being. *Journal of Personality,* 65:529–566.

Sparrow, R., Liden, R., Wayne, S., & Kraimer, M. (2001). Social networks and the performance of individuals and groups. *Academy of Management Journal,* 44:316–325.

Thayer, R.E. (1989). *The biopsychology of mood and arousal.* New York: Oxford University Press.

Tsai, W., & Ghoshal, S. (1998). Social capital and value creation: The role of intrafirm networks. *Academy of Management Journal,* 41:464–476.

Uzzi, B. (1997). Social structure and competition in interfirm networks: The paradox of embeddedness. *Administrative Science Quarterly,* 42:35–67.

Wasserman, S., & Faust, K. (1994). *Social network analysis: Methods and applications.* Cambridge: Cambridge University Press.

Watson, D., Clark, L.A., & Tellegen, A. (1988). Development and validation of brief measures of positive and negative affect: The PANAS scales. *Journal of Personality and Social Psychology,* 54:1063–1070.

Wellman, B., & Frank, K. (2001). Network capital in a multi-level world: Getting support from personal communities. In Lin, N., Burt,

R., & Cook, K. (Eds.), *Social capital: Theory and research* (pp.233–274). New York: Aldine de Gruyter.

Chapter 22

Argyris, C. (1957). *Personality and organization: The conflict between system and the individual.* New York: Harper & Row.

Barzelay, M. (1992). *Breaking through bureaucracy.* Berkeley: University of California Press.

Behn, R. (1998). The new public management and the search for democratic accountability. *International Public Management Journal* 1(2):131–164.

Berry, J.M., Portney, K., & Thompson, K. (1993). *The rebirth of urban democracy.* Washington, DC: Brookings Institution.

Boas, F. (1966). *Kwakiutl ethnography.* Ed. H. Codere. Chicago: University of Chicago Press.

Boje, D.M., & Rosile, G.A. (2001). Where's the power in empowerment? *Journal of Applied Behavioral Science* 37(1):90–117.

Box, R. (1998). *Citizen governance: Leading American communities into the twenty-first century.* Thousand Oaks, CA: Sage.

Bozeman, B. (1993). *Public management: The state of the art.* San Francisco: Jossey-Bass.

Bryson, J. (1995). *Strategic planning for public and nonprofit organizations: A guide to strengthening and sustaining organizational achievement.* San Francisco: Jossey-Bass.

Bryson, J.M., Cunningham, G.L., & Lokkesmoe, K.J. (2002). What to do when stakeholders matter: The case of problem formulation for the African American Men Project of Hennepin County, Minnesota. *Public Administration Review,* 65(5):568–584.

Carnevale, D.G. (1995). *Trustworthy government: Leadership and management strategies for building trust and high performance.* San Francisco: Jossey-Bass.

Collins, R. (1993). Emotional energy as the common denominator of rational action. *Rationality and Society,* 5(2):203–230.

Conger, J.A., & Kanungo, R.N. (1988). The empowerment process: Integrating theory

440

and practice. *Academy of Management Review,* 13(3):471–482.

Dixon, N.M. (1998). The responsibilities of members in an organization that is learning. *The Learning Organization: An International Journal,* 5:161–167.

Emirbayers, M., & Mische, A. (1998). What is Agency? *American Journal of Sociology,* 103:962–1023.

Feldman, M.S. (2002). Resources in emerging structures and processes of change. Unpublished manuscript.

Feldman, M.S., & Khademian, A.M. (2000). Managing for inclusion: Balancing control and participation. *International Journal of Public Management,* 3(2):149–168.

_____(2002). To manage is to govern. *Public Administration Review,* 62(5):529– 541.

Follett, M.P. (1924). *Creative experience.* New York: Longmans, Green.

_____(1940). *Dynamic administration: The collected papers of Mary Parker Follett.* Eds.

H.C. Metcalf and L. Urwicks. New York: Harper and Row.

Fredericksen, P., & and London, R. (2000). Disconnect in the hollow state: The pivotal role of organizational capacity in community based organizations. *Public Administration Review,* 60(3): 230–239.

IAP2 (International Association for Public Participation) (2000). Public participation spectrum. Available at www.iap2.org/practitio nertools/spectrum.html (accessed December 2002).

Ingraham, P.W., Thompson, J.R., & Sanders, R.P. (1998). *Transforming government: Lessons from the reinvention laboratories.* San Francisco: Jossey-Bass.

Ingram, H., & Smith, S.R. (1993). *Public policy for democracy.* Washington, DC: Brookings Institution.

Jarrar, Y.F., & Zairi, M. (2002). Employee empowerment: A UK survey of trends and best practices. *Managerial Auditing Journal,* 17(5):266–271.

Jones, L., & Thompson, F. (1999). *Public management: Institutional renewal for the twenty-first century.* Stamford, CT: JAI Press.

Kanter, R.M. (1983). *The change masters: Innovation and enterpreneurship in the American corporation.* New York: Simon & Schuster.

Kanter, R.M. (1979). *Men and women of the corporation.* New York: Basic Books.

Kettl, D.F. (2000). *The global public management revolution: A report on the transformation of governance.* Washington, DC: Brookings Institution.

Khademian, A. (2002). *Working with culture: How the job gets done in public programs.* Washington, DC: Congressional Quarterly Press.

Kim, S. (2002). Participative management and job satisfaction: Lessons for management leadership. *Public Administration Review,* 62(2):231–241.

Kreisberg, S. (1992). *Transforming power: Domination, empowerment, and education.* Albany, NY: State University of New York Press.

Kouzes, J., & Posner, B. (1995). *The leadership challenge :How to keep getting extraordinary things done in organizations.* San Francisco: Jossey-Bass.

LaBonte, R. (1999). Social capital and community development: practitioner emptor. *Australian and New Zealand Journal of Public Health,* 23(4):93– 96.

Lappe, F., & Dubois, P. (1994). *The quickening of America: Rebuilding our nation, remaking our lives.* San Francisco: Jossey-Bass, Inc.

Leblebici, H., Salancik, G.R., Copay, A., & King, T. (1991). Institutional change and the transformation of interorganizational fields: An organizational history of the U.S. radio broadcasting industry. *Administrative Science Quarterly,* 36(3):333–363.

Lichtenstein, B.B., & Brush, C. (2001) How do "resource bundles" develop and change in new ventures? A dynamic model and longitudinal exploration. *Entrepreneurship Theory and Practice,* 25(3):37–58.

Light, P. (1998). *Sustaining innovation: Creating nonprofit and government organizations that innovate naturally.* San Francisco: Jossey-Bass.

Likert, R. (1961). *New patterns in management.* New York: McGraw-Hill.

Marans, S., with Adnopos, J., Berkman, M., Esseman, D., MacDonald, D., Nagler, S., Randall, R., Schaefer, M., & Wearing, M. (1995). *The police–mental health partnership: A community-based response to urban violence.* New Haven, CT: Yale University Press.

Markus, G. (2002). Civic participation in American cities. Report of the Civic Engagement Study, University of Michigan.

McKinsey and Company (2001). *Effective capacity building in nonprofit organizations.* Washington, DC: Venture Philanthropy Partners, Inc.

Moe, T. (1989). The politics of bureaucratic structure. In Chubb, J., & Peterson, P. (Eds.), *Can the government govern?* (pp.267–329). Washington, DC: Brookings Institution.

O'Connor, E. (2001). Back on the way to empowerment: The example of Ordway Tead and industrial democracy. *Journal of Applied Behavioral Science,* 37(1):15–32.

OECD (Organization for Economic Cooperation and Development) (2001). Engaging citizens in policy making: Information, consultation, and public participation. Public management policy brief, July.

Parr, J., & Lampe, D. (1996). Empowering citizens. In Perry, J. (Ed.), *Handbook for public administration* (pp.196–209). San Francisco: Jossey-Bass.

Peccei, R., & Rosenthal, P. (2001). Delivering customer-orientated behaviour through empowerment: An empirical test of HRM assumptions. *Journal of Management Studies,* 38(6):831–857.

Peters, T., & Waterman, R. (1982). *In search of excellence: Lessons from America's best run companies.* New York: Harper & Row.

Prasad, A. (2001). Understanding workplace empowerment as inclusion. *Journal of Applied Behavioral Science,* 37(1):51–69.

Prasad, P., & Eylon, D. (2001). Where's the power in empowerment: Answers from Follett and Clegg. *Journal of Applied Behavioral Science,* 37(1):90–117.

Pratt, M.G., & Ashforth, B.E. (2003). Fostering meaningfulness in working and at work. In Cameron, K.S., Dutton, J.E., & Quinn, R.E. (Eds.), *Positive organizational scholarship.* San Francisco: Berrett-Koehler.

Putnam, R. (2000). *Bowling alone: The collapse and revival of American community.* New York: Simon and Schuster.

Putnam, R. (1995). Bowling alone: America's declining social capital. *Journal of Democracy* 6:65–78.

Quinn, R., & Dutton, J. (2002). Coordination as energy-in-conversation: A process theory of organizing. Unpublished manuscript, revised and resubmitted for the *Academy of Management Review.*

Rabe, B. (1994). *Beyond NIMBY: Hazardous waste sitting in Canada and the United States.* Washington, DC: Brookings Institution.

Randolph, W.A., & Sashkin, M. (2002). Can organizational empowerment work in a multinational setting? *Academy of Management Executive,* 16(1):102–115.

Reardon, K. (1998). Enhancing the capacity of community based organizations in East St. Louis. *Journal of Planning and Educational Research,* 17:323–333.

Reich, R. (1988a). Policy making in a democracy. In Reich, R. (Ed.), *The power of public ideas* (pp.123–156). Cambridge: Harvard University Press.

_____(Ed.) (1988b). *The power of public ideas.* Cambridge: Harvard University Press.

Ryan, R.M., & Bernstein, J.H. (2002). Vitality/zest/enthusiasm/vigor/energy. In Peterson, C., & Seligman, M., Values in Action (VIA) classification of strengths. Unpublished manuscript, Values in Action Institute.

Sahlins, M. (1989). The cosmology of capitalism: The trans-Pacific sector of the world system. *Proceedings of the British Academy for 1988.*

Sandel, M.. (1996). *Democracy's discontent: America in search of a public philosophy.* Cambridge: Harvard University Press.

Senge, P. (1990). *The fifth discipline: The art and practice of the learning organization.* New York: Doubleday Currency.

Sewell, W. (1992). A theory of structure: Duality, agency, and transformation. *American Journal of Sociology,* 98(1):1–29.

Spreitzer, G. (1995). Psychological empowerment in the workplace: Dimensions measurement and validation. *Academy of Management Journal,* 38(5): 1442–1465.

Spreitzer, G.M., & Sonenshein, S. (2003). Positive deviance and extraordinary organizing. In Cameron, K.S., Dutton, J.E., & Quinn, R.E. (Eds.), *Positive organizational scholarship.* San Francisco: Berrett-Koehler.

Stone, C., Henig, J., Jones, B., & Pierannunzi, C. (2001). *Building civic capacity: The politics of reforming urban schools.* Lawrence: University Press of Kansas.

Tead, O. (1918). *Instincts in industry: A study of working-class psychology.* Boston: Houghton Mifflin, Co.

Tead, O. (1945). *Democratic administration.* New York: Association Press.

Tead, O. (1951). *The art of administration.* New York: McGraw-Hill.

Thacher, D. (2001). Equity and community policing: A new view of community partnerships. *Criminal Justice Ethics,* 20:3–16.

Thompson, F. (1991). Management control and the Pentagon: The organizational strategy-structure mismatch. *Public Administration Review,* 51(1):52–66.

Vicenzi, R., & Adkins, G. (2000). A tool for assessing organizational vitality in an era of complexity. *Technological Forecasting and Social Change,* 64:101–113.

Vigoda, E. (2002). From responsiveness to collaboration: Governance, citizens, and the next generation of public administration. *Public Administration Review,* 62(5):527–540.

Warwick, D. (1975). *A theory of public bureaucracy.* Cambridge: Harvard University Press.

Weber, E. (1998). *Pluralism by the rules: Conflict and cooperation in environmental regulation.*

450

Washington, DC: Georgetown University Press.

Weber, M. (1946). *From Max Weber: Essays in sociology.* Gerth, H., & Wright Mills, C. (Eds. and Trans.). New York: Oxford University Press.

Wrzesniewski, A. & Dutton, J. (2001). Crafting a job: Revisioning employees as active crafters of their work. *Academy of Management Review,* 26(2):179– 201.

Chapter 23

Baumeister, R.F., Bratslavsky, E., Finkenauer, C., & Vohs, K.D. (2001). Bad is stronger than good. *Review of General Psychology,* 5:323–370.

Cameron, K.S., & Quinn, R.E. (1999). *Diagnosing and changing organizational culture.* Reading, MA: Addison-Wesley.

Gottman, J. (1994). *Why marriages succeed and fail.* New York: Simon & Schuster.

Losada, M. (1999). The complex dynamics of high performance teams. *Mathematical and Computer Modelling,* 30:179–192.

About the Contributors

Blake E. Ashforth' s research concerns the ongoing dance between individuals and organizations. He is interested in processes that mediate between the two, particularly socialization and identification. Blake is also interested in the dark side of organizational life, from burnout to helplessness. He is the Jerry and Mary Ann Chapman Professor of Business at Arizona State University.

Bruce Avolio currently holds the Donald and Shirley Clifton Chair in Leadership at the University of Nebraska in the College of Business Administration and is Director of the Gallup Leadership Institute. Professor Avolio has an international reputation as a researcher in leadership, having published over eighty articles and five books. His latest books are titled *Transformational and Charismatic Leadership: The Road Ahead* (Oxford Press: Elsevier Science, 2002) and *Made/Born: Leadership Development in Balance* (forthcoming from Erlbaum). His last two published books were *Full Leadership Development: Building the Vital Forces in Organizations* (Sage, 1999) and *Developing Potential Across a Full Range of Leadership: Cases on Transactional and Transformational Leadership* (Erlbaum, 2000).

Richard P. Bagozzi studies emotions in organizations and everyday life and their relationship to goal setting and goal striving. His research explores the representation and measurement of emotions, the relationship between social identity and emotions, the effects of emotions on in-role and extra-role performance in organizations, the effects of culture and the self-construal on coping with emotions, and the role of emotions in decisionmaking, with special emphasis on anticipated emotions, desires, and self-regulation. He holds the J. Hugh Liedtke Professor of Management and is also professor of psychology at Rice University.

Wayne Baker is professor of organizational behavior and professor of sociology at the University of Michigan, and faculty associate at the Institute for Social Research. He is directing the 2003 Detroit Area Study and the Detroit Arab American Study. His research interests include economic sociology, social networks, organizations, and culture.

Thomas S. Bateman studies motivation and work behavior, often by learning from unique individuals or people in intriguing job situations. Recent studies with collaborators explore top executives' goal hierarchies, the distinguishing outlooks or characteristics of scientists who pursue super-longterm goals, champions of the natural environment in business organizations, the impact of extrinsic rewards on intrinsic motivation, and proactive behavior in organizations. He holds the Bank of America chair in the McIntire School of Commerce at the University of Virginia.

Kim S. Cameron is professor of organizational behavior in the School of Business and professor of higher education in the School of Education at the University of Michigan. His research centers on organizational virtuousness, especially forgiveness after downsizing, and its effects on performance. A key aspiration is to establish positive organizational scholarship in the mainstream of the organizational sciences.

Arran Caza is interested in the differences between novice and expert performance, and particularly how organizational and contextual factors influence the development of expertise. Because expert performance relies on more than cognitive understanding, his research addresses issues such as the role of emotion, principle, and intuition in skilled performances. He is a doctoral student at the University of Michigan, in both the School of Business and organizational psychology programs.

Donald O. Clifton is the past chairman of the Gallup Organization and the current chairman of the Gallup International Research and Education Center in Lincoln, Nebraska. Dr. Clifton has created more than 200 personnel selection interviews for salespeople, managers, army generals, CEOs, priests, teachers, physicians, nurses, dentists, professional athletes, lawyers, accountants, and support staff. He is a widely published author, and his articles have appeared in many professional journals including the *Journal of Educational Psychology, Compensation and Benefits Management,* and *Teacher Education and Practice,* the journal of the Texas Association of Colleges for Teacher Education. Dr. Clifton coauthored the best-selling book *Now, Discover Your Strengths* with Marcus Buckingham, as well as *Soar With Your Strengths* with Paula Nelson. He is the chief designer of the Strengths-Finder® profile and lives in Lincoln, Nebraska.

David L. Cooperrider is professor of organizational behavior at Case Western Reserve University and chairman of the SIGMA Program for Human Cooperation and Global Action. He is cofounder of the Taos Institute and editor of Sage Publication's book series on Human Dimensions of Global Change. Most importantly, David was instrumental in developing and introducing appreciative inquiry as a new approach to organizational change, and his consulting and writing have been widely recognized worldwide. He has been the recipient of the Academy of Management's Innovation and Best Paper of the Year Award, and one of his consulting interventions using appreciative inquiry was recognized as the best organizational change program in the country by American Society for Training & Development.

Rob Cross is an assistant professor of management in the University of Virginia's McIntire School of Commerce and a research fellow with IBM's Institute for Knowledge-Based Organizations, where he directs the social network research program. His research focuses on knowledge creation and sharing, specifically how relationships and informal networks in organizations can provide competitive advantage in knowledge-intensive work. Current research projects include a series of studies on the role of social networks in knowledge creation and sharing, a functional theory of workbased relations, assessment of the role of trust in knowledge exchange, and emerging work on the role of energy in social networks.

Jane E. Dutton' s research focuses on how high-quality relationships affect individuals and work organizations. She is interested in the transformative potential of relationships as they enable growth, identity, knowledge, and change for individuals. She also studies how organizational contexts enable relational capabilities of firms that heal, build resilience, and foster human flourishing. She is the William Russell Kelly Professor of Business Administration and professor of psychology at the University of Michigan.

Amy Edmondson' s research focuses on how psychological safety affects learning in teams and organizations. In field studies in hospitals, factories, and other work organizations, she investigates what organizations and managers can do to create environments conducive to collaborative problem solving and positive change. She is associate professor of business administration at Harvard University's School of Business.

Robert A. Emmons is professor of psychology at the University of California, Davis. He is the author of nearly eighty original publications in peerreviewed journals or chapters in edited volumes, including the books *The Psychology of Ultimate Concerns: Motivation and Spirituality in Personality* (Guilford Press, 1999), *Words of Gratitude for the Body, Mind, and Soul* (Templeton Foundation Press, 2001), and *The Psychology of Gratitude* (forthcoming from Oxford University Press). His research focuses on personal goals, spirituality, the psychology of gratitude and thankfulness, and subjective well-being.

Martha S. Feldman' s research is in organization theory, public management, and qualitative research methods. She is currently working on the application of practice theories and structuration to understanding changes in routines and other processes in organizations. She has done ethnographic research in the U.S. court system, in the U.S. Department of Energy, and in the housing division of a large state university. Her current research sites are the city administrations of Charlotte, North Carolina; Grand Rapids, Michigan; and San Jose, California. She is associate dean of the Ford School of Public Policy and professor of political science and public policy at the University of Michigan.

Barbara L. Fredrickson is associate professor of psychology at the University of Michigan. Fredrickson is a pathfinder in the emerging field of positive psychology. She first presented her "broaden-and-build" theory of positive emotions in the 1998 publication "What Good Are Positive Emotions?" *Review of General Psychology,* 2:300–319. She has since presented applications of this theory for cultivating health and well-being in a 2000 publication in *Prevention and Treatment,* 3, available at www.journ als.apa.org/prevention , and empirical support for it in a 2001 publication in *American Psychologist,* 56:218–226. Her research, supported by the National Institute of Mental Health, suggests that positive emotions broaden people's modes of thinking, speed recovery from the potentially heart-damaging effects of fear and anxiety, and enhance individuals' physical, intellectual, and social resources.

Jody Hoffer Gittell' s work focuses on co-ordination within and across organizations. She has developed a theory of relational coordination—coordinating work through relationships of shared goals, shared knowledge, and mutual respect. She has identified quality and efficiency outcomes of relational coordination, and a set of organizational practices and contextual factors that foster it. She is assistant professor of management at the Heller School for Social Policy and Management of Brandeis University, and a faculty member of the MIT Global Airline Industry Program.

James K. Harter' s research focuses on estimating the practical effect of various human resource initiatives, particularly in the areas of employee engagement, strengths development, and employee selection. He is director of workplace research for the Gallup Organization. He holds a Ph.D. in psychological and cultural studies (quantitative and qualitative methods) from the University of Nebraska, Lincoln, and serves as an adjunct faculty member at the University of Nebraska, and faculty and council member for the Gallup International Research and Education Center.

Emily D. Heaphy' s research focuses on how high-quality relationships and social identity affect organizational and interpersonal processes. She is a doctoral student of organizational behavior and human resource management at the University of Michigan.

Anne M. Khademian, together with coauthor Martha Feldman, is interested in the ways public managers are using inclusion, shared resources, transparency, and the creation and development of relationships to address complex public problems in a democracy. She is also interested in the relationship between management efforts and the development and impact of cultures in public organizations for public policy. She has focused much of her research efforts on financial regulatory agencies of the federal government. She is currently a visiting senior fellow with the Robert A. Fox Leadership Program at the University of Pennsylvania.

Fiona Lee is associate professor of psychology and associate professor of organizational behavior and human resource management at the University of Michigan. Professor Lee holds a Ph.D. in social psychology from Harvard University in Cambridge, Massachusetts, and a B.A. in economics and psychology from Scripps College in Claremont, California. Her research focuses on how complex events are understood and communicated within organizations, and how these interpretations affect working relationships, risk-taking, learning, impressions, and performance.

Fred Luthans' s theory-building and research has evolved from organizational behavior modification to social cognition/self-efficacy to positive organizational behavior and leadership. In particular, his recent interests are in positive psychological states (rather than fixed traits), such as confidence, hope, and resiliency, that are open to development and lead to authentic leadership and performance improvement in the workplace. He is a professor at the University of Nebraska and holds the George Holmes Distinguished Professor of Management. In addition, he is a senior research scientist with Gallup, Inc., editor of *Organizational Dynamics,* coeditor of the *Journal of Leadership and Organization Studies,* and coeditor-in-chief of the *Journal of World Business.*

Nansook Park' s main research interest is the promotion of positive mental health in children and adolescents. Using cross-cultural and developmental perspectives, she is interested in investigating the structures, correlates, and influence of positive experiences and understanding how character strengths promote positive development, resiliency, and mental health among youth. She is an assistant professor of psychology at the University of Rhode Island and a certified school psychologist.

Christopher M. Peterson has been at the University of Michigan since 1986, where he is presently professor of psychology and acting director of clinical training. He recently held a three-year appointment as an Arthur F. Thurnau Professor, in recognition of contributions to undergraduate teaching. His doctoral training (1972–1976) was in social and personality psychology at the University of Colorado, where he became interested in individual differences in cognitive characteristics. He maintained this interest during postdoctoral re-specialization in clinical psychology (1979–1981) at the University of Pennsylvania, where he began to use the perspective of the learned helplessness model to investigate psychopathology, specifically depression, and physical well-being. He is currently turning his attention to positive psychology, working with Martin Seligman on a project describing and measuring such positive traits as curiosity, hope, kindness, playfulness, and teamwork.

Christine Porath' s research focuses on how individuals effectively self-manage, and how self-determined behavior can override constraining factors and affect extraordinary (positive) change. She also studies how negative interpersonal behavior, specifically workplace incivility, affects individuals and organizations. She is an assistant professor at the University of Southern California in the Marshall School of Business.

Michael G. Pratt is interested in positive organizational scholarship and the processes through which individuals create various forms of attachments with collectives (e.g., organizations and professions). He is especially interested in how individuals find meaning in and at work, and how organizations facilitate this process. His work addresses topics such as identification, identity, emotions, socialization, and sensemaking. He is an associate professor in the College of Business at the University of Illinois at Urbana–Champaign.

Robert E. Quinn is interested in positive organizational scholarship and the processes of change. He focuses his research, teaching, and practice on unleashing human potential. He specifically addresses topics such as leadership, vision, and the transformation of people, groups, and organizations. He holds the Margaret Elliot Tracy Collegiate Professorship at the University of Michigan and teaches in the School of Business.

Ryan W. Quinn is an assistant professor in the Olin School of Business at Washington University in St. Louis, Missouri. His research focuses on the emotional and communicative dynamics of coordination. He is interested in how individuals can work with others in ways that bring out the best in all of the people involved, and in the collectives they participate in. He uses theories of communication, affect, and coordination to study phenomena such as collective flow, principled action, and organizational change. He has a Ph.D. in organizational behavior and human resource management from the University of Michigan's School of Business.

Leslie E. Sekerka is an assistant professor in the Management Group at the Graduate School of Business and Public Policy at the Naval Postgraduate School in Monterey, California. Her research focuses on processes leading to organizational development and change. She is presently investigating how organizational interventions influence individuals' emotions, cognitive resources, identity, and relationships, and how changes at this level contribute to sustained systemic change. Her recent publications and conference presentations address topics that advance positive organizational scholarship and include the psychophysiology of appreciative thinking, the benefits of peer-coaching, and a theory of positive organizational change. Leslie received her Ph.D. from the Department of Organizational Behavior at Case Western Reserve University, Cleveland, Ohio.

Martin E.P. Seligman works on positive psychology, learned helplessness, depression, ethnopolitical conflict, and optimism. He is Fox Leadership Professor of Psychology at the University of Pennsylvania. Among his books are *Learned Optimism* (Pocket Book, 1998), *What You Can Change and What You Can't* (Knopf, 1994), *The Optimistic Child* (Houghton Mifflin, 1995), and *Helplessness* (W.H. Freeman, 1991). His latest book, *Authentic Happiness,* is published by Free Press, 2002. He received both the American Psychological Society's William James Award (for basic science) and the Cattell Award (for the application of science). The National Institute of Mental Health, the National Science Foundation, the Guggenheim Foundation, the Templeton foundation, and the MacArthur Foundation have supported Dr. Seligman's research. In 1997 he was elected president of the American Psychological Association by the largest vote in modern history. He is the director of the Positive Psychology Network, and his current mission is the attempt to transform social science to work on the best things in life—virtue, positive emotion, and positive institutions—and not just on healing pathology.

Scott Sonenshein' s research focuses on understanding how moral values and organizational norms affect workplace behaviors. His current projects include positive deviance, organizational integrity and business ethics.

Scott is a doctoral student in the Department of Organizational Behavior at the University of Michigan's School of Business. Before starting Michigan's program, Scott received a B.A. in business ethics from the University of Virginia and a M.Phil. from the University of Cambridge.

Gretchen M. Spreitzer' s research focuses on how to develop the full potential of individuals in the workplace. She studies how organizational contexts can enable individual empowerment, hope, and positive action. She is especially interested in the transformative potential of leadership and organizational change. Gretchen is clinical professor of organizational behavior and human resource management at the University of Michigan's School of Business, after spending nine years on the faculty at the University of Southern California's Marshall School of Business.

Kathleen M. Sutcliffe is associate professor of organizational behavior and human resource management at the University of Michigan. Her current research focuses on processes associated with team and organizational resilience, high-reliability organizing, and investigation of the social and organizational underpinnings of medical mishaps.

Stefan Thomke' s research focuses on managing flexibility, experimentation, and learning in the development of new products and services. An important part of his research examines the impact of new and rapidly advancing technologies (such as computer simulation) on the economics of innovation in general, and development performance and organization in particular. He is an associate professor at Harvard University's School of Business and teaches in the area of technology and operations management.

Timothy J. Vogus' s research focuses on the organizational structures and practices underlying high performance. He is interested in these structures and practices as mechanisms that enable collective mindfulness, resilience, and high reliability. He also studies the micro and political dynamics of institutional emergence and change. He is a doctoral candidate in organizational behavior and human resource management at the University of Michigan's School of Business.

Karl E. Weick is the Rensis Likert Collegiate Professor of Organizational Behavior and Psychology, and professor of psychology at the University of Michigan's School of Business. Interests include collective sensemaking under pressure, medical errors, handoffs in extreme events, high-reliability performance, improvisation, and continuous change. In addition, his current writing is distributed across a variety of projects that include sensemaking and meaning-making in complex and ambiguous environments; mechanisms for intellectual renewal used by organizational scholars; lessons learned about leadership from wildland fire tragedies; and generalizations from research on high-reliability organizations to individual and organizational performance.

Melissa Wooten, a doctoral student in organizational behavior and human resource management at the University of Michigan, conducts research on social structure and organizations, focusing on the ability of the legal environment to influence organizational structure and practices. Currently, she studies the connection between the legal environment and its implications for the employment and advancement of women and racial minorities. She also investigates the extent to which legal regulations can sufficiently deter an organization from engaging in discriminatory practices.

Monica C. Worline is an interdisciplinary organizational scholar who has spent several years studying the notions of courage and compassion in organizations and the social dynamics that these positive dynamics engender. After completing her dissertation entitled "Dancing the Cliff Edge: Courage in Organizational Life" in Organizational Psychology at the University of Michigan, in the Fall of 2003 Ms. Worline will join the faculty of Goizueta

Business School at Emory University. Prior to graduate school, Ms. Worline worked in Silicon Valley and was involved in a successful software startup venture. She graduated from Stanford University with honors and majors in English and Feminist Studies.

Amy Wrzesniewski' s research focuses on how people make meaning of their work in challenging contexts (e.g., stigmatized occupations, temporary work assignments, absence of work), and the experience of work as a job, career, or calling. Her current research involves studying how employees shape their interactions and relationships with others in the workplace to change both their work identity and the meaning of the job. She is assistant professor of management and organizational behavior at New York University.

Berrett-Koehler Publishers

Berrett-Koehler is an independent publisher of books and other publications at the leading edge of new thinking and innovative practice on work, business, management, leadership, stewardship, career development, human resources, entrepreneurship, and global sustainability.

Since the company's founding in 1992, we have been committed to creating a world that works for all by publishing books that help us to integrate our values with our work and work lives, and to create more humane and effective organizations.

We have chosen to focus on the areas of work, business, and organizations, because these are central elements in many people's lives today. Furthermore, the work world is going through tumultuous changes, from the decline of job security to the rise of new structures for organizing people and work. We believe that change is needed at all levels—individual, organizational, community and global—and our publications address each of these levels.

To find out about our new books, special offers, free excerpts, and much more, subscribe to our free monthly eNewsletter at www.bkconnection.com

More books from Berrett-Koehler Publishers

The Appreciative Inquiry Summit

A Practitioner's Guide for Leading Large-Group Change

The first book to provide a comprehensive practitioner's guide to the AI Summit—the preferred method when applying whole-scale change to large groups—*The Appreciative Inquiry Summit* provides step-by-step guidance for planning and running an AI Summit.

The Power of Appreciative Inquiry

Diana Whitney and Amanda Trosten-Bloom

The Power of Appreciative inquiry is a comprehensive and practical guide to using Appreciative Inquiry for strategic large-scale change. Written by pioneers in the field, the book provides detailed examples along with practical guidance for using AI in an organizational setting.1

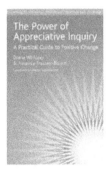

Change Is Everybody's Business

Pat McLagan

Change Is Everybody's Business challenges readers to realize the power they have to make things happen—to support, stymie, or redirect change, Pat McLagan draws on her 30 years of experience consulting on change projects worldwide to outline the beliefs, character traits, and actions that will enable anyone to welcome change and take e of it rather than fear and resist it. She shows readers precisely what they need to know to become more conscious participants in determining their own destiny at work—and in life.

Leadership and Self-Deception

Getting Out of the Box
The Arbinger Institute

Leadership end Self-Deception reveals that there are only two ways for leaders to be: the source of leadership problems or the source of leadership success. The authors examine this surprising truth, identify self-deception as the underlying cause of leadership failure, and show how any leader can overcome self-deception to become a consistent catalyst of success.

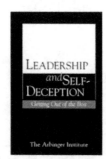

Empowerment Takes More Than a Minute

Second Edition
Ken Blanchard, John Carlos, and Alan Randolph

Empowerment Takes More Than a Minute shows managers how to achieve true, lasting results in their organizations. These expert authors explain how to empower the workforce by moving from a command-and-control mindset to a supportive, responsibilitycentered environment in which ail employees have the opportunity and responsibility to do their best. They explain how to build ownership and trust using three essential keys to making empowerment work in large and small organizations.

The 3 Keys to Empowerment

Release the Power Within People for Astonishing Results

Ken Blanchard, John Carlos, and Alan Randolph

This user-friendly action guide examines and expands on the three keys to empowerment originally presented in *Empowerment Takes More Than a Minute*—sharing information with everyone, creating autonomy through boundaries, and replacing the hierarchy with teams. It provides managers with thought-pro-voking questions, clear advice, effective activities, and action tools that will help them create a culture of empowerment.

Spread the word!

Berrett-Koehler books and audios are available at quantity discounts for orders of 10 or more copies.

Positive Organizational Scholarship

Foundations of a New Discipline

Kim S. Cameron, Jane E. Dutton, and Robert E. Quinn, Editors

To find out about discounts on orders of 10 or more copies for individuals, corporations, institutions, and organizations, please call us toll-free at (800) 929-2929.

To find out about our discount programs for resellers, please contact our Special Sales

476

department at (415) 288-0260; Fax: (415) 362-2512. Or email us at bkpub@bkpub.com.

Subscribe to our free e-newsletter!

To find out about what's happening at Berrett-Koehler and to receive announcements of our new books, special *offers,* free excerpts, and much more, subscribe to our free monthly e-newsletter at www.bkconnection.com.

494

Books For ALL Kinds of Readers

At ReadHowYouWant we understand that one size does not fit all types of readers. Our innovative, patent pending technology allows us to design new formats to make reading easier and more enjoyable for you. This helps improve your speed of reading and your comprehension. Our EasyRead printed books have been optimized to improve word recognition, ease eye tracking by adjusting word and line spacing as well as minimizing hyphenation. Our EasyRead SuperLarge editions have been developed to make reading easier and more accessible for vision-impaired readers. We offer Braille and DAISY formats of our books and all popular E-Book formats.

We are continually introducing new formats based upon research and reader preferences. Visit our web-site to see all of our formats and learn how you can Personalize our books for yourself or as gifts. Sign up to Become A RHYW Registered Reader.

www.readhowyouwant.com

CPSIA information can be obtained
at www.ICGtesting.com
Printed in the USA
LVHW062315130319
610605LV00021B/609/P